Time Out
SHORTLIST

Paris
2014

WHAT'S NEW | WHAT'S ON | WHAT'S BEST

www.timeout.com/paris

Contents

Don't Miss: 2014

Itineraries

Paris by Area

Essentials

Published by Time Out Guides Ltd
Universal House
251 Tottenham Court Road
London W1T 7AB
Tel: + 44 (0)20 7813 3000
Fax: + 44 (0)20 7813 6001
Email: guides@timeout.com
www.timeout.com

Editorial Director Sarah Guy
Management Accountant Margaret Wright

Time Out Guides is a wholly owned subsidiary of Time Out Group Ltd.

This edition first published in Great Britain in 2013 by Ebury Publishing
A Random House Group Company
Company information can be found on www.randomhouse.co.uk
Random House UK Limited Reg. No. 954009
10 9 8 7 6 5 4 3 2 1

Distributed in the US and Latin America by Publishers Group West (1-510-809-3700)

For further distribution details, see www.timeout.com

ISBN: 978-1-84670-377-5

A CIP catalogue record for this book is available from the British Library.

Printed and bound in Germany by Appl.

The Random House Group Limited supports the Forest Stewardship Council® (FSC®), the leading international forest-certification organisation. Our books carrying the FSC label are printed on FSC® - certified paper. FSC is the only forest-certification scheme supported by the leading environmental organisations, including Greenpeace. Our paper procurement policy can be found at www.randomhouse.co.uk/environment

FSC
www.fsc.org
MIX
Paper from responsible sources
FSC® C004592

Paris Shortlist

The **Time Out Paris Shortlist 2014** is one of a series of annual guides that draws on Time Out's background as a magazine publisher to keep you current with everything that's going on in town. As well as Paris's key sights and the best of its eating, drinking and leisure options, it picks out the most exciting venues to have opened in the last year and gives a full calendar of annual events from October 2013 to December 2014. It also includes features on the important news, trends and openings, all compiled by locally based editors and writers. Whether you're visiting for the first time in your life or the first time this year, you'll find the *Time Out Paris Shortlist* contains all you need to know, in a portable and easy-to-use format.

The guide divides central Paris into ten areas, each containing listings for Sights & Museums, Eating & Drinking, Shopping, Nightlife and Arts & Leisure, and maps pinpointing their locations. At the front of the book are chapters rounding up these scenes city-wide, and giving a shortlist of our overall picks. We also include itineraries for days out, plus essentials such as transport information and hotels.

Our listings give phone numbers as dialled within France. From abroad, use your country's exit code followed by 33 (the country code for France) and the number given, dropping the initial '0'.

We have noted price categories by using one to four euro signs (€-€€€€), representing budget, moderate, expensive and luxury. Major credit cards are accepted unless otherwise stated. We also give **Event highlights**.

All our listings are double-checked, but places do sometimes close or change their hours or prices, so it's a good idea to call a venue before visiting. While every effort has been made to ensure accuracy, the publishers cannot accept responsibility for any errors that this guide may contain.

Venues are marked on the maps using symbols numbered according to their order within the chapter and colour-coded as follows:

- 1 Sights & Museums
- 1 Eating & Drinking
- 1 Shopping
- 1 Nightlife
- 1 Arts & Leisure

Map Key

Major sight or landmark	
Hospital or college	
Railway station	
Park	
River	
Autoroute	
Main road	
Main road tunnel	
Pedestrian road	
Arrondissement boundary	
Airport	✈
Church	✚
Métro station	Ⓜ
RER station	RER
Area name	LES HALLES

Time Out **Paris** Shortlist 2014

EDITORIAL
Editor Dominic Earle
Proofreader Marion Moisy

DESIGN
Senior Designer Kei Ishimaru
Picture Editor Jael Marschner
Deputy Picture Editor Ben Rowe

ADVERTISING
Sales Director St John Betteridge
Head of French Advertising Sales Charlie Sokol

MARKETING
Senior Publishing Brand Manager Luthfa Begum
Head of Circulation Dan Collins

PRODUCTION
Production Controller Katie Mulhern-Bhudia

CONTRIBUTORS
This guide was researched and written by the writers of *Time Out Paris*.

PHOTOGRAPHY
7, 28 Stéphane Monier; 11, 126, 129 Heloise Bergman; 21, 41, 42, 43, 47, 50, 53, 63, 82 Oliver Knight; 22, 44, 70, 87, 119, 122, 141, 153, 158 Shutterstock.com; 29, 30, 90, 93, 98, 100, 132 (top) Olivia Rutherford; 39 Zherui WU; 45 Elena Shchipkova; 48, 55 Elan Fleisher; 49, 145, 180 Jean-Christophe Godet; 51, 56, 116, 132 (bottom) Karl Blackwell; 64 (top) flickr.com/photos/yorgda; 104 Food Snob (www.foodsnobblog.wordpress.com); 110 Manuelle Gautrand Architecture – Vincent Fillon; 163, 169 Patrick Lazic.

The following images were supplied by the featured establishments: pages 8, 14, 26, 34, 36, 64 (bottom), 75, 78, 114, 125, 137, 148, 156, 161, 164, 173.

Cover photograph: Musée du Louvre by Francisco Hidalgo.

MAPS
JS Graphics (john@jsgraphics.co.uk).

About **Time Out**

Founded in 1968, Time Out has expanded from humble London beginnings into the leading resource for those wanting to know what's happening in the world's greatest cities. As well as our influential what's-on weeklies in London, New York and Chicago, we publish nearly 30 other listings magazines in cities as varied as Beijing and Mumbai. The magazines established Time Out's trademark style: sharp writing, informed reviewing and bang up-to-date inside knowledge of every scene.

Time Out made the natural leap into travel guides in the 1980s with the City Guide series, which now extends to over 50 destinations around the world. Written and researched by expert local writers and generously illustrated with original photography, the full-size guides cover a larger area than our Shortlist guides and include many more venue reviews, along with additional background features and a full set of maps.

Throughout this rapid growth, the company has remained proudly independent, still owned by Tony Elliott four decades after he started Time Out London as a single fold-out sheet of A5 paper. This independence extends to the editorial content of all our publications, this Shortlist included. No establishment has been featured because it has advertised, and no payment has influenced any of our reviews. And, for our critics, there's definitely no such thing as a free lunch: all restaurants and bars are visited and reviewed anonymously, and Time Out always picks up the bill.
For more about the company, see www.timeout.com.

Don't Miss 2014

Islamic Arts Gallery, Musée du Louvre

WHAT'S BEST

Sights & Museums

A decade ago, a weekend for many in the French capital would have meant a quick dash round the Louvre and Musée d'Orsay, a hike up the Eiffel Tower and a twilight cruise on the Seine, followed by *steak-frites* and a carafe of Bordeaux in a cramped, smoky St-Germain bistro. Fast-forward to 2013 and the Louvre is now home to a dramatic subterranean Islamic Arts Gallery (see p74), the Musée d'Orsay has had a dynamic revamp (see p133), and the Eiffel Tower (see p122) is putting the finishing touches to a new glass floor. And thanks to Mayor Delanoë's courageous Berges de Seine project, the Seine is having a makeover too, with a stretch of the Left Bank between Musée d'Orsay and Pont de l'Alma pedestrianised for 'culture, sport and walks'.

Come 2014, there will be more new or good-as-new cultural treats awaiting arts-lovers, including a renovated Musée Picasso and the new Fondation Jérôme Seydoux-Pathé showcase of film memorabilia.

Paris, of course, already reigns supreme when it comes to sights and museums, with three of the world's top ten most visited art museums within its clutch – the Louvre holds an unassailable lead with 8.8 million visitors per year, some three million ahead of its closest rival the British Museum, while the Pompidou (see p100) and newly revamped Musée d'Orsay squeeze in at no.8 and no.10 respectively. Across the rest of the city, the list of sights worth your time is almost endless – from iconic treasures such as the Arc de Triomphe (see p56) to lesser-known gems like the Musée Fragonard (see p160). All this, and much more that we haven't yet mentioned, in a city that's a manageable size and boasts one of the best transport networks anywhere in the world.

Neighbourhood culture

As well as these exciting revamps in central Paris, culture is also migrating around the capital. Western Paris is now home to the Musée Belmondo (see p160) – not an *hommage* to the Nouvelle Vague heartthrob, but rather to Jean-Paul's father, Paul, one of France's most important 20th-century sculptors. Up north, meanwhile, Larry Gagosian (www.gagosian.com) and Thaddaeus Ropac (www.ropac.net) have both headed out to the *banlieue* to open galleries with the sort of space they could only have dreamed of in the Marais. Also worth a mention is the Maison de Jean Cocteau (see p159) to the south, a fitting tribute to one of France's finest artists.

The lie of the land

Parisians identify parts of their city by two systems: there are the named districts, whose frontiers aren't always clear – the Marais, the Latin Quarter, Montparnasse and so on – and the 20 numbered arrondissements that spiral out, clockwise and in ascending order, from the Louvre. Together they comprise an urban jigsaw. Each piece has a particular connotation or function: the fifth is academic; the sixth is arty and chic; the 16th is wealthy and dull; while the 18th, 19th and 20th arrondissements are riotously multicultural. Residents are frequently assessed, on first meeting at least, by their postcode, and as a consequence often develop

SHORTLIST

Best new/revamped
- Docks en Seine (see p150)
- Institut du Monde Arabe (see p144)
- Musée du Louvre Islamic Arts Gallery (see p74)
- Musée d'Orsay (see p133)
- Musée Zadkine (see p133)

Best secret
- La Collection 1900 (see p70)
- Musée Valentin Haüy (see p127)

Best art
- Centre Pompidou (see p100)
- Musée du Louvre (see p74)
- Musée d'Orsay (see p133)
- Musée de l'Orangerie (see p74)
- Palais de Tokyo (see p61)

Best dead
- Cimetière du Montparnasse (see p154)
- Cimetière du Père-Lachaise (see p101)

Best outdoors
- Jardin du Luxembourg (see p130)
- Bois de Boulogne (see p160)
- Parc des Buttes-Chaumont (see p96)

Best views
- Arc de Triomphe (see p56)
- Cathédrale Notre-Dame de Paris (see p118)
- Eiffel Tower (see p122)
- Institut du Monde Arabe (see p144)
- Sacré-Coeur (see p91)
- Tour Montparnasse (see p154)

Best tours
- Vedettes de Paris (see p122)

The most comfortable and modern boats in Paris

vedettes de paris

The sightseeing cruise of Paris
Get the best in 1 hour

www.vedettesdeparis.com

Location:
At the foot of the Eiffel Tower
Port de Suffren, 7th district + 00 33 (0)1 44 18 19 50
M° Bir-Hakeim & Trocadero; RER C Champ de Mars

This Parisian sightseeing cruise has to be at the top of your list of things to do when you are in the French capital.

Ideally located at the foot of the Eiffel Tower, its charming boats enhance the pleasure of a guided cruise on the Seine.

Listed by UNESCO as World Heritage, the river banks offer you some of the most well-known monuments such as the Eiffel Tower, the Louvre, the Orsay Museum and Notre Dame Cathedral amongst others.

Recorded multilingual commentary and a bar service on board.

Departures :
Everyday every 30/45min from 11am to 10pm. Times vary depending on the season. Check out our website for exact times.

Sightseeing or «by Night» cruise:
€13: Adult; €5: Children 5-12s; free under 4s

Exclusive :
Sparkling cruise, Sugar cruise or Snacking cruise
from €18 to €22

Special **Time Out** offer *

€3 OFF

On this guide's presentation
On both cruises on each adult ticket (VDP: 86)

*** Except on French Bank Holidays / Offer valid until 1st september 2014. Terms and conditions apply.**

Sparkling cruise

The magic of Paris by Night

Snacking cruise

Get a sample of the best monuments

Exclusive: a bar on board

a fierce sense of local pride. Indeed, many will tell you Paris isn't so much a city as a jumble of villages.

We've divided this book into areas, though not necessarily into shapes that residents would recognise; we've imagined the city as a series of visitor-friendly concentrations of shops, sights, restaurants and bars. The Champs-Elysées & Western Paris section has the famous avenue as its spine, lined with high-end shops. It also contains fashion's most glamorous thoroughfare, avenue Montaigne, which is almost matched in terms of lustre and allure by rue du Fbg-Saint-Honoré.

Montmartre & Pigalle has, at its northern end, picturesque Montmartre with its vertiginous flights of steps, narrow winding streets and the massive bulk of Sacré-Coeur (see p91). To the south lies Pigalle, famous for the Moulin Rouge and its strip clubs and scuzzy bars (though it's a far more salubrious proposition today than it once was).

Opéra to Les Halles used to be the centre of royal power in Paris, and you can get a sense of this by taking a stroll around the Palais-Royal (see p74). Today, however, it's the city's commercial and cultural powerhouse: it's home to the Les Halles shopping complex, to the jewellers and fashion houses of place Vendôme, and to the Louvre, Palais Garnier (see p86) and Monet showcase Musée de l'Orangerie (see p74).

North-eastern Paris is the area visitors from the UK are likely to see first: Eurostar trains terminate at the Gare du Nord (see p95) in the tenth arrondissement. The area is on the up, with its main artery, the charming Canal St-Martin, lined with boutiques and cafés. Further north and east of here is the magnificently odd Parc des Buttes-Chaumont (see p96), a warren of cliffs and grottoes carved out of a former quarry. Marais, Bastille & Eastern Paris is barfly territory, especially along rue Oberkampf, rue Jean-Pierre Timbaud and rue

Sacré-Coeur

Cultural exhibitions
In and around Paris
Events | Nightlife
Must See | Gourmet
Come and join us
| new-paris-idf.com
| facebook / Paris Tourisme
le nouveau Par!s
Île-de-France
The very best of Paris and its region
is here for you to discover and to share

St-Maur. The ever-trendy Marais is chock-full of independent galleries and quirky shops, and is also the centre of gay life in Paris.

The Islands – the Ile de la Cité, the oldest part of the city and home to Notre-Dame cathedral (see p118), and the more elegant Ile St-Louis – are essential ports of call. Notre-Dame celebrated its 850th anniversary in 2013 with a set of nine new, sweetly tuned bells.

Undeniably, the main attraction of the affluent 7th & Western Paris area is the Eiffel Tower, universal emblem of the French capital. Its ironwork is most alluring at night, when it is lit up by thousands of shimmering lightbulbs. This is also the best time to climb it, because the queues are at their shortest.

For many years, St-Germain-des-Prés was the intellectual heartland of the city. But these days it's more about fashion than philosophy, and the cafés are no place for starving writers. The city's most beautiful park, the Jardin du Luxembourg (see p130), won't cost you a *sou*, however; and the Musée d'Orsay is still excellent value, and gleaming after its recent revamp. Due east, the Latin Quarter is home to several august academic institutions, including the Sorbonne. And to the south, Montparnasse, although no longer the artistic stronghold it was in the 1920s, still boasts excellent cafés and restaurants, and the resting place of some of France's most illustrious dead, the Cimetière du Montparnasse (see p154).

The missing piece in Paris's cultural jigsaw is the Musée Picasso, which has been closed since 2009 to upgrade facilities and increase exhibition space for a reopening in late 2013. But Paris still provides opportunities aplenty to view the works of its famed former resident, from the Pompidou to the Musée de l'Orangerie.

Getting around

Vélib', the municipal bike hire scheme that puts some 20,000 bicycles at the disposal of residents and visitors, continues to flourish. Emboldened by the bikes' runaway success, Mayor Bertrand Delanoë launched another green transport innovation: an eco-friendly car hire system, which began operating in December 2011. Dubbed 'Autolib', the new project allows subscribers to pick up and drop off a car at any one of approximately 700 stations. The scheme has a fleet of 1,800 green (100 per cent electric) cars, and subscription fees range from €12 per month for an annual pass to €10 for a one-off daily pass. The half-hourly rate, meanwhile, ranges from €5 to €7. Each vehicle is tracked in real time, and when drivers have finished their hire period, they are guided to the nearest available parking spot.

If you don't feel confident about your chances in Paris traffic, the métro and RER are extensive and reliable, and buses are clean, frequent and cheap. Some of the bus routes are worth riding just for the sightseeing opportunities they offer: no.24 takes you through St-Germain-des-Prés and the Latin Quarter; no.69 runs all the way from Gambetta in the east, via the Louvre, to the Champ de Mars in the west; and no.73 connects the Champs-Elysées to the futuristic concrete jungle of La Défense.

But when all is said and done, you really can't beat walking for getting around the capital. Paris is compact enough to be navigated fairly easily on foot, and this is undoubtedly the best way to hear the heartbeat of the city.

For a selection of fascinating self-guided tours around the city, check out the Itineraries section of the guide (pp41-54).

Candelaria p17

WHAT'S BEST

Eating & Drinking

A surprising number of new restaurants are thriving in the difficult economic climate, from snob-free gastronomy at Cobéa (see p155), to Starck substance and style at Ma Cocotte (see p161) in the Puces de St-Ouen. Except for the simplest restaurants, it's wise to book ahead. This can usually be done on the same day as your visit, although top-notch establishments require bookings well in advance.

Bistro boom

Thankfully, the French continue to love classic bistro style. Many are old favourites, but the last few years have also seen the rise of the neo-bistro scene, updated for a new generation. At the very centre is Le Chateaubriand (see p108), the *coeur d'artichaut* of this dining trend, which the categorisers call 'bistronomy' (not a word necessarily embraced by the chefs themselves).

So, what are the magic ingredients of the bistronomy boom? First, take the same flair long associated with Parisian gastronomy but use a little less finesse and significantly more innovation; next, add world-beating raw ingredients of thoroughly researched provenance and chefs who are generally young auto-didacts enjoying success with their first business (Inaki Aizpitarte, Le Chateaubriand's Basque chef-owner was previously a *paysagiste*, his sommelier an actor, his olive oil supplier a tight-rope walker). Finally, sprinkle with reasonable prices and an atmosphere that's relaxed and intentionally unbourgeois.

The Chateaubriand's kitchen buys many of its delectable treats locally. The olive oil comes from La Tête dans les Olives (2 rue Ste-Marthe, 10th, 09.51.31.33.34, www.latetedanslesolives.com), a tiny shop in a pretty street. Owner Cedric Casanova goes to Sicily every six weeks, where he organises and advises 26 farmers on how to make the fruit of their 20,000 olive trees attractive to the Paris market. Should you wish to sample more of his Sicilian products, including pasta made by his fishing buddy, Cedric has opened a restaurant with one table next door. It only seats six and works out at roughly €30 per head. Booking is by email and there's a three-month waiting list to enjoy his tomatoes, figs and extraordinarily heady oregano.

Aizpitarte's other big opening is the Rem Koolhaus-designed Le Dauphin (see p108), a tapas-style restaurant/bar a few doors down at 131 avenue Parmentier, where dishes include *magret séché* and *tempura de gambas*. As at Le Chateaubriand, sourcing is all-important. Bread comes from Du Pain et des Idées (see p112), voted best baker in Paris a few years ago.

Such is the hoopla that Aizpitarte has created, there is inevitably talk of a new scene in the 11th: the proprietors of *branché* Chez Jeanette and Chez Justine chose a site opposite Le Chateaubriand and Le Dauphin for their new catering venture, Le Floréal (see p109) – an American-style diner serving up hamburgers and cupcakes.

Another Chateaubriand success story of the past couple of years has been former sommelier David Loyola's Aux Deux Amis (45 rue Oberkampf, 11th, 01.58.30.38.13). This tiny bar is permanently packed with a hipster crowd, but it's a different vibe from the student hangouts around the Oberkampf metro nearby. Vodka caramel is

SHORTLIST

Best recent openings
- Blend (see p76)
- Cobéa (see p155)
- Le Dauphin (see p108)
- Le Floréal (see p109)
- Ma Cocotte (see p161)

Best value
- Le Camion qui Fume (see p19)
- L'Encrier (see p109)
- Le Hangar (see p109)

Most glamorous
- Alain Ducasse au Plaza Athénée (see p62)
- L'Arpège (see p127)
- Café de la Paix (see p77)
- Jules Verne (see p128)
- Lapérouse (see p146)
- Le Meurice (see p79)

Bars with character
- Café Charbon (see p107)
- Chez Jeanette (see p96)
- Chez Prune (see p96)
- La Fourmi (see p91)
- La Palette (see p135)
- La Perle (see p111)

Cocktail classics
- Café Marly (see p77)
- Candelaria (see p108)
- Le Crocodile (see p146)
- Le Fumoir (see p77)
- Lizard Lounge (see p111)

Best for nighthawks
- L'Alimentation Générale (see p106)
- Harry's New York Bar (see p79)
- Le Tambour (see p80)

Bistronomic stars
- Le Chateaubriand (see p108)
- Frenchie (see p77)
- Granterroirs (see p62)
- La Maison Mère (see p91)

interdit – instead, customers enjoy organic wines and simple dishes such as *tortilla de Jeannine*.

And if you're headed up to the Marché aux Puces de St-Ouen, don't miss out on sampling Starck's new bistro, Ma Cocotte, perfect for a post-browse brunch.

Brasserie classics

The spectacle of sitting amid art nouveau extravagance, as waiters in black and white rush between tables serving platters of oysters and choucroute, comes at a price, but is cheaper at lunchtime or late at night. Bofinger (see p107) and La Coupole (see p157), both part of the Flo chain, pull in locals and tourists. The Costes brothers set the standard for the modern brasserie experience with stylish restaurants such as Georges (6th floor, Centre Pompidou, 19 rue Beaubourg, 4th, 01.44.78.47.99); they have also taken over a few old bistros, such as Chez Julien (1 rue du Pont Louis-Philippe, 4th, 01.42.78.31.64).

Top tables

To crank it up a notch, you could opt for a spot of all-out luxury in one of the city's haute cuisine restaurants. And it doesn't come much more haute than Jules Verne (see p128), Alain Ducasse's classy venue perched in its eyrie on the second floor of the Eiffel Tower. For once, the food is as good as the views, with dishes such as turbot with champagne zabaglione. Other sumptuous dining experiences are to be had at Le Meurice (see p79), Stella Maris (see p65) and Alain Passard's L'Arpège (see p127).

Restaurants where you can easily spend €200 or more a head often have lunch menus for €75-€80 – still a lot of money, but for this you are treated to a full-blown experience from *amuse-bouches* to *mignardises*. Ordering the lunch menu often means having a more limited choice of dishes, but staff are likely to draw on the freshest ingredients from the market. A notch down from haute cuisine, restaurants such as Le Restaurant (see p135) and Pétrelle (see p92) offer sumptuous dining experiences for less than €100 per person.

In the mix

Having lagged behind London and New York for years in the cocktail stakes, Paris is now being flooded with a host of cool new mixology bars. The trend was started by the Experimental Cocktail Club a few years ago, and the new wave includes Sherry Butt, Candelaria and L'Entrée des Artistes, all run by ex-Experimental bartenders. Each has its speciality – Candelaria (see p108) is a taqueria specialising in tequila cocktails; Sherry Butt (20 rue Beautreillis, 4th, 09.83.38.47.80, www.sherrybuttparis.com) favours a whisky base, as its name subtly suggests; and L'Entrée des Artistes (8 rue de Crussol, 11th, 09.50.99.67.11) is embracing the aged cocktails trend started by molecular pioneer Tony Conigliaro.

What they all have in common is that they are small, tucked away and packed with a new breed of imbiber who approaches cocktails as if they were fine wines. The icing on the cake is the fact that Conigliaro himself, star of the London cocktail scene, has now opened a bar in Paris, Le Coq (12 rue du Château d'Eau, 10th, 01.42.40.85.68, www.barlecoq.com).

Café culture

While Paris excels when it comes to café culture, from sitting out on the terrace of the Café de Flore (see

p134) to popping into your local for a *grand crème* and croissant, until now that culture has not extended to the quality of the coffee itself. All that's changing fast, though, with a new generation of cafés opening up, many run by Australian and American baristas who take their espresso skills very seriously.

Caféothèque (52 rue de l'Hotel de Ville, 4th, 01.53.01.83.84, www.lacafeotheque.com) is where the coffee revolution in Paris kicked off a few years ago, created by the doyenne of 'coffeeology' Gloria Montenegro. A former ambassador of Guatemala, today she's an unofficial ambassador for quality coffee from all over the world. At the moment, Caféothèque stocks and roasts coffee from 23 countries.

The Marché d'Aligre has become the hottest weekend rendezvous for foodies, and there's no shortage of trendy hangouts for coffee-lovers. But to feel the authentic pulse of Aligre, and taste some great coffee, nothing compares to stopping off at tiny Café Aouba (30 rue d'Aligre, 12th, 01.43.43.22.24). Opened in 1938 by a Portuguese butcher, this is the ultimate market bar, packed with stallholders, shoppers and curious tourists. The friendly *patronne* flits between making coffee for everyone, checking her beans on the big coffee roaster, and selling everything from artisan honey to homemade jam. Don't expect any designer deco here, just a red Formica counter with elbow room for half-a-dozen customers, and a shining Faema espresso machine. While the house brand is a mixture of beans from Colombia and Brazil, there are brews from Cuba, Mexico, Kenya and Uganda.

If you're after something stronger, the tenth and 11th, especially around rue Oberkampf, continue to be the most happening areas for bars. Café Charbon (see p107), both a restaurant and a pre-club cocktail bar, and L'Alimentation Générale (see p106), whose excellent concerts give stage space to up-and-coming musicians, are places to be seen. Also worth a trip is the area of St-Blaise, in the 20th, where a handful of buzzing venues have turned the area into a hub of urban subculture.

Breton and beyond

There are several decent crêperies around Montparnasse, where the Bretons originally settled, or you could try gourmet crêperie Breizh Café (109 rue Vieille-du-Temple, 3rd, 01.42.72.13.77, www.breizhcafe.com) in the Marais.

The streets around Belleville (20th) and the southern end of the 13th are crammed with decent Chinese, Vietnamese and Laotian restaurants; the second, around rue Ste-Anne, is flourishing with Japanese eateries, including the excellent Kaï (see p79). Rue des Rosiers in the Marais is a centre for Jewish cooking, and Italian, Indian, Moroccan and Lebanese cuisines can be found across the city.

US food has been getting a look-in, too, with gourmet burger van Le Camion qui Fume (www.lecamionquifume.com) one of the great success stories of 2012, and burger joints Blend (see p76), Big Fernand (see p91) and La Maison Mère (see p91) fuelling the trend.

In the know

Many venues close for their annual break during August, and some close at Christmas too. All bills include service charge, but an additional tip of a few euros (for the whole table) is polite unless you're unhappy with the service. Finally, try to avoid anywhere displaying a sign saying '*menu touristique*' or 'We speak English'.

Diptyque

WHAT'S BEST

Shopping

Paris shopping has never been in better shape. Where else in the world can you find so many independent boutiques and specialist shops, right in the middle of some of the most picturesque areas of the city? Whether you're tasting cheeses at Alléosse (see p66), sniffing candles at Diptyque (see p147) or selecting a pair of Tropézienne sandals at K Jacques (see p113), shopping in the French capital is a sensual pleasure based around quality, not quantity. Where we have window-shopping, they have window-licking (*lèche-vitrine*).

And now, even the chain stores are looking pretty fly with a slew of mainstream fashion brands – Banana Republic, Levi's, Hugo Boss, Abercrombie & Fitch (see p65) and even Marks & Spencer (see p67) – opening exciting new flagship stores on the Champs-Elysées, luring Parisians back to their long-neglected heartland of consumer chic.

Different areas of the city have different specialities. There are clusters of antiques shops in the seventh arrondissement, and second-hand and rare book outlets in the fifth; crystal and porcelain manufacturers still dot rue de Paradis in the tenth; furniture craftsmen as well as children's clothes shops inhabit rue du Fbg-St-Antoine; bikes and cameras are clustered on boulevard Beaumarchais; and the world's top jewellers can be found on place Vendôme. The historic covered passages in the second and ninth are also fun places in which to shop, with chic stores mixed in with philatelists and booksellers.

Family-run food shops have thankfully not been eroded by supermarket culture, and tend to cluster in 'market streets' such as rue des Martyrs and rue Mouffetard, as well as around the many covered and open-air food markets. Here, everything from a vintage bottle of armagnac to a single praline chocolate is lovingly presented, served and wrapped. Informed discussion is still very much part of the purchasing process, and beautiful, old-style shops, unchanged for decades, add to the pleasure.

Green, organic and ethical have also become sexy concepts to the French. Not-for-profit concept store Merci (see p113) offers guilt-free clothes shopping, and Designpack Gallery (24 rue de Richelieu, 1st, 01.44.85.86.00, www.designpack gallery.fr) recycles packaging into funky objects for the home.

Concept kings

The concept shop trend is a central feature of the scene, crossing the boundaries between clothes, music and product design. The capital's concept kings have very different personalities. There's cosmopolitan, metropolitan, glamorous but down-with-the-kids Colette (see p81); bobo I-probably-care-more-about-my-home-than-my-wardrobe Merci; and sophisticated, avant-garde L'Eclaireur (see p112). And then the smaller ones such as tomboyish Spree (16 rue de La Vieuville, 18th, 01.42.23.41.40, www.spree.fr), full of music and film industry cool. But what they all have in common is a product range that is both entertainingly diverse and seductively scarce.

At Colette, you can find Zippo lighters a few feet away from Smythson diaries, a few feet away from Ladurée macaroons, all one flight of stairs away from Alexander Wang and Valentino. At Merci, perfume and porcelain sit happily alongside each other on the main floor. And in Spree, antique furniture at the entrance gives way to a corridor with Dr Hauschka cleansers and toners, which in turn opens on to a room with racks of cute designer clothes. On the high-tech front, Sony opened its first European concept store, Sony Style,

Galeries Lafayette p81

at 39 avenue George V, and Apple has opened a gloriously indulgent store by the Opéra Garnier (see p80).

Boutique chic

The stretch of rue St-Honoré and rue du Fbg-St-Honoré from the Hôtel Costes to the Hôtel Bristol is wall-to-wall fashion boutiques, with Givenchy (see p66), Lanvin (see p83) and Jimmy Choo (376 rue St-Honoré, 8th, 01.58.62.50.40) the three major highlights.

Nearby rue Boissy d'Anglas has a branch of L'Eclaireur with its Fornassetti café (10 rue Boissy d'Anglas, 8th, 01.53.43.03.70, www.leclaireur.com).

Avenue Montaigne's headliners include Fendi at no.22, the Roberto Cavalli flagship at no.53 and, next door at no.52, Ralph Lauren's three-floor womenswear store. The small streets criss-crossing the Golden Triangle also have a few surprises, such as Lola.J (15 rue Clément Marot, 8th, 01.47.23.87.40).

Palais-Royal & around

If you're visiting Colette, don't miss a detour to the Marché St-Honoré. This former food market, rebuilt in glass by Ricardo Bofill, combines bistros and boutiques, with Marc by Marc Jacobs (see p83) a big attraction.

Easily reached on foot from here, the Palais-Royal gets better and better. On the eastern side, galerie du Valois has Stella McCartney (see p84), cult Swedish brand Acne Jeans at no.124, and the covetable and racy gloves of Maison Fabre at no.128. Opposite, with the idyllic gardens in between, is galerie de Montpensier, containing Marc Jacobs (see p84) and vintage wear from Didier Ludot (see p81), as well as Martin Margiela in the road behind (see p84). Also in the area

SHORTLIST

Best recent openings
- Causses (see p92)
- Storie (see p157)
- WAIT (see p113)

Best concept stores
- Colette (see p81)
- L'Eclaireur (see p112)
- LE66 (see p66)
- Merci (see p113)

Best hand-picked fashion
- L'Eclaireur (see p112)
- Kokon To Zai (see p83)

Best for accessories
- Colette (see p81)
- Marc by Marc Jacobs (see p83)

Best for eveningwear
- Lanvin (see p83)
- Yves Saint Laurent (see p140)

Best souvenirs
- Arty Dandy (see p138)
- Diptyque (see p147)

Best food and wine
- Alléosse (see p66)
- Christian Constant (see p138)
- Lavinia (see p83)
- Du Pain et des Idées (see p112)
- Pierre Hermé (see p139)
- Première Pression Provence (see p113)

Literary life
- La Hune (see p139)
- I Love My Blender (see p112)
- Shakespeare & Company (see p149)

The classics
- Le Bon Marché (see p138)
- Galeries Lafayette (see p81)
- Printemps (see p84)

is Kitsuné (52 rue de Richelieu, 1st, 01.42.60.34.28), the record label now selling its own-brand clothing.

Further east, the Etienne-Marcel area is the centre for club and streetwear, with boutiques and chains such as All Saints (49 rue Etienne-Marcel, 1st, 01.44.88.91.30) and Kiliwatch (see p83).

Marais mode

From second-hand T-shirt bargain bins to vintage designer pieces for hundreds of euros, the Marais is the place to head for everything pre-loved. The cavernous Kilo Shop (69-71 rue de la Verrerie, 4th, 09.67.13.79.54, www.kilo-shop.fr) sells bags, shoes, furs, knits and more by weight; Vintage Bar (16 rue de la Verrerie, 4th, 01.42.74.56.95), complete with decommissioned beer taps, stocks scarlet-soled Louboutins; Plus Que Parfait (23 rue des Blancs Manteaux, 4th, 01.42.71.09.05) sells on your unwanted threads for a commission.

Going Gauche

St-Germain tends to be more conservative, but is increasingly offering a mirror image of the Right Bank, with brands insisting on a presence on both sides of the Seine. These include Paul & Joe (see p139) and Vanessa Bruno (see p140), plus a stunning Hermès store (see p138) set in an old swimming pool. Shoe heaven is found along rue de Grenelle with all the top brands. Other highlights include bobo bags in colourful fabrics and denim from the former prêt-à-porter designer Jérome Dreyfuss (1 rue Jacob, 6th, 01.43.54.70.93); Hélène Lamey's nightwear and childrenswear at Bluet (18 rue du Pré-aux-Clercs, 7th, 01.45.44.00.26); and multi-brand shop Kyrie Eleison (15 carrefour de l'Odéon, 6th, 01.46.34.26.91) with lush creations by Orla Kiely, Eros-Erotokritos and La Fée Parisienne.

On the luxury scene, opium-coloured walls and lacquered ceilings provide a showcase for Stephane Pilati's creations at Yves Saint Laurent (see p140), while at Sonia Rykiel's St-Germain flagship (see p140) black mosaics, smoked glass and multiple mirrors evoke a '70s nightclub. And if you're in the market for jewellery, head to Marie-Hélène de Taillac's store (see p139), a Tom Dixon-designed space.

Further south, new Montparnasse shop Storie (see p157) is drawing curious, creatively bent shoppers to the area, offering an eclectic mix of homewares from around the world.

Edible delights

The layout of Fauchon (24-26 pl de la Madeleine, 8th, 01.70.39.38.00, www.fauchon.com), with different areas (pâtisserie, bakery, fruit and vegetables, etc) and chefs on hand at each to offer advice and recipes, provides an excuse to indulge at this luxury store. Food markets are found in all arrondissements – two of the most popular are the historic Marché d'Aligre in the 12th, and the Marché des Enfants Rouges in the 3rd, which focuses on organic produce. Near the Marché d'Aligre, pop into Première Pression Provence (see p113), an olive oil paradise. Causses (see p92), SoPi's (South Pigalle) new *alimentation générale extraordinaire*, is well worth a visit.

Practicalities

Shops generally open from 10am to 7pm Monday to Saturday. Sunday opening is found in the Marais, on the Champs-Elysées, at Bercy Village and the Carrousel du Louvre. Many shops on the Champs-Elysées stay open until midnight. Thursday is late closing at department stores.

WHAT'S BEST

Nightlife

Serious nighthawks may have migrated long ago to more happening cities such as London, New York and Berlin, but the French capital is fighting back with a string of great new leftfield Left Bank venues pumping out everything from gypsy jazz to electro-tropical candomblé to the Seine-side party crowds.

Go early if you want to avoid the queues, but bear in mind that Parisians tend to go out clubbing late and most venues will be pretty empty if you turn up before midnight. Also look out for flyers, join the MySpace and Facebook groups of your favourite venues, and most importantly, make friends with people in the places you go to: it's the best way to hear about cool underground parties coming up. Many of these new nightlife stars double up as gig venues, too, giving much-needed stage space to the city's up-and-coming bands.

Nightclubs

The 13th is Paris's new nightlife central. The long-delayed Cité de la Mode et du Design on the quai d'Austerlitz has opened its doors, and its first on-site clubs are setting tongues wagging. Wanderlust and Nüba have joined the likes of Petit Bain and Batofar (for all, see p152) along the banks of the Seine, making the 13th arrondissement the undisputed clubbing capital. Spread across a vast space, Wanderlust includes a wooden terrace perfect for sunset drinks (although you'll need deep pockets – a beer costs €8 and a bottle of rosé €35), an open-air cinema, art installations and a restaurant run by TV chef Benjamin Darnaud with dishes such as *steak-frites* and poached cod with lemongrass.

Running the venue is the ultra-hip Savoir Faire team (the brains behind Le Social Club and Silencio), so it should come as no surprise that the dress code is designer, the bouncers are unforgiving and the queues are long (come very early or late). You'll also find ping pong tables, weekend yoga lessons and chill-out areas dotted with chaises longues. Music is minimal techno and house on a top-notch sound system, getting the crowd going to the point where, if you're outside, you can watch a sea of well-dressed backsides gyrating together in the club's street-level bay windows.

The big name on Paris's nightlife scene in the past few years has been André Sareiva. Having gone from underground street artist to head of a multinational brand, he has redefined the meaning of cool in under a decade. Much hype surrounded L'Appartement, an ephemeral project launched by Sareiva and Lionel Bensemoun, aka La Clique. Hidden away in a Left Bank *hôtel particulier*, invite-only L'Appartement allowed the chosen few to party in a 3,000 sq ft flat, with everything arranged to make them feel at home: you could pour your own drink, tuck into a gourmet buffet and rifle through the collection of old vinyl. The only rule was to keep the address a secret and let the rumour spread.

La Clique's latest project, Nüba, is once again grabbing the hip headlines with its rooftop clubbing and supremely relaxed vibe.

Other Sareiva successes include Le Baron (see p67) and Le Montana (see p140), an even smaller venue near Café de Flore, revamped by La Clique and preferred by those who deem the Baron too passé.

SHORTLIST

Best new/revamped
- Nüba (see p152)
- Wanderlust (see p152)

Best bands
- Le Bataclan (see p115)
- L'International (see p115)
- Point Ephémère (see p99)

Best sound systems
- Panic Room (see p115)
- Rex (see p85)

All night long
- Batofar (see p152)
- Mix Club (see p157)

Best for chanson
- LesTrois Baudets (see p94)

Perfect for posing
- Le Baron (see p67)
- Le Montana (see p140)
- Silencio (see p86)

Best for star DJs
- Rex (see p85)

Seine-side partying
- Petit Bain (see p152)
- Wanderlust (see p152)

Best gay club
- Queen (see p68)

Best for jazz
- Caveau de la Huchette (see p149)
- Au Duc des Lombards (see p85)
- New Morning (see p99)

Killer cocktails
- Panic Room (see p115)

Life is a cabaret
- Le Lido (see p67)
- Moulin Rouge (see p94)

L'International

If it's more mainstream, big-room clubbing you're after, Queen (see p68) is a gay-friendly club known for its wild disco nights, while Rex (see p85) offers up mainstream and experimental electro on one of the best sound systems in Europe.

If you prefer your clubbing cosy, plenty of bars around Bastille, Oberkampf and Grands Boulevards are willing to oblige. Panic Room (see p115) is one of the hippest, with a stream of French electro nights. Traditionalists can choose their poison too; a host of school disco-type nights where the DJ is no superstar take place at the twice-monthly Bal at Elysée Montmartre (72 bd de Rochechouart, 18th, 01.44.92.45.36), and salsa and world music get a good hammering at Le Divan du Monde (see p94).

Because Paris clubs don't really get going until 2am, people usually hit a DJ bar before, and diehards finish their evening at an 'after' on Sunday morning. Free passes can be found on various flyers (see www.flyersweb.com). Other good sites are www.radiofg.com and www.lemonsound.com. Also look out for one-off events in venues like Rex and Point Ephémère (see p99).

The last métro leaves at around 12.45am (1.45am on Friday and Saturday), and the first gets rolling at 5.45am; in between you'll have to use a night bus, Vélib or taxi.

Rock, roots & jazz

Paris's music scene is bubbling with talent, and the emergence of some great new bands speaks volumes about the creativity of today's up-and-coming artists. The capital is brimming with authentic gig venues, and venues such as L'International (see p115) give precious stage space to those on the way up the ladder.

Chanson française is still going strong, helped by the revival of Les Trois Baudets (see p94), a government-subsidised *chanson* hall in the heart of Pigalle. Jazz is having a mini revival too: after the disappearance of old flames like Le Slow Club, Le Bilboquet and Les 7 Lézards, a handful of new joints have opened up, while flagship clubs Au Duc des Lombards (see p85), New Morning (see p99) and Le Sunset/Le Sunside (60 rue des Lombards, 1st, 01.40.26.46.60) continue to book top-notch acts.

Paris is also a European leader for world music, particularly African and Arab acts. And don't forget that every 21 June, the city turns into one giant music venue for the Fête de la Musique.

Website www.gogoparis.com selects regular concert highlights and features a decent concert list for the coming months; www.infoconcert.com is also well worth a look. The weekly magazine *Les Inrockuptibles* is a decent resource. Alternatively, try reliable, bi-monthly gig bible *Lylo*, free in bars and branches of Fnac. The Fnac (see p66) and Virgin Megastore ticket offices (see p67) also display details of up-and-coming concerts. For reduced-price tickets try www.billetreduc.com.

Prices for gigs vary according to a group or artist's pulling power, but several excellent venues, like La Bellevilloise (19-21 rue Boyer, 20th, 01.46.36.07.07), host regular free nights – ideal if you're feeling adventurous and/or are on a budget. For concerts, it's best to turn up at the time stated on the ticket: noise curfews mean that times are adhered to pretty closely.

Cabaret

The promise of busty babes slinking across stage in frilly knickers has turned glamour cabarets into some of the hottest spots around. The Moulin Rouge (see p94) popularised the skirt-raising concept during the 19th century, and since then venues such as Le Lido (see p67) have institutionalised garter-pinging.

These days, a cabaret is an all-evening, smart-dress affair, with a pre-show meal and champers. The Moulin Rouge is the most traditional revue and the only place with cancan. Toulouse-Lautrec posters, glittery lamp-posts and fake trees lend tacky charm, while 60 Doriss dancers cover the stage with faultless synchronisation.

For space go to Le Lido. With 1,000 seats, this classy venue is the largest cabaret: high-tech touches optimise visibility. The slightly tame show, with 60 Bluebell Girls, has boob-shaking and wacky costumes. For a more risqué performance, try Crazy Horse (12 av George V, 8th, 01.47.23.32.32, www.lecrazyhorseparis.com).

Moulin Rouge

Louxor

WHAT'S BEST

Arts & Leisure

A number of major cultural developments and innovations, and several new sites, have given a significant lift to Paris's cultural scene in the last couple of years. The revamped Théâtre de la Gaîté Lyrique (see p115) reopened in 2011 after a ten-year renovation as the capital's first digital cultural centre, and the completion of the extension of the Palais de Tokyo (see p61) in early 2012 has now created the largest contemporary art centre in Europe.

Construction has also finished on the Cité Européenne du Cinéma in the northern suburb of St-Denis. Backed by maverick French film director Luc Besson, the vast complex houses eight studios and promises to give the national film industry a massive boost – not that it really needs a boost after the raging success of *The Artist* and *Intouchables* in 2011. Between them, they garnered a raft of awards and hugely impressive box office takings.

Another major building project is the much-vaunted Philharmonie, which is rising near the Cité de la Musique. Architect Jean Nouvel's 2,400-seat concert hall is now due to open in 2015 and will give the city a major venue for the classical repertoire, as well as hosting jazz and world music.

What's especially good about the arts here is the accessibility: there are any number of festivals and discount promotions on offer throughout the year, many organised by the city council, that bring what the Brits often consider to be 'elitist' art forms within reach of the public.

Film

Cinema-going is a serious pastime in Paris. In any given week there's a choice of some 350 movies – not including the numerous festivals (see pp34-40), many of which offer free or discounted entry. The city houses some 90 cinemas and around 400 screens, almost a quarter of which show nothing but arthouse. Even the multiplexes regularly screen documentaries and films from Eastern Europe, Asia and South America. This vibrant scene is constantly evolving, with new multi-screen complexes under construction and classic picture houses constantly under renovation.

Visiting one of the city's many picture palaces is an experience in itself – from the glorious faux-oriental Pagode (see p128) to the innovative surroundings of the Forum des Images (see p86). And 2013 has seen the reopening of the revamped Louxor (see p94) in all its glorious Egyptian-inspired art deco glory.

Opera & classical

The Opéra National de Paris (see p86) continues to thrive under director Nicolas Joel, who came to the capital after 18 years at Toulouse Opera. With a reputation for traditional values, Joel favours a classical repertoire, while music director Philippe Jordan offers some youthful energy. Major productions for 2014 include *Madama Butterfly* and *La Traviata*. The Théâtre National de l'Opéra Comique (see p86), meanwhile, continues to capitalise on new financial security following its promotion to National Theatre status by offering a crowd-pleasing season of revivals and classics, including Viardot's *Cendrillon* and Reynaldo Hahn's *Ciboulette*.

SHORTLIST

Wonderful settings
- Louxor (see p94)
- Palais Garnier (see p86)
- Théâtre des Champs-Elysées (see p69)
- Théâtre Marigny (see p69)

Most innovative
- International opera at Festival d'Automne (see p34)

Most romantic
- Candlelit recitals for the Festival Chopin (see p38)
- Lovers' seats at MK2 Bilbliothèque (see p99)

Best bargains
- €3.50 film tickets, Printemps du Cinéma (see p35)
- Free concerts at Paris Jazz Festival (see p38)

Best alfresco
- Cinéma en Plein Air (see p38)
- Festival Classique au Vert (see p39)
- Fête de la Musique (see p38)

Best film venues
- Forum des Images (see p86)
- Louxor (see p94)
- La Pagode (see p128)

Best opera venues
- Palais Garnier (see p86)
- Théâtre National de l'Opéra Comique (see p86)

Original creations
- 104 (see p159)
- Gaîté Lyrique (see p115)

Culture after dark
- Palais de Tokyo (see p61)
- Nuit Blanche (see p34)
- Nuit des Musées (see p36)

MOULIN ROUGE®
PARIS
THE SHOW OF THE MOST
FAMOUS CABARET IN THE WORLD !
DINNER & SHOW AT 7PM FROM 180€
SHOW AT 9PM & 11PM : 109€
Féerie
MONTMARTRE
82, BLD DE CLICHY - 75018 PARIS
TEL : 33(0)1 53 09 82 82
WWW.MOULIN-ROUGE.CO
FACEBOOK.COM/LEMOULINROUGEOFFICI

Elsewhere, at the Châtelet (see p86) director Jean-Luc Choplin's populist programming has included a string of retro musicals recently, including big-hitters *West Side Story* and *Carousel*.

The main musical provider in summer is the Paris Quartier d'Eté festival (01.44.94.98.00, www.quartierdete.com), with concerts in gardens across the city. The Festival de Saint-Denis (01.48.13.06.07, www.festival-saint-denis.com) also offers top names in a spectacular setting.

Many venues offer cut-rate tickets to students (under 26) an hour before curtain-up. During the Fête de la Musique (21 June) all events are free, and freebies crop up at the Maison de Radio France and the Conservatoire de Paris.

Dance

Paris is home to a thriving dance scene, with sumptuous ballet productions at the Palais Garnier and international companies at Châtelet. Highlights at the Palais Garnier in 2014 include Gluck's *Orphée et Eurydice* and John Cranko's adaptation of *Onéguine*.

The Centre National de la Danse (1 rue Victor-Hugo, 93507 Pantin, 01.41.83.27.27, www.cnd.fr) is an impressive headquarters for France's 600-plus regional dance companies. Every season sees some kind of contemporary dance festival in or near Paris; the Festival d'Automne (see p34) has been a star fixture on the circuit for more than 40 years.

Theatre

French-speaking theatre buffs can choose from some 450 productions every week: from offbeat shows in small, independent venues to high-brow classics in grandiose auditoriums like the Comédie Française (2 rue Richelieu, 1st, 08.25.10.16.80, www.comedie-francaise.fr), whose staple shows feature the giants of French drama: the 2013-14 season includes the likes of Jean Anouilh's *Antigone* and Candide's *Voltaire*.

Fortunately for Anglophones, the Paris theatre scene is becoming ever more international, with translations of English and American plays firmly in vogue. The restored and re-baptised Odéon Théatre de l'Europe (pl de l'Odéon, 6th, 01.44.85.44.00, www.theatre-odeon.fr) offers plays in a number of languages, including at least one per season in English. Anglophone performances are occasionally programmed at the Théatre des Bouffes du Nord (37bis bd de la Chapelle, 10th, 01.46.07.34.50, www.bouffesdunord.com), while the cutting-edge MC93 Bobigny (1 bd Lénine, 93000 Bobigny, 01.41.60.72.72, www.mc93.com) regularly hosts international companies performing in their mother tongue.

Meanwhile, the Improfessionals (www.improfessionals.com) stage regular improvised performances in English, and Shakespeare in English is performed every summer at the Bois de Boulogne's Théâtre de Verdure du Jardin Shakespeare by London's Tower Theatre Company (www.towertheatre.org.uk).

What's on

For listings, the best sources are the weekly magazines *L'Officiel des Spectacles* and *Pariscope*. When it comes to films, take note of the two letters printed near the title: VO (*version originale*) means a screening in the original language with French subtitles; VF (*version française*) means that it's been dubbed into French. Cinema seats can be reserved at www.allocine.fr.

WHAT'S ON

Calendar

This is the pick of events as we went to press. On public holidays, or *jours feriés*, banks, many museums, most businesses and a number of restaurants close. New Year's Day, May Day, Bastille Day and Christmas Day are the most piously observed holidays. Dates in **bold** show public holidays.

October 2013

Until 13 Oct **Festival Paris Ile-de-France**
Various venues
www.festival-ile-de-france.com
Classical, contemporary and world music festival set in various venues.

Until 4 Nov **Roy Lichtenstein: Une Rétrospective**
Centre Pompidou
www.centrepompidou.fr.

Until 12 Jan 2014
Festival d'Automne
Various venues
www.festival-automne.com
This major annual arts festival focuses on bringing challenging theatre, dance and modern opera to Paris.

Until 6 Jan 2014 **Claude Simon: L'Inépuisable Chaos du Monde**
Centre Pompidou
www.centrepompidou.fr.

Until 6 Jan 2014 **Georges Braque**
Grand Palais
www.grandpalais.fr

Until 13 Jan 2014 **Frida Kahlo/ Diego Rivera: L'Art en Fusion**
Musée de l'Orangerie
www.musee-orangerie.fr

5 **Nuit Blanche**
Various venues
www.nuitblanche.paris.fr
Galleries, museums, swimming pools, bars and clubs stay open till very late for one night only.

5-6 **Prix de l'Arc de Triomphe**
Hippodrome de Longchamp
www.prixarcdetriomphe.com

France's richest flat race attracts the elite of horse racing.

9-13 **Fête des Vendanges de Montmartre**
Various venues
www.fetedesvendanges demontmartre.com
The modest 1,000-bottle harvest of the Clos Montmartre vineyard is the pretext for a weekend of street parties.

15 **Peter Gabriel**
Palais Omnisports de Paris Bercy
www.bercy.fr

15 Oct 2013-19 Jan 2014
Europunk: Une Révolution Artistique
Cité de la Musique
www.citedelamusique.fr

22 Oct-13 Nov **Così Fan Tutte**
Palais Garnier
www.operadeparis.fr

24-27 **FIAC**
Various venues
www.fiac.com
The Grand Palais is the main venue for this week-long contemporary art fair, with *hors les murs* works around town.

November 2013

Ongoing Claude Simon, Così Fan Tutte, Europunk, Festival d'Automne, Frida Kahlo/Diego Rivera, Georges Braque, Roy Lichtenstein (see Oct)

1 **Toussaint (All Saints' Day)**

6-12 **Festival des Inrockuptibles**
Various venues
www.lesinrocks.com
This festival attracts top indie, rock, techno and trip hop acts. Bill-toppers in 2013 include Foals and Suede.

11 **L'Armistice (Armistice Day)**
Arc de Triomphe
The President lays wreaths to honour the French combatants who died during the World Wars.

Mid Nov **Beaujolais Nouveau**
Various venues
www.beaujolaisgourmand.com
The new vintage is launched to packed cafés and wine bars.

16-19 **Written on Skin**
Salle Favart, Opéra Comique
www.opera-comique.com

16 Nov-22 Dec **Africolor**
Various venues in St-Denis
www.africolor.com
African music festival with a spirited wrap party.

December 2013

Ongoing Claude Simon, Europunk, Festival d'Automne, Frida Kahlo/ Diego Rivera, Georges Braque (see Oct); Africolor (see Nov)

Dec-Mar **Paris sur Glace**
Various venues
www.paris.fr
Paris opens up its outdoor ice rinks.

5 Dec 2013-1 Jan 2014
My Fair Lady
Théâtre du Châtelet
www.chatelet-theatre.com

24-25 **Noël (Christmas)**

31 **New Year's Eve**
Jubilant crowds swarm along the Champs-Elysées, and restaurants hold expensive soirées.

January 2014

Ongoing Claude Simon, Europunk, Festival d'Automne, Frida Kahlo/ Diego Rivera, Georges Braque (see Oct); My Fair Lady, Paris sur Glace (see Dec)

1 **Jour de l'An (New Year's Day)**
The Grande Parade de Paris brings floats, bands and dancers.

4-10 **Bolshoi Ballet**
Palais Garnier
www.operadeparis.fr

6 **Fête des Rois (Epiphany)**
Pâtisseries all sell *galettes des rois*, frangipane-filled cakes in which a *fêve*, or tiny charm, is hidden.

Mid Jan **Mass for Louis XVI**
Chapelle Expiatoire
Royalists and right-wing crackpots mourn the end of the monarchy.

29 **Depeche Mode**
Palais Omnisports de Paris Bercy
www.bercy.fr

February 2014

Ongoing Paris sur Glace (see Dec)

Early Feb **Paris Face Cachée**
Various venues
www.parisfacecachee.fr
Paris Face Cachée lifts the lid on places you might not have known existed, and gives participants a chance to experience Paris at work behind the scenes.

1 **Six Nations: France/England**
Stade de France
www.rbs6nations.com

8 **Bryn Terfel**
Salle Pleyel
www.sallepleyel.fr

9 **Six Nations: France/Italy**
Stade de France
www.rbs6nations.com

11 Feb-11 May **Gustave Doré: L'Imaginaire au Pouvoir**
Musée d'Orsay
www.musee-orsay.fr

13 **Nouvel An Chinois**
Various venues
Lion and dragon dances, and lively martial arts demonstrations.

14 Feb-12 Mar **Madama Butterfly**
Opéra Bastille
www.operadeparis.fr

17-25 **Pelléas et Mélisande**
Salle Favart, Opéra Comique
www.opera-comique.com

March 2014

Ongoing Paris sur Glace (see Dec); Gustave Doré, Madama Butterfly, Six Nations (see Feb)

Early Mar-Apr **Banlieues Bleues**
Various venues in Seine St-Denis
www.banlieuesbleues.org
Featuring five weeks of top-quality jazz, blues, R&B and soul.

Paris Face Cachée

11 Mar-24 Aug **Great Black Music**
Cité de la Musique
www.citedelamusique.fr

15 **Six Nations: France/Ireland**
Stade de France
www.rbs6nations.com

End Mar **Printemps du Cinéma**
Various venues
www.printempsducinema.com
Film tickets are cut to a bargain €3.50.

End Mar-end June **Festival de l'Imaginaire**
Various venues
www.festivaldelimaginaire.com
This festival covers everything from Balinese dance to lute music.

29 **Le Chemin de la Croix (Way of the Cross)**
Square Willette
Good Friday pilgrimage as crowds follow the Archbishop of Paris from the bottom of Montmartre to Sacré-Coeur.

31 **Pâques (Easter Sunday)**

April 2014

Ongoing Gustave Doré (see Feb); Banlieues Bleues, Festival de l'Imaginaire, Great Black Music (see Mar)

Early Apr-end May **Foire du Trône**
Pelouse de Reuilly
www.foiredutrone.com
France's biggest funfair.

6 **Marathon de Paris**
Av des Champs-Elysées to av Foch
www.parismarathon.com

End Apr-early May **Grand Marché d'Art Contemporain**
Place de la Bastille
www.joel-garcia-organisation.fr
Annual arts fair.

May 2014

Ongoing Gustave Doré (see Feb); Festival de l'Imaginaire,

Loud and proud

Fanfare is the soundtrack to many a street party.

A cacophonous hybrid of Baltic brass band, New Orleans marching band and student rag day parade, *fanfare* is the true sound of the Paris streets. If you're in the capital for Fête de la Musique, Beaujolais Nouveau, a rugby match, political protest or just about any other mass gathering, you're sure to hear and see one. Though they take many strange forms today, Paris's *fanfares* – or *fanfares des beaux-arts* – have their roots in the carnivalesque antics of the city's architecture students. Every spring from 1892 to 1966, the students held a Bal des Quat'z'arts, a costumed procession through the streets followed by an orgiastic 'pagan' ball accompanied by *fanfares*, originally playing *bigotphones* (a kind of papier mâché kazoo), and later moving on to brass and woodwind instruments.

'A *fanfare* should be *faux, fort et pas en place* – false, loud and with no rhythm,' says Raphael Pluot, trombonist with the Chili Kipu's, whose costumes include Rod Stewart wigs, leopardskin Spandex and drag. One of the 30 or so Paris fanfares, they have their HQ at Le Square bar (165 rue du Temple, 3rd).

Paris's funkiest *fanfare* is the Tarace Boulba collective (www.taraceboulba.com), formed by two members of Les Négresses Vertes in 1993. With 1,000 members, it turns out in groups of anything from ten to 70, playing funk and Afrobeat in an atmosphere of crazed abandon.

Great Black Music (see Mar); Foire du Trône, Grand Marché d'Art Contemporain (see Apr)

1 **Fête du Travail (May Day)**
Unions march in eastern Paris.

3-21 **Orphée et Eurydice**
Palais Garnier
www.operadeparis.fr

8 **Victoire 1945 (VE Day)**

9 **Jour de l'Ascension**

Mid May **Le Printemps des Rues**
Various venues
www.leprintempsdesrues.com
Annual street-theatre festival.

Mid May **La Nuit des Musées**
Various venues
www.nuitdesmusees.culture.fr
For one night, major museums stay open late and put on special events.

Mid May **Art St-Germain-des-Prés**
Various venues
www.artsaintgermaindespres.com
More than 50 galleries get together.

Mid May **Festival Jazz à St-Germain-des-Prés**
Various venues
www.espritjazz.com
A ten-day celebration of jazz and blues.

Mid-late May **Quinzaine des Réalisateurs**
Forum des Images
www.quinzaine-realisateurs.com
The Cannes Directors' Fortnight programme comes to Paris.

20 **Bobby McFerrin**
Théâtre du Châtelet
www.chatelet-theatre.com

20 **Lundi de Pentecôte (Whit Monday)**

Late May-late June **Festival de St-Denis**
Various venues in St-Denis
www.festival-saint-denis.com
Four weeks of concerts showcasing top-quality classical music.

End May-early June **French Open**
Stade Roland Garros
www.rolandgarros.com
Paris plays host to the most prestigious clay court competition in the world. Rafael Nadal and Serena Williams will be defending champions in 2014.

June 2014

Ongoing Festival de l'Imaginaire, Great Black Music (see Mar); Festival de St-Denis, French Open (see May)

Early June **Fête du Vélo**
Across Paris
www.tousavelo.com
Cycling tours and activities as Paris's two-wheelers take to the streets.

Early June-July **Paris Jazz Festival**
Parc Floral de Paris
www.parisjazzfestival.fr
Two months of free jazz weekends at the lovely Parc Floral.

June-July **Festival Chopin à Paris**
Orangerie de Bagatelle
www.frederic-chopin.com
Romantic candlelit piano recitals in the Bois de Boulogne.

2-20 **La Traviata**
Opéra Bastille
www.operadeparis.fr

21 **Fête de la Musique**
Various venues
www.fetedelamusique.fr
Free gigs take place across the city.

24 June-30 Sept **Jean-Baptiste Carpeaux**
Musée d'Orsay
www.musee-orsay.fr

Late June **Gay Pride March**
www.inter-lgbt.org
Outrageous floats and costumes parade towards Bastille, followed by an official party and various club events.

Gay Pride March

Late June **Solidays**
Hippodrome de Longchamp
www.solidays.org
A music bash for AIDS charities.

Late June-early July **Festival Paris Cinéma**
Various venues
www.pariscinema.org
This festival features over 200 French and international films.

July 2014

Ongoing Great Black Music (see Mar); Festival Chopin à Paris, Festival Paris Cinéma, Jean-Baptiste Carpeaux, Paris Jazz Festival (see June)

Early-late July **Etés de la Danse**
Théâtre du Chatêlet
www.lesetesdeladanse.com
International dance festival. The San Francisco Ballet will guest in 2014.

July-Aug **Cinéma en Plein Air**
Parc de la Villette
www.villette.com
Free films screened under the stars.

3 **Daniel Barenboim**
Salle Pleyel
www.sallepleyel.fr

14 **Quatorze Juillet (Bastille Day)**
Various venues
France's national holiday commemorates the Revolution. At 10am, crowds line the Champs-Elysées. By night, the Champ de Mars fills for fireworks.

Mid July-mid Aug **Paris, Quartier d'Eté**
Various venues
www.quartierdete.com
Classical and jazz concerts, plus dance and theatre, in outdoor venues.

Mid July-mid Aug **Paris-Plages**
Various venues
www.paris.fr
Palm trees, huts, hammocks and 2,000 tonnes of sand on both banks of the Seine lend a seaside vibe to the city.

Late July **Tour de France**
Av des Champs-Elysées
www.letour.fr
The ultimate endurance test reaches a climax on the Champs-Elysées.

August 2014

Ongoing Great Black Music (see Mar); Jean-Baptiste Carpeaux (see June); Cinéma en Plein Air, Paris-Plages, Paris Quartier d'Eté (see July)

15 **Fête de l'Assomption (Assumption Day)**
Cathédrale Notre-Dame de Paris

Late Aug **Rock en Seine**
Domaine National de St-Cloud
www.rockenseine.com
Three days, one world-class line-up of rock and indie groups.

September 2014

Ongoing Jean-Baptiste Carpeaux (see June)

Early Sept **Jazz à la Villette**
Parc de la Villette
www.jazzalavillette.com
This is one of the best jazz festivals in a city that loves jazz music.

Early Sept-mid Oct **Festival Paris Ile-de-France**
See Oct 2013.

Sept **Festival Classique au Vert**
Parc Floral de Paris
www.classiqueauvert.fr
Free classical recitals take place in a delightful park setting.

Mid Sept **Techno Parade**
Various venues
www.technoparade.fr
This parade (finishing up at Bastille) marks the start of electronic music festival Rendez-vous Electroniques.

Mid Sept **We Love Green Festival**
Parc de Bagatelle, Bois de Boulogne
www.welovegreen.fr
This eco festival is held in the Parc de Bagatelle. Highlights for 2012 included Norah Jones and Django Django.

Mid Sept-late Dec **Festival d'Automne**
See Oct 2013.

Mid Sept **Journées du Patrimoine**
Various venues
www.journeesdupatrimoine.culture.fr
Embassies, ministries, scientific establishments and corporate headquarters open their doors to the public.

Late Sept **Fête de la Gastronomie**
Various venues
www.fete-gastronomie.fr.
This festival celebrates French cuisine.

October 2014

Ongoing Festival d'Automne, Festival Paris Ile-de-France (see Sept)

Early Oct **Nuit Blanche**
See Oct 2013.

Early Oct **Prix de l'Arc de Triomphe**
See Oct 2013.

Early Oct **Fête des Vendanges de Montmartre**
See Oct 2013.

Mid Oct **FIAC**
See Oct 2013.

November 2014

Ongoing Festival d'Automne (see Sept)

1 **Toussaint (All Saints' Day)**

Early Nov **Festival des Inrockuptibles**
See Nov 2013.

11 **L'Armistice (Armistice Day)**
See Nov 2013.

Mid Nov **Beaujolais Nouveau**
See Nov 2013.

Nov-Dec **Africolor**
See Nov 2013.

December 2014

Ongoing Africolor (see Nov); Festival d'Automne (see Sept)

Dec-Mar **Paris sur Glace**
See Dec 2013.

24-25 **Noël (Christmas)**

31 **New Year's Eve**

Itineraries

Comédie Française

Dead Famous

The French capital has some of history's most influential characters buried on its soil; the Montparnasse cemetery alone shelters hundreds of writers and artists within its confines, including the likes of Baudelaire, Beckett and Man Ray. But these are the lucky ones. Other historical figures did not always get to their final resting place in one piece – their bones, hair or innards led to great traffic back in the day. This trip around central Paris gives you the chance to get up close and personal with some of the city's more macabre relics.

Start on place du Palais-Royal, 1st (M° Palais Royal Musée du Louvre). Turn your back on the Louvre and walk into the **Comédie Française** (2 rue de Richelieu, 1st). Founded in 1640 by Louis XIV with Molière as its lead playwright, 'La Comédie' is still the only state theatre with a permanent troupe of actors. In the foyer, look out for an old armchair inside a glass cage. It is believed to be the one from which Molière delivered his last lines at a performance of *Le Malade Imaginaire* in 1673. He died shortly after the curtain fell. As a tribute to the playwright, the seat is put back on stage every 15 January, the anniversary of his birth.

In the same room, the statue of an old man regards theatregoers with a sarcastic smile. You may have recognised Voltaire, the French Enlightenment philosopher, immortalised here by sculptor Jean-Antoine Houdon. But it is a lesser-known fact that the statue serves as reliquary for the philosopher's brain, sealed inside its pedestal.

After Voltaire's death in 1778, the apothecary who performed the autopsy removed his brain and heart and put them in boiling alcohol to solidify them. Voltaire's brain then passed through many hands before finally ending up at the Comédie in 1924.

As for his heart, it remained on display for a long time at the Château de Ferney, where Voltaire died. It was only when the philosopher's body was declared 'property of the state' in 1791 that the heart was given to Napoléon III, who decided to keep it at the Imperial Library, now the **Bibliothèque Nationale – Richelieu**. Walk to the entrance – currently at 5 rue de Vivienne, as the site is under renovation until 2017 – and ask to see the *salon d'honneur*, a stunning oak-veneered room presided over by a statue of Voltaire identical to the one at the Comédie. The heart is enclosed in its wooden pedestal.

The next destination is on the Left Bank, a perfect opportunity to test out Vélib, Paris's hugely popular municipal bike scheme. There is a *borne* opposite the library, at 71 rue de Richelieu.

Head south and turn left into rue des Petits Champs. Cycle across place des Victoires and turn right into rue du Louvre. Follow the traffic all the way down to the river, and turn left on to quai du Louvre, a section of riverbank lined with *bouquinistes*. Carry on to Pont au Change, where you can use the bus lane to cycle across the bridge. Once on the island, keep going

Bibliothèque Nationale – Richelieu

Eglise St-Etienne-du-Mont

south, passing the impressive gates of the Palais de Justice, and turn left on to quai du Marché Neuf. Go straight ahead until you're facing Notre-Dame cathedral. You can drop your bike at the *borne* on the side of the square, on rue d'Arcole.

Head south across Pont au Double. On quai de Montebello, walk around the small park in front of you and take rue de la Bûcherie. If you're feeling peckish after all that cultural dissection, you can indulge yourself with a dish of gently sautéed brains at offal specialist **Ribouldingue** (see p147) around the corner.

With rested feet and a full stomach, you're ready for more relic-hunting. Find rue St-Jacques at the end of rue de la Bûcherie and walk down to rue Soufflot. The columns of the **Panthéon** (see p146) should be clear to see on your left. As the last home of many French *grands hommes*, the Panthéon could be seen as the ultimate reliquary, even though there's not much to peep at in terms of old bones. The crypt gathers the shrines of over 70 illustrious French figures, including Victor Hugo, Alexandre Dumas and our old friend Voltaire, whose carcass – or what remains of it – can finally rest in peace here.

A somewhat more sensational relic can be found in the **Eglise St-Etienne-du-Mont** (see p142), just around the corner from the Panthéon. The church, a masterpiece of Flamboyant Gothic architecture, displays a finger bone belonging to Sainte Geneviève, the patron saint of Paris, in a glass reliquary next to her sarcophagus.

Next, retrace your steps towards boulevard St-Michel and brace yourself for a creepy rendezvous. You can pick up a Vélib from the *borne* at 174 rue St-Jacques or cross through the Jardin du Luxembourg for some much-needed greenery.

From boulevard St-Michel, take rue de Médicis, followed by rue de Vaugirard which hugs the north side of the Jardin du Luxembourg. After passing the Sénat, turn right into rue Garancière, then left into rue St-Sulpice. Carry on along rue du Vieux Colombier until you reach

Panthéon

rue de Sèvres. Look out for Vaneau métro station and the Vélib *borne* around the corner.

Find the **Chapelle des Lazaristes**, identifiable by its tall green doors next to no.95 rue de Sèvres, and climb up the stairs to the side of the altar. Here lies the surprisingly fresh-looking corpse of Saint Vincent de Paul, patron saint of the poor. While his skeleton was preserved in its entirety, his face and hands were covered in wax and moulded to resemble the deceased, giving the disturbing impression that he passed away only minutes ago. The people of Paris, very attached to Saint Vincent de Paul, clubbed together to pay for the sumptuous silver and gold coffin in which the body lies.

Pick up a Vélib on rue Vaneau and head north. Turn left into rue de Babylone and then right into boulevard des Invalides. Keep cycling towards the Seine, with the golden dome of **Les Invalides** (see p124) on your left, the last resting place of Napoléon I. The emperor could easily win the title of most scattered cadaver in history. While his heart and innards are in Austria, you will need to travel to the US to get anywhere near his penis.

After such intense reflections, you should arrive on quai d'Orsay, by the Seine. Cross the Pont Alexandre III and turn left on to cours Albert I. At place de l'Alma, where other pilgrims are gathered by the Princess Diana memorial, take avenue du Président Wilson on your right. Carry on until you reach place du Trocadéro. A Vélib *borne* on avenue d'Eylau will allow you to dispose of your bike.

The **Musée de l'Homme** (17 place du Trocadéro, 16th, closed for refurbishment until 2015) is home to philosopher René Descartes' skull. The rest of his body is buried on the Left Bank, which makes the perfect start to another trek. But by now you will probably have had your share of gravestones for the day. Take a pew on the steps and enjoy one of the best views there is of the city. Chances are you've never felt more alive.

ITINERARIES

Castel Béranger

Meet the Moderns

In stark contrast with its current rather snooty image (the area is the epitome of thorough bourgeois respectability), during the early 1900s the 16th arrondissement was a hotbed of avant-garde architecture and experimentation, and is today home to some of the capital's seminal modernist buildings. This walk explores the artists' studios, apartment blocks and luxury villas that sprang up in a district that had only recently been incorporated into Paris proper.

START: On rue La Fontaine at **Castel Béranger** (no.14), the art nouveau masterpiece of Hector Guimard, before dropping in for an early coffee break at the whimsically pretty **Café Antoine** (no.17, 01.40.50.14.30), inserted into another Guimard building with clever wraparound corners. Next admire the rampart tendrils sprouting from the wrought-iron fence of the **Hôtel Mezzara** at no.60, which was also designed by Guimard, for textile manufacturer Paul Mezzara. Further along at no.65, don't miss the 1920s Studio Building designed by modernist maverick Henri Sauvage.

Turning right into avenue Mozart, you'll stumble across Guimard's former home at no.122, where he lived with his American artist wife, Adeline Oppenheim. On the corner as you turn left into rue Jasmin stands an imposing Beaux Arts-style apartment building – exactly the sort of neo-Renaissance frippery against which Guimard was rebelling.

Turn right into rue Henrich Heine, then left on rue du Dr Blanche. Here you'll find the **Fondation Le Corbusier** (8 square du Dr Blanche, 01.42.88.75.72, www.fondationlecorbusier.fr), which is housed in two villas designed by the architect in 1923. The interior reveals his mastery of multiple viewpoints, fluidity of space and surprising use of colour.

Just off rue du Dr Blanche, turning right into Rue Mallet-Stevens, stand six exclusive Cubist houses by Robert Mallet-Stevens, the glamorous architect and designer who best combined the elegance of art deco with the rigours of modernism. Back at 5 rue du Dr Blanche are artists' studios by Pierre Patout, who also decked out the luxury cruise liner *Normandie* (art deco was known as *'le style paquebot'*).

Head right down rue de l'Assomption, then turn left on to avenue Mozart and right on to rue de Passy at La Muette métro station, with glitzy art deco brasserie **La Rotonde** (12 chaussée de la Muette, 16th, 01.45.04.01.32) on the corner. Next to the Passy covered market, take rue Duban, then rue Singer towards the river on to rue Raynouard. Nos.51-55 were designed by Auguste Perret in reinforced concrete, cunningly tinted golden yellow to match the traditional Paris stone. Best known for housing the Théâtre des Champs-Elysées, this building contained apartments and Perret's architectural offices. Turn left on rue Raynouard, past the Maison de Balzac, and cross place du Costa Rica into rue Benjamin-Franklin.

There's more Perret at no.25bis (a) where, behind the leaf motif tiles, the 1904 building was one of the first to be constructed around a concrete frame. The revolutionary structure freed up the floor plan from load-bearing walls, creating the light, airy spaces associated with modernism – as well as giving all the occupants a view of the Seine. The walk ends at Trocadéro with the **Palais de Chaillot**, an example of gigantesque 1930s state classical revival. It was designed by Léon Azéma, Louis-Hippolyte Boileau and Jacques Carlu for the 1937 Exposition Universelle, with two curved wings, giant bronze sculptures by Henri Bouchard and Pommier, and quotations by Paul Valéry. Pop into the **Cité de l'Architecture** (see p57), in the east wing, for a more thorough tour of French architecture past, present and future.

Fondation Le Corbusier p47

Vintage on a Vespa

Vintage shops in London and New York have been adding retro flair to wardrobes for years, but it has taken Paris – the city of 'serious' haute couture – a little longer to jump on the bandwagon. Today, though, the city is dripping in everything your vintage heart could desire, from rare 1920s Chanel accessories and art deco lighting to '60s rock LPs and '80s kitten boots. And the good news is that many of the best vintage boutiques are condensed on the Right Bank between Palais-Royal and Faidherbe Chaligny (east of Bastille) – an easy distance to cover in one well-planned afternoon.

To really look the part, and for whizzing between the shops for maximum rifling time, hire a vintage-style Vespa from **Left Bank Scooters** (06.78.12.04.24, www.leftbankscooters.com; over-20s only). There are two models to choose from, each with a handy compartment for stashing your shopping: the metallic green, 1955-style Vespa LXV 125cc with chrome trimmings and leather seats (€80 a day) or the red Vespa S 50cc (€70 a day), which is based on the 1962 Primavera model. Both can be delivered to and picked up from your hotel at no extra cost.

French law now stipulates that you need a motorcycle licence to drive a 125cc scooter, but your standard driving licence will do for the 50cc. And don't worry too much about parking. Where possible, look out for parking bays for motorbikes (*parking moto*). But if you can't find room under the official parking sign, the traffic police are generally pretty lenient, as long as you don't block the road or pavement.

START: Park your Vespa at the *parking moto* area on the corner of rue Paul Bert and rue Faidherbe, 11th (M° Faidherbe Chaligny).

Most vintage boutiques on this tour only open in the afternoon, so start with a retro lunch on rue Paul Bert. If you're looking for old school Paris, **Bistrot Paul Bert** (see p107) never fails to deliver, with its zinc bar, 1930s tiles and lip-smacking dishes such as suckling pig with potato gratin. Alternatively, for a mix of hippy chic and slabs of Argentinean steak, try **Unico** (15 rue Paul Bert, 11th, 01.43.67.68.08, www.resto-unico.com), a former 1970s butcher's shop that has kept its original orange and white tiles.

After lunch, leave your Vespa and walk down rue Faidherbe, stopping off briefly to admire **Les Années Scooter** (23 rue Faidherbe, 11th, 01.46.59.47.90, www.lesanneesscooter.com), a den of mid 20th-century scooters, table lights, clocks, jukeboxes and street signs. Philippe, the passionate owner, can tell you the story behind every piece on display. A few doors further down, **Restaur'Bronze** (41 rue Faidherbe, 01.43.71.44.25, www.restaurbronze.com) is one of the last places in Paris to specialise in metal objects from the 1930s and '40s, including some show-stopping art deco lights, all perfectly restored by owner Marc Arguence, who learned the trade from his father.

One thing's for sure: you can't scoot around town with a 1932 crystal candelabra in tow, so head back to your Vespa. Drive back down rue Faidherbe and turn left down rue de Charonne. Park up opposite the Bistrot du Peintre café (where you'll be coming back for coffee in a while) – there are usually a few free *moto* spots available. Take a right down bohemian rue Keller, lined with galleries, bars and emerging clothes designers.

Turn left on to rue de la Roquette and walk to **Adöm** (35 & 56 rue de la Roquette, 01.48.07.15.94), which is split into two small boutiques. Girls head to no.56 for 1970s and '80s jeans and '60s shift dresses, while boys drop into no.35 for 1950s baseball jackets, cowboy boots and a selection of sneakers.

Bistrot Paul Bert

Continue along rue de la Roquette, then turn right into rue Saint-Sabin. **Born Bad** (11 rue Saint-Sabin, 11th, 01.43.38.41.78, www.bornbad.fr) is an Aladdin's cave of second-hand new wave, soul, 1950s rock and '60s surf LPs and CDs that attracts music-savvy Parisians from across town.

Now retrace your steps to the art nouveau surroundings of **Le Bistro du Peintre** (116 av Ledru-Rollin, 11th, 01.47.00.34.39, www.bistrotdupeintre.com), where you can peruse your purchases over a fortifying *café au lait*.

Sustenance over, the boutique-filled Haut Marais beckons. Return to your Vespa and head south down av Ledru-Rollin, then right on to car-clogged rue du Faubourg-St-Antoine. At place de la Bastille, take a right up bd Beaumarchais and park near St-Sébastien Froissart métro station.

During the last few years, this previously forgotten northern stretch of the Marais has been transformed into one of Paris's hottest shopping areas, with numerous one-off boutiques – including two wonderful vintage finds. The first is aesthete William Moricet's tiny **Studio W** (6 rue du Pont-aux-Choux, 3rd, 01.44.78.05.02), a sparsely stocked vintage shop where quality is king. There are clothes – mostly rare designer vintage dresses by YSL and Chanel – but it's the accessories that shine: 1970s boots, '80s stilettos and enough dinky '60s leather clutch bags to make your heart swoon. The second shop, **Matières à Reflexion** (19 rue de Poitou, 3rd, 01.42.72.16.31, www.matieresareflexion.com), is the ultimate vintage bag-maker – a place where old leather jackets and clothes are crafted into one-off bags and satchels fastened with aged brass hardware.

From here, hop back on the bike and whizz down rue du Pont-au-Choux, turn left on to rue de Turenne and then right on to rue St-Antoine. Park near St-Paul métro station. Walk up rue Pavée and turn left on to rue du Roi de Sicile, and you'll find two vintage hotspots. For punky London retro style, try **Noir Kennedy** (see p113), which is chock full of leather coats, lumberjack shirts, ripped jeans and funky 1980s T-shirts. If '40s fashion is more your style, try **Mam'Zelle Swing** (35 rue du Roi de Sicile, 4th, 01.48.87.04.06, www.mamzelle-swing.com), where Bérénice stocks well-selected pieces, many with price tags under €100.

Back on your Vespa, drive all the way down rue de Rivoli, turn right up rue de l'Echelle and right down rue St-Honoré, then park wherever you can at Palais-Royal. From here, take a stroll under the arcades of the Palais-Royal gardens to Paris's ultimate temple of luxury vintage, **Didier Ludot** (see p81). You just have to catch a glimpse of the window displays to see there is something special about Ludot's pieces, many of which look like they could have been cast-offs from Audrey Hepburn or Marilyn Monroe.

If you're daring enough to go in, you'll find outfits by today's up-and-coming designers too – or the vintage pieces of tomorrow, as the owner likes to call them.

Shopping over for the afternoon, head back east for a fittingly retro-style dinner at red- and white-checked **Astier** (44 rue Jean-Pierre Timbaud, 11th, 01.43.57.16.35, www.restaurant-astier.com), where Cyril Boulet and Nicolas Frezel revive vintage French dishes such as smoked herring, braised Charolais beef, and vanilla cream with sophisticated flair.

Didier Ludot

Paris by Area

Champs-Elysées & Western Paris

In truth, *'la plus belle avenue du monde'* is not especially beautiful and it heaves with cars and crowds at pretty much any time of the day. The hordes aren't here for beauty, though. They're here for the shops, which the avenue, after years in the retail doldrums, now supplies in abundance thanks to an influx of megabrands such as Banana Republic, Abercrombie & Fitch, and Levi's. Fortunately, amid all this rampant consumerism are a good number of museums covering such cerebral topics as architecture, human evolution and life on the ocean waves, plus a greatly extended Palais de Tokyo that now lays claim to the title of Europe's largest contemporary art centre.

The western end of the Champs-Elysées is dominated by the Arc de Triomphe towering above place Charles-de-Gaulle, also known as L'Etoile. Built by Napoleon I, the arch was modified to celebrate the Revolutionary armies. From the top, visitors can gaze over the square (commissioned later by Haussmann), with 12 avenues radiating out in all directions. South of the arch, avenue Kléber leads to the monumental buildings of the panoramic Trocadéro.

Sights & museums

Arc de Triomphe

Pl Charles-de-Gaulle, 8th (01.55.37. 73.77). M° Charles de Gaulle Etoile.
Open *Oct-Mar* 10am-10.30pm daily. *Apr-Sept* 10am-11pm daily.
Admission €9.50; free-€6 reductions.
Map p58 B2 ❶
The Arc de Triomphe has long been one of the capital's quintessential landmarks, drawing in 1.5 million visitors a year. But until recently, the interior was unimpressive, having changed little since the 1930s. After a revamp by

architect Christophe Girault and artist Maurice Benayouna, a new museum opened with interactive screens and multimedia displays allowing visitors to look at other arches around Europe and the world, as well as screens exploring the Arc's tumultuous 200-year history. But the main reason to head up here is the rooftop view, one of the finest in the city.

Bateaux-Mouches

Pont de l'Alma, 8th (01.42.25.96.10, www.bateaux-mouches.fr). M° Alma-Marceau. **Tickets** €11.50; free-€5.50 reductions. **Map** p58 C4 ❷

If you're after a whirlwind tour of the sights and don't mind tourists and schoolchildren, this, the oldest cruise operation on the Seine, is a good option.

Cinéaqua

2 av des Nations Unies, 16th (01.40.69.23.23, www.cineaqua.com). M° Trocadéro. **Open** 10am-7pm daily. **Admission** €19.50; free-€15.50 reductions. **Map** p58 B5 ❸

This aquarium and three-screen cinema is a wonderful attraction and a key element in the renaissance of the once moribund Trocadéro.

Cité de l'Architecture et du Patrimoine

Palais de Chaillot, 1 pl du Trocadéro, 16th (01.58.51.52.00, www.citechaillot.fr). M° Trocadéro. **Open** 11am-7pm Mon, Wed, Fri-Sun; 11am-9pm Thur. **Admission** €8; free-€5 reductions. **Map** p58 A4 ❹

Opened in 2007 in the east wing of the Palais de Chaillot, this architecture and heritage museum impresses by its scale. The ground floor is filled with mock-ups of cathedral façades and heritage buildings, and interactive screens place the models in context. Upstairs, darkened rooms house full-scale copies of medieval and Renaissance murals and stained-glass windows. The highlight of the modern architecture section is the walk-in replica of an apartment from Le Corbusier's Cité Radieuse in Marseille. Temporary exhibitions are housed in the basement.

Galerie-Musée Baccarat

11 pl des Etats-Unis, 16th (01.40.22.11.00, www.baccarat.fr). M° Boissière or Iéna. **Open** 10am-6pm Mon, Wed-Sat. **Admission** €5; free-€3.50 reductions. **Map** p58 B3 ❺

Philippe Starck has created a neo-rococo wonderland in the former mansion of the Vicomtesse de Noailles. See items by Georges Chevalier and Ettore Sottsass, services made for princes and maharajahs, and show-off items made for the great exhibitions of the 1800s.

Galeries Nationales du Grand Palais

3 av du Général-Eisenhower, 8th (01.44.13.17.17, www.grandpalais.fr). M° Champs-Elysées Clemenceau. **Open** times vary. **Admission** €11-€12; free-€8 reductions. **Map** p59 E4 ❻

The Grand Palais was built for the 1900 Exposition Universelle and the design was the work of three different architects. During World War II, it played the role of reluctant host to Nazi tanks. In 1994, the glass-roofed central hall was closed when bits of metal started falling off. After major restoration, the Palais reopened in 2005 and now hosts major exhibitions.

Musée d'Art Moderne de la Ville de Paris

11 av du Président-Wilson, 16th (01.53.67.40.00, www.mam.paris.fr). M° Alma Marceau or Iéna. **Open** 10am-6pm Tue-Sun. **Admission** free. *Temporary exhibitions* €5-€11; free-€5.50 reductions. No credit cards. **Map** p58 B4 ❼

This monumental 1930s building, housing the city's modern art collection, is strong on the Cubists, Fauves, the Delaunays, Rouault and Ecole de Paris artists Soutine and van Dongen. The museum was briefly closed in May 2010 after the theft of

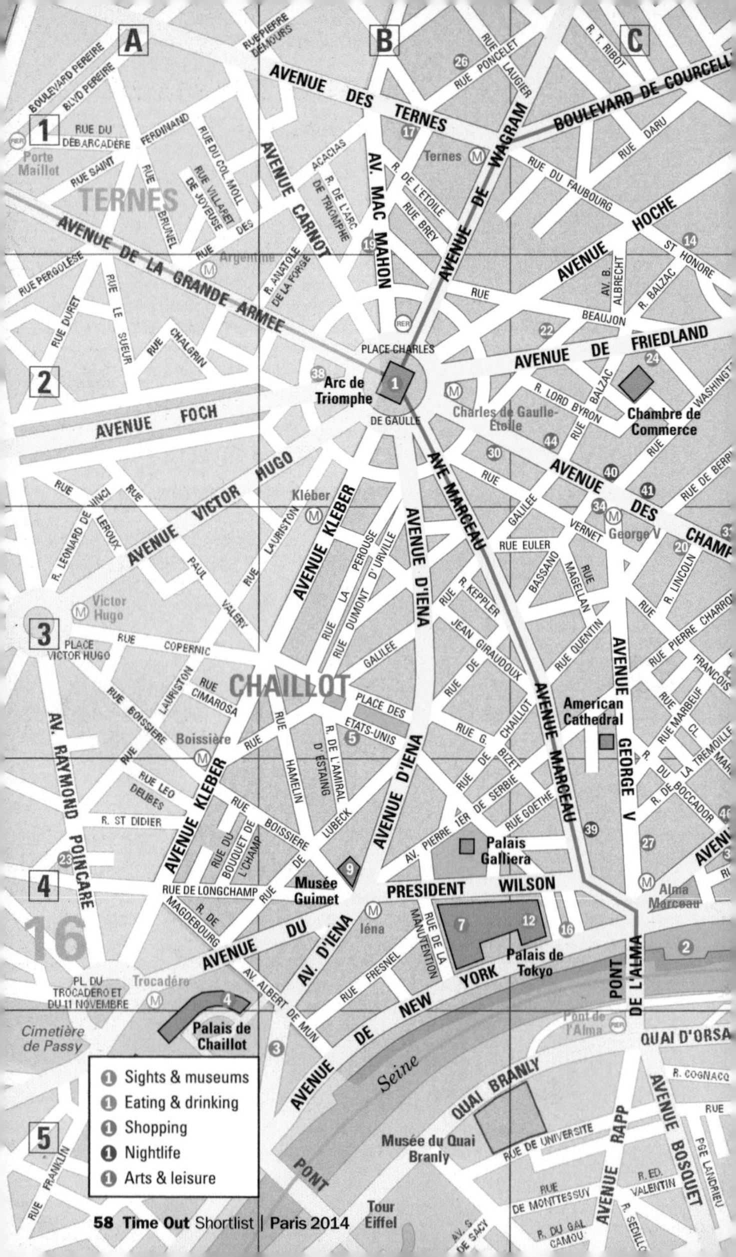
A
B
C
1
2
3
4
5
AVENUE DES TERNES
BOULEVARD PEREIRE
BLVD PEREIRE
RUE PIERRE DEMOURS
RUE PONCELET
RUE LAUGIER
R. T. RIBOT
BOULEVARD DE COURCELLES
RUE DU DÉBARCADÈRE
Porte Maillot
RUE SAINT FERDINAND
RUE BRUNEL
RUE DU COL. MOLL
RUE VILLARET DE JOYEUSE
TERNES
AVENUE CARNOT
ACACIAS
R. DE L'ARC DE TRIOMPHE
AV. MAC MAHON
R. DE L'ETOILE
RUE BREY
Ternes
AVENUE DE WAGRAM
RUE DARU
RUE DU FAUBOURG
ST HONORE
AVENUE HOCHE
AVENUE DE LA GRANDE ARMEE
RUE DES
Argentine
RUE PERGOLESE
RUE LE SUEUR
RUE DURET
R. ANATOLE DE LA FORGE
RUE CHALGRIN
AV. B. ALBRECHT
R. BALZAC
RUE BEAUJON
PLACE CHARLES DE GAULLE
Arc de Triomphe
AVENUE DE FRIEDLAND
Chambre de Commerce
R. LORD BYRON
RUE BALZAC
WASHINGTON
Charles de Gaulle-Etoile
AVENUE FOCH
AVENUE VICTOR HUGO
RUE DE VINCI
RUE LEROUX
R. LEONARD DE
RUE PAUL VALERY
Kléber
RUE LAURISTON
AVENUE KLEBER
AVENUE D'IENA
AVE MARCEAU
RUE GALILEE
AVENUE DES CHAMPS
RUE DE BERRI
RUE VERNET
George V
RUE EULER
RUE BASSANO
RUE MAGELLAN
R. LINCOLN
RUE LA PEROUSE
RUE DUMONT D'URVILLE
R. KEPPLER
RUE JEAN GIRAUDOUX
RUE QUENTIN
RUE PIERRE CHARRON
Victor Hugo
PLACE VICTOR HUGO
RUE COPERNIC
CHAILLOT
RUE DE CHAILLOT
AVENUE MARCEAU
AVENUE GEORGE V
American Cathedral
RUE FRANCOIS
RUE MARBEUF
RUE CL. MAROT
R. DU BOCCADOR
LA TREMOILLE
AV. RAYMOND POINCARE
RUE CIMAROSA
RUE LAURISTON
RUE BOISSIERE
Boissière
PLACE DES ETATS-UNIS
R. DE L'AMIRAL D'ESTAING
RUE HAMELIN
RUE G. BIZET
RUE DE SERBIE
RUE GOETHE
RUE LEO DELIBES
R. ST DIDIER
RUE DU BOUQUET DE L'CHAMP
RUE DE LUBECK
AV. PIERRE 1ER DE SERBIE
Palais Galliera
Musée Guimet
RUE DE LONGCHAMP
R. DE MAGDEBOURG
PRESIDENT WILSON
Iéna
RUE DE LA MANUTENTION
Alma Marceau
16
AVENUE DU
AV. D'IENA
RUE FRESNEL
Palais de Tokyo
AVENUE DE NEW YORK
PONT DE L'ALMA
PL. DU TROCADERO ET DU 11 NOVEMBRE
Trocadéro
AV. ALBERT DE MUN
Cimetière de Passy
Palais de Chaillot
Pont de l'Alma
QUAI D'ORSAY
Seine
QUAI BRANLY
R. COGNACQ
AVENUE BOSQUET
Sights & museums
Eating & drinking
Shopping
Nightlife
Arts & leisure
Musée du Quai Branly
RUE DE UNIVERSITE
AVENUE RAPP
RUE FRANKLIN
PONT
RUE DE MONTTESSUY
R. ED. VALENTIN
PGE LANDRIEU
Tour Eiffel
R. DU GAL CAMOU
AV. DE SACY
R. SEDILLOT

Champs-Elysées & Western Paris

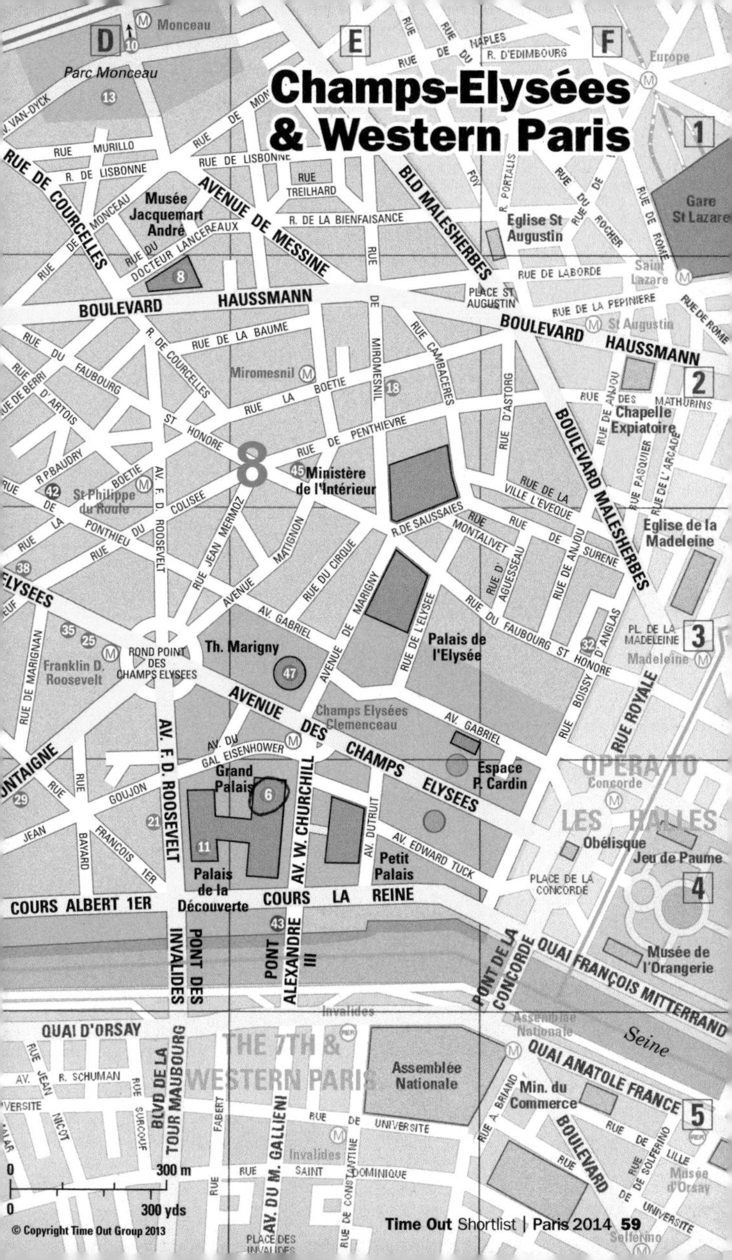

five masterpieces. The €100-million haul netted paintings by Picasso, Matisse, Braque, Modigliani and Léger.
Event highlights Pierre Henry: Autoportrait en 53 tableaux (until 1 Dec 2013)

Musée Jacquemart-André

158 bd Haussmann, 8th (01.45.62. 11.59, www.musee-jacquemart-andre. com). M° Miromesnil or St-Philippe-du-Roule. **Open** 10am-6pm daily (until 9pm Mon & Sat during exhibitions). **Admission** €11; free-€9.50 reductions. **Map** p59 D2 ❽
A stern pair of stone lions usher visitors into this grand 19th-century mansion, home to a collection of stately *objets d'art* and fine paintings. The collection was assembled by Edouard André and his artist wife Nélie Jacquemart, using money inherited from his rich banking family. The mansion was built to order to house their art hoard, which includes Rembrandts, Tiepolo frescoes and paintings by Italian masters Uccello, Mantegna and Carpaccio.

Musée National des Arts Asiatiques – Guimet

6 pl d'Iéna, 16th (01.56.52.53.00, www. museeguimet.fr). M° Iéna. **Open** 10am-6pm Mon, Wed-Sun. **Admission** €7.50; free-€5.50 reductions. **Map** p58 B4 ❾
The museum houses 45,000 objects from Neolithic times onwards, in a voyage across the diverse Asian religions and civilisations. Lower galleries focus on India and South-east Asia, centred on Hindu and Buddhist Khmer sculpture from Cambodia. Don't miss the Giant's Way, part of the entrance to a temple complex at Angkor Wat. Upstairs, Chinese antiquities include mysterious jade discs. Afghan glassware, Tibetan mandalas and Moghul jewellery also feature.

Musée National Jean-Jacques Henner

43 av de Villiers, 17th (01.47.63.42.73, www.musee-henner.fr). M° Malesherbes. **Open** 11am-6pm Mon, Wed-Sun (until 9pm 1st Thur of mth). **Admission** €5; free-€3 reductions. **Map** p59 D1 ❿
The Musée Jean-Jacques Henner traces the life of one of France's most respected artists, from his humble beginnings in Alsace in 1829 to his rise as one of the most sought-after painters in Paris. On the first floor, Alsatian landscapes and family portraits are a reminder of the artist's lifelong attachment to his native region. What brought the artist most acclaim (and criticism), however, was his trademark nymph paintings. The museum is set to close until spring 2014 for renovations.

Palais de la Découverte

Av Franklin-D-Roosevelt, 8th (01.56. 43.20.21, www.palais-decouverte.fr). M° Champs-Elysées Clemenceau or Franklin D. Roosevelt. **Open** 9.30am-6pm Tue-Sat; 10am-7pm Sun (last entry 30mins before closing). **Admission** €8; free-€6 reductions. *Planetarium* €3. **Map** p59 D4 ⓫
This science museum houses designs dating from Leonardo da Vinci's time to the present day. Models, real apparatus and audio-visual material bring the displays to life, and exhibits cover astrophysics, astronomy, biology, chemistry, physics and earth sciences. There are shows at the Planetarium, and 'live' experiments take place at weekends and during school holidays.

Palais de Tokyo: Site de Création Contemporaine

13 av du Président-Wilson, 16th (01.81. 97.35.88, www.palaisdetokyo.com). M° Alma Marceau or Iéna. **Open** noon-midnight Mon, Wed-Sun. **Admission** €8; free-€6 reductions. **Map** p58 C4 ⓬
See box p64.

Parc Monceau

Bd de Courcelles, av Hoche, rue Monceau, 8th. M° Monceau. **Open** *Nov-Mar* 7am-8pm daily. *Apr-Oct* 7am-10pm daily. **Admission** free. **Map** p59 D1 ⓭

Monceau is a favourite with well-dressed children and their nannies. It was laid out in the 18th century for the Duc de Chartres in the English style, with a lake, lawns and follies: an Egyptian pyramid, a Corinthian colonnade, a Venetian bridge and sarcophagi.

Eating & drinking

Les 110 de Taillevent

NEW *195 rue du Faubourg Saint-Honoré, 8th (01.40.74.20.20, www.taillevent.com). M° Ternes.* **Open** 12.15-2.30pm, 7.30-10.30pm daily. **€€€. Brasserie. Map** p58 C1 ⑭

Elegant design and French cuisine go hand in hand at the Gardinier brothers' new brasserie, with 110 wines from the Taillevent vaults on offer. As befits a restaurant where wine is so important, chef Emile Cotte's menu concentrates on flavour: calamari topped with fine slices of chorizo and espelette pepper; roasted duckling and caramelised endives with gingerbread; iced nougat melting beneath strawberries spiked with balsamic vinegar.

Alain Ducasse au Plaza Athénée

Hôtel Plaza Athénée, 25 av Montaigne, 8th (01.53.67.65.00, www.alain-ducasse.com). M° Alma Marceau. **Open** 7.45-10.15pm Mon-Wed; 12.45-2.15pm, 7.45-10.15pm Thur, Fri. Closed late July-late Aug & 1wk Dec. **€€€€. Haute cuisine. Map** p58 C4 ⑮

The sheer glamour would be enough to recommend this restaurant, Alain Ducasse's most lofty Paris undertaking. The ceiling drips with 10,000 crystals. An *amuse-bouche* of a single langoustine in a lemon cream with a touch of Iranian caviar starts the meal off beautifully. Cheese is delicious, as is the *rum baba comme à Monte-Carlo.*

Antoine

10 av de New York, 16th (01.40.70.19.28, www.antoine-paris.fr). M° Alma-Marceau or Trocadéro. **Open** noon-2.45pm, 7.30-10.45pm daily. **€€€. Seafood. Map** p58 C4 ⑯

Antoine is Paris's newest shrine to the sea. Chic, moneyed crowds gather to sample oysters and extravagant dishes such as whole roasted lobster with winter vegetables *en cocotte*, plump St-Jacques scallops with creamy purée, and wonderful vanilla millefeuille. The fixed-price lunch menu is good value.

Le Dada

12 av des Ternes, 17th (01.43.80.60.12). M° Ternes. **Open** 6am-2am Mon-Sat; 7am-10pm Sun. **€€. Café. Map** p58 B1 ⑰

Perhaps the hippest café in this stuffy part of town, Le Dada is best known for its well-placed, sunny terrace. Inside, the wood-block carved tables and red walls provide a warm atmosphere for a crowd that tends towards the well-heeled, well-spoken and, well, loaded. That said, the atmosphere is friendly; if terracing is your thing, you could happily spend a summer's day here.

Granterroirs

30 rue de Miromesnil, 8th (01.47.42.18.18, www.granterroirs.com). M° Miromesnil. **Open** 9am-4pm Mon, Fri; 9am-8pm Tue; 9am-7pm Wed; 9am-10pm Thur. *Food served* noon-3pm Mon-Fri & 7-9.30pm Thur (reserve in advance). Closed 2wks Aug. **€€. Bistro. Map** p59 E2 ⑱

The walls of this *épicerie* heave with more than 600 enticing specialities originating from southern France, including Périgord foie gras, charcuterie from Aubrac and a fine selection of wines. They make great gifts – but why not try sampling some of the goodies by enjoying the midday *table d'hôte* feast? Come in early to ensure that you can choose from the five succulent *plats du jour.*

Le Hide

10 rue du Général-Lanrezac, 17th (01.45.74.15.81, www.lehide.fr). M° Charles de Gaulle Etoile. **Open**

PARIS BY AREA

Galerie-Musée Baccarat p57

Bigger picture

The expanded Palais de Tokyo still pushes the boundaries.

Paris's most happening art space since it opened in 2002, the **Palais de Tokyo** (see p61) has now virtually tripled in size to become the largest contemporary art centre in Europe. The organisation is known for its highly international approach, and for blurring boundaries between art, music, science and politics – as well as for its artist-designed Tokyo Eat restaurant and Black Block shop. Architects Lacaton & Vassal, who transformed the 1937 building in 2002, employing a deliberately raw, distressed style (as much for budget reasons as aesthetics), have now tackled the vast remaining spaces, many of them unused for over 30 years. And it's symbolic that the Triennale, previously held in the Grand Palais, has moved here, under art director Okwui Enwezor.

Some people fear the extension heralds the museification of the Palais de Tokyo – that it will lose its contemporaneity and spirit of independence as it becomes part of the big state machine, with shows by established and 'mid-generation' artists and an express mission to promote French art. However, new president Jean de Loisy argues: 'True to its genetic code, the Palais de Tokyo above all supports the most experimental, the newest and the most intense artists, whatever their age.'

Autumn 2012 saw a group show, 'Imaginary Detours', and a solo show by Fabrice Hyber, in a rhythm where large exhibitions are punctuated by *modules* (small exhibitions by emerging artists) and *alertes*, where artists react to current events at short notice. 'This is not an institution preoccupied by art history but a laboratory experimenting with the best of our time, when art is impregnated by and sometimes revises the boundaries of other disciplines,' says de Loisy. Perhaps not quite so much the organised shelves of a laboratory as the hubble bubble of an artistic cauldron.

noon-2pm, 7-10pm Mon-Fri; 7-10pm Sat. €€. **Bistro**. **Map** p58 B1 ⑲

This bistro is packed with a happy crowd that appreciates Japanese-born chef Hide Kobayashi's superb cooking. Expect dishes such as duck foie gras terrine with pear-and-thyme compôte to start, followed by tender faux-filet steak in a light foie gras sauce. Desserts are excellent: perfect tarte tatin comes with crème fraîche from Normandy.

Ladurée

75 av des Champs-Elysées, 8th (01.40. 75.08.75, www.laduree.fr). M° Franklin D. Roosevelt or George V. **Open** 7.30am-11.30pm Mon-Fri; 8.30am-midnight Sat; 8.30am-10pm Sun. €€. **Café**. **Map** p58 C3 ⑳

Decadence permeates this elegant tea-room. While you bask in the glow of bygone wealth, indulge in tea, pastries and, above all, hot chocolate. It's a rich, velvety tar that will leave you in the requisite stupor for a lazy afternoon.

Lasserre

17 av Franklin-Roosevelt, 8th (01.43. 59.02.13, www.restaurant-lasserre. com). M° Franklin D Roosevelt. **Open** 7-10pm Tue, Wed, Sat; noon-2pm, 7-10pm Thur, Fri. €€€€. **Haute cuisine**. **Map** p59 D4 ㉑

Lasserre's rich history is definitely a part of the dining experience: Audrey Hepburn, André Malraux and Salvador Dalí were regulars. But its illustrious past is nothing next to the food: chef Christophe Moret (ex-Plaza Athénée) and his pastry chef Claire Heitzler (ex-Ritz) create lip-smacking delicacies to die for. The upstairs dining room, accessed by a bellboy-operated lift, is a sumptuous affair in taupe and white, with solid silver table decorations and a retractable roof that opens just enough for you to see the stars at night.

Stella Maris

4 rue Arsène-Houssaye, 8th (01.42.89. 16.22, www.stellamaris-paris.com). M° Charles de Gaulle Etoile. **Open** 12.30-2.30pm, 7.30-10pm Mon-Fri; 7.30-10pm Sat. Closed 2wks Aug. €€€€. **Haute cuisine**. **Map** p58 B2 ㉒

Trained by Robuchon and Troisgros, Tateru Yoshino turns out food that is resolutely French. You might float your way through foie gras with carrots, truffles and pistachio oil, pan-fried sea bass with saffron risotto, and perfectly lopsided Grand Marnier soufflé.

La Table Lauriston

129 rue de Lauriston, 16th (01.47.27. 00.07, www.restaurantlatablelauriston. com). M° Trocadéro. **Open** noon-2.30pm, 7-10.30pm Mon-Fri; 7-10.30pm Sat. Closed 3wks Aug & 1wk Dec. €€€. **Bistro**. **Map** p58 A4 ㉓

In spring, stalks of asparagus from the Landes are trimmed to avoid stringiness and served with the simplest *vinaigrette d'herbes*. More extravagant is *foie gras cuit au torchon*, in which the duck liver is wrapped in a cloth and poached in a bouillon. Order a dessert with attitude: the giant *baba au rhum*.

Taillevent

15 rue Lamennais, 8th (01.44.95. 15.01, www.taillevent.com). M° George V. **Open** 12.15-1.30pm, 7.15-9.30pm Mon-Fri. Closed Aug. €€€€. **Haute cuisine**. **Map** p58 C2 ㉔

Rémoulade de coquilles St-Jacques is a technical feat, with slices of raw, marinated scallop wrapped in a tube shape around a diced apple filling, encircled by a *rémoulade* sauce. An earthier and lip-smacking dish is the trademark *épeautre* – an ancient wheat – cooked 'like a risotto' with bone marrow, black truffle, whipped cream and parmesan, and topped with sautéed frog's legs.

Shopping

Abercrombie & Fitch

NEW *23 av des Champs-Elysées, 8th (08.05.11.15.59, www.abercrombie. com). M° Franklin D Roosevelt.* **Open** 10am-8pm Mon-Sat; 11am-7pm Sun. **Map** p59 D3 ㉕

The US brand's flagship store has been causing a stir on the Champs since it opened in 2011, with banging tunes and topless male models standing in the doorway at all times. Like its sister stores in London and New York, the box-hedged garden, dimmed lighting and scent of aftershave make the place feel more like a club than a shop. Whether you're into A&F's preppy ranges or not, it's worth a detour.

Alléosse

13 rue Poncelet, 17th (01.46.22.50.45, www.fromage-alleosse.com). Mº Ternes. **Open** 9am-1pm, 4-7pm Tue-Thur; 9am-1pm, 3.30-7pm Fri, Sat; 9am-1pm Sun. **Map** p58 B1 ㉖

People cross town for these cheeses – wonderful farmhouse camemberts, delicate st-marcellins, a choice of *chèvres* and several rarities.

Balenciaga

10 av George V, 8th (01.47.20.21.11, www.balenciaga.com). Mº Alma Marceau or George V. **Open** 10am-7pm Mon-Sat. **Map** p58 C4 ㉗

The Spanish fashion house is ahead of Japanese and Belgian designers in the hip stakes. Floating fabrics contrast with dramatic cuts, producing a sophisticated style that the fashion *haut monde* can't wait to slip into.

PARIS BY AREA

Balmain

44 rue François 1er, 8th (01.47. 20.57.58, www.balmain.com). Mº George V. **Open** 10.30am-7pm Mon-Sat. **Map** p58 C3 ㉘

A portrait of the late Pierre Balmain surveys the scene at his eponymous shop. What would he have made of the clothes around him? Long gone are the afternoon dresses with perfectly positioned waists, full skirts and trapezoidal necklines. The racks are these days lined with bondage trousers, studded jackets and animal print drainpipes. There hasn't been such a good display of grungy punk glamour since London's Kensington Market closed its doors.

Dior

26-30 av Montaigne, 8th (01.40.73. 73.73, www.dior.com). Mº Franklin D. Roosevelt. **Open** 10am-7pm Mon-Sat. **Map** p59 D4 ㉙

The Dior universe is here on avenue Montaigne, from the main prêt-à-porter store and jewellery, menswear and eyewear to Baby Dior, where rich infants are coochy-cooed by drooling assistants.

Drugstore Publicis

133 av des Champs-Elysées, 8th (01.44.43.79.00, www.publicis drugstore.com). Mº Charles de Gaulle Etoile. **Open** 8am-2am Mon-Fri; 10am-2am Sat, Sun. **Map** p58 B2 ㉚

On the ground floor there's a newsagent, pharmacy, bookshop and upmarket deli. The basement is a macho take on Colette, keeping selected design items and lifestyle mags, and replacing high fashion with wines and a cigar cellar.

Fnac

74 av des Champs-Elysées, 8th (08.25. 02.00.20, www.fnac.com). Mº George V. **Open** 10am-11.45pm Mon-Sat; noon-11.45pm Sun. **Map** p58 C3 ㉛

Fnac is a supermarket of culture: books, DVDs, CDs, audio kit, computers and photo equipment. Most branches stock everything; others specialise. All branches operate as a concert box office.

Givenchy

28 rue du Fbg-St-Honoré, 8th (01.42.68.31.00, www.givenchy.com). Mº Madeleine or Concorde. **Open** 10am-7pm Mon-Sat. **Map** p59 F3 ㉜

This flagship store for men's and women's prêt-à-porter and accessories incorporates surreal rooms within rooms – cut-out boxes filled with white, black or mahogany panelling – providing a contemporary art gallery setting.

LE66

66 av des Champs-Elysées, 8th (01.53. 53.33.80). Mº George V. **Open** 11am-8.30pm Mon-Fri; 11.30am-9pm Sat; 1-8pm Sun. **Map** p59 D3 ㉝

This fashion concept store is youthful and accessible, with an ever-changing selection of hip brands. Assistants, who are also the buyers and designers, make for a motivated team. The store takes the form of three transparent modules, the first a bookstore run by Black Book of the Palais de Tokyo, and the second two devoted to fashion.

Louis Vuitton

101 av des Champs-Elysées, 8th (01.53.57.52.00, www.vuitton.com). M° George V. **Open** 10am-8pm Mon-Sat; 11am-7pm Sun. **Map** p58 C2 34

The 'Promenade' flagship sets the tone for Vuitton's global image, from the 'bag bar', bookstore and new jewellery department to the women's and men's ready-to-wear.

Marks & Spencer

100 av des Champs-Elysées & 1 rue de Berri, 8th (www.marksandspencer.fr). M° George V. **Open** 10am-10pm daily. **Map** p58 C2 35

Marks opened its new Paris store in late 2011. While most French people love nothing more than criticising British food, give them an M&S chicken tikka sarnie and the superlatives flow like wine from a barrel. They're also secret admirers of British fashion, and M&S offers cuts, colours and fabrics not readily available in France.

Prada

10 av Montaigne, 8th (01.53.23.99.40, www.prada.com). M° Alma Marceau. **Open** 10am-7pm daily. **Map** p58 C4 36

The high priestess of European chic, Miuccia Prada's elegant stores pull in fashion followers of all ages. Handbags of choice are complemented by the coveted ready-to-wear range.

Sephora

70 av des Champs-Elysées, 8th (01.53.93.22.50, www.sephora.fr). M° Franklin D. Roosevelt. **Open** 10am-midnight Mon-Thur, Sun; 10am-1am Fri, Sat. **Map** p58 C3 37

The flagship of the cosmetic supermarket chain houses around 12,000 brands of scent and slap. Sephora Blanc (14 cour St-Emilion, 12th, 01.40.02.97.79) features beauty products in a minimalist interior.

Virgin Megastore

52-60 av des Champs-Elysées, 8th (01.49.53.50.00, www.virginmega.fr). M° Franklin D. Roosevelt. **Open** 10am-10pm Mon-Thur; 10am-midnight Fri, Sat; noon-10pm Sun. **Map** p59 D3 38

The luxury of perusing CDs and DVDs until late every day of the week makes this a choice spot, and the listening posts let you sample any CD. Tickets for concerts and sports events are available here too. This main branch has the best book selection.

Nightlife

Le Baron

6 av Marceau, 8th (01.47.20.04.01, www.clublebaron.com). M° Alma Marceau. **Open** 11pm-6am daily. **Admission** free. **Map** p58 C4 39

This small but supremely exclusive hangout for the international jet set only holds 150, most of whom are regulars you'll need to befriend in order to get past the door. But if you manage to get in, you'll be rubbing shoulders with celebrities and super-glossy people.

Le Lido

116bis av des Champs-Elysées, 8th (01.40.76.56.10, www.lido.fr). M° Franklin D. Roosevelt or George V. **Dinner** 7pm. **Shows** 9.30pm, 11.30pm daily. **Admission** *9.30pm show* (incl champagne) €105. *11.30pm show* (incl champagne) €145. *Dinner & show* €160-€300. *Show & backstage tour* prices vary. **Map** p58 C2 40

This is the largest cabaret of them all: high-tech touches optimise visibility, and chef Philippe Lacroix provides fabulous gourmet nosh. On stage, 60 Bluebell Girls slink around, shaking their boobs with panache.

PARIS BY AREA

My museum in Paris...
SIGHTSEEING CRUISE, LUNCH CRUISE, DINNER CRUISE
Bateaux Parisiens
Information and booking : +33(0)1 76 64 14 45
Le Paris d'un grand
Boarding at the foot of the Eiffel Tower
Bateaux Parisiens, a sodexo Company

Queen

102 av des Champs-Elysées, 8th (01.53.89.08.90, www.queen.fr). M° George V. **Open** midnight-7am Mon-Thur, Sun; midnight-8am Fri, Sat. **Admission** €15 Mon-Thur, Sun; €20 Fri, Sat. **Map** p58 C2 41

Once the city's most fêted gay club and the only venue that could hold a torch to the Rex, with a roster of top local DJs holding court, Queen's star faded in the early noughties but is now starting to shine more brightly again.

Le Régine

49 rue de Ponthieu, 8th (01.40.39.07.07, www.leregine.com) M° St-Philippe-du-Roule. **Open** 7pm-5am Thur; midnight-6am Fri, Sat. **Admission** €10-€20. **Map** p59 D2 42

Régine was once a key figure on the Paris nightlife scene, and the club she created is experiencing a rejuvenation. Her portrait still sits by the entrance for a touch of '70s nostalgia, but the revamped venue has shifted from disco to sophisticated electro, inviting the cream of international DJs to the decks.

Showcase

Underneath Pont Alexandre III, 8th (01.45.61.25.43, www.showcase.fr). M° Champs-Elysées Clemenceau. **Open** 11.30pm-dawn Fri, Sat. **Admission** free-€15. **Map** p59 E4 43

This vast venue is where music-crazed insomniacs come on weekends to discover up-and-coming bands and dance until daybreak. The club has lost some of its hype over the last couple of years, but high-profile guest DJs have been setting the bar higher lately: Carol Cox, will.i.am and Calvin Harris have made appearances in the past couple of years.

Arts & leisure

Le Balzac

1 rue Balzac, 8th (01.45.61.10.60, www.cinemabalzac.com). M° George V. **Admission** €10; €6.50-€8 reductions. No credit cards. **Map** p58 C2 44

Built in 1935 and boasting a mock ocean-liner foyer, the Balzac scores highly for design and programming. Manager Jean-Jacques Schpoliansky often welcomes punters in person.

Salle Pleyel

252 rue du Fbg-St-Honoré, 8th (01.42.56.13.13, www.sallepleyel.fr). M° Ternes. **Box office** noon-7pm Mon-Sat; 2hrs before show Sun. *By phone* 11am-7pm Mon-Sat; 11am-5pm Sun & 1hr before performance. **Admission** €10-€190. **Map** p59 E2 45

Home to the Orchestre de Paris, this restored concert hall looks splendid. If the improved acoustics are only partially successful, the venue has nevertheless regained its status as the capital's leading venue for large-scale symphonic concerts.

Théâtre des Champs-Elysées

15 av Montaigne, 8th (01.49.52.50.50, www.theatrechampselysees.fr). M° Alma Marceau. **Box office** noon-7pm Mon-Sat; 2hrs before show Sun. *By phone* 11am-6pm Mon-Fri; 2-6pm Sat. **Admission** €5-€160. **Map** p58 C4 46

This beautiful art nouveau theatre with bas-reliefs by Bourdelle celebrated its centenary in 2013, having hosted the première of Stravinsky's *Le Sacre du Printemps* in 1913. It remains the favourite venue for touring foreign orchestras, with a prestigious line-up of visiting maestros.

Théâtre Marigny

Av de Marigny, 8th (08.92.22.23.33, www.theatremarigny.fr). M° Champs-Elysées Clemenceau or Franklin D. Roosevelt. **Box office** 11am-6.30pm Mon-Sat. **Admission** €25-€79. **Map** p59 E3 47

Théâtre Marigny boasts a location off the Champs-Elysées, a deluxe interior conceived by Charles Garnier (of Opéra fame), high-profile casts and an illustrious pedigree stretching back more than 150 years.

Palais Garnier p86

Opéra to Les Halles

In centuries gone by, these two adjoining central districts – bounded by the Grands Boulevards to the north and the river to the south – were the city's commercial and provisioning powerhouses, home to most of the newspapers, banks and major mercantile institutions. Nowadays, although there is still a strong financial slant, thanks to the presence of the two stock exchanges and the Banque de France, the focus is on shopping: mass-market stuff in and around **Les Halles**, shading into more exclusive brands the further one moves west, in particular on and just off rue St-Honoré.

Les Halles itself was, famously, the city's wholesale food market until 1969, when the Second Empire iron-framed buildings that housed it were ripped out. The soulless shopping centre that filled the gap in the 1970s has been one of the city's least liked features, and is currently being uprooted itself, to be replaced by a 21st-century glory of gardens, glass, open spaces and retail opportunities aplenty.

A short distance west of Les Halles is the **Louvre**, no longer the centre of French power though it still exerts considerable influence: first as a grandiose architectural ensemble, a palace within the city; and, second, as a symbol of the capital's cultural pre-eminence. Across rue de Rivoli from the Louvre stands the elegant **Palais-Royal**. After a stroll in its quiet gardens, it's hard to believe this was the starting point of the French Revolution. Today, its arcades house a mix of antiques dealers, philatelists and fashion showcases.

Sights & museums

La Collection 1900

Maxim's, 3 rue Royale, 8th (01.42.65.30.47, www.maxims-musee-art nouveau.com). M° Madeleine. **Open** *Guided tours* (reservations essential)

2pm Wed-Sun (English); 3.15pm, 4.30pm Wed-Sun (French). **Admission** €15. No credit cards. **Map** p72 A3 ❶

Couturier Pierre Cardin has owned belle époque restaurant Maxim's since 1981, and now he has added a museum of art nouveau, which he has been collecting since the age of 18. There are rooms and rooms of exhibits, arranged so as to evoke a 19th-century courtesan's boudoir. Read Zola's *Nana* before your visit to grasp the full effect of the dreamy lake maidens sculpted in glistening faience, pewter vanity sets in the shape of reclining nudes, and beds inlaid with opium flowers to promote sleep. Dinner settings on display include Gustave Eiffel's own chunky tureens, just crying out for turtle soup.

Eglise de la Madeleine

Pl de la Madeleine, 8th (01.44.51. 69.00, www.eglise-lamadeleine.com). M° Concorde or Madeleine. **Open** 9.30am-7pm daily. **Admission** free. **Map** p72 A2 ❷

The building of a church on this site began in 1764; in 1806 Napoleon sent instructions from Poland for Barthélémy Vignon to design a 'Temple of Glory' dedicated to his Grand Army. After the emperor's fall, construction slowed and the building, by now a church again, was finally consecrated in 1845. The exterior is ringed by fluted Corinthian columns, with a double row at the front, and a frieze of the Last Judgement above the portico. Inside are giant domes, an organ and pseudo-Grecian marble side altars.

Forum des Halles

1st. M° Les Halles/RER Châtelet Les Halles. **Map** p73 E4 ❸

The labyrinthine mall and transport interchange extend for three levels underground and include the Ciné Cité multiplex and Forum des Images, as well as fashion chains and the Forum des Créateurs, a section dedicated to young designers. But all is changing with a new landscaping of the area due to be completed by 2016.

Jardin des Tuileries

Rue de Rivoli, 1st. M° Concorde or Tuileries. **Open** *Apr, May* 7am-9pm daily; *June-Aug* 7am-11pm daily; *Sept-Mar* 7.30am-7.30pm daily. **Map** p72 B4 ❹

The gravelled alleyways of these gardens have been a chic promenade ever since they opened to the public in the 16th century. André Le Nôtre created the prototypical French garden with terraces and central vista running down the Grand Axe through circular and hexagonal ponds. As part of Mitterrand's Grand Louvre project, sculptures such as Coysevox's winged horses were transferred to the Louvre and replaced by copies, and the Maillol sculptures were returned to the Jardins du Carrousel; a handful of modern sculptures have been added, including bronzes by Moore, Ernst, Giacometti, and Dubuffet's *Le Bel Costumé*. A funfair sets up along the rue de Rivoli side during the summer.

Jeu de Paume

1 pl de la Concorde, 8th (01.47.03.12.50, www.jeudepaume.org). M° Concorde. **Open** 11am-9pm Tue; 11am-7pm Wed-Sun (last admission 30mins before closing). **Admission** €8.50; free-€5.50 reductions. **Map** p72 A3 ❺

The Centre National de la Photographie moved into this site in 2005. The building, which once served as a tennis court, has been divided into two white, almost hangar-like galleries. It is not an intimate space, but it works well for showcase retrospectives. A video art and cinema suite in the basement shows new digital installation work.

Event highlights Erwin Blumenfeld (15 Oct 2013-26 Jan 2014)

Musée des Arts Décoratifs

107 rue de Rivoli, 1st (01.44.55. 57.50, www.lesartsdecoratifs.fr). M° Palais Royal Musée du Louvre or Pyramides. **Open** 11am-6pm Tue, Wed, Fri-Sun; 11am-9pm Thur (late opening during exhibitions only).

Opéra to Les Halles

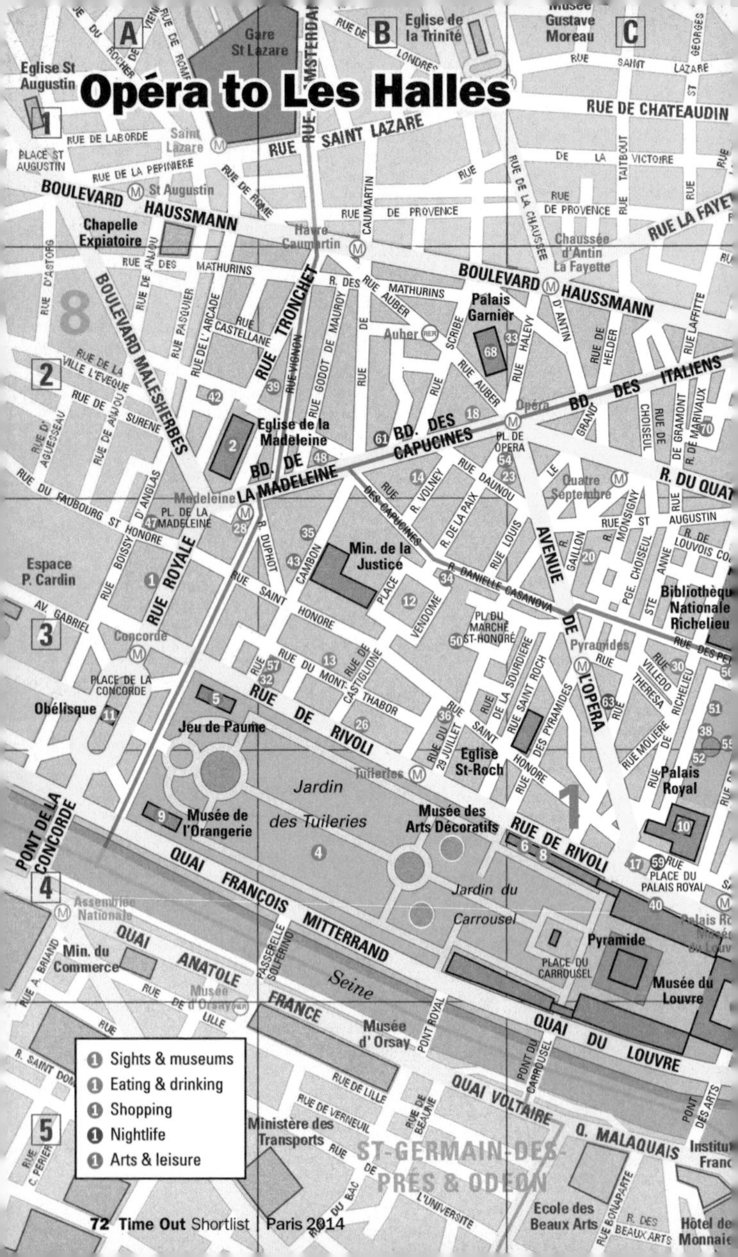

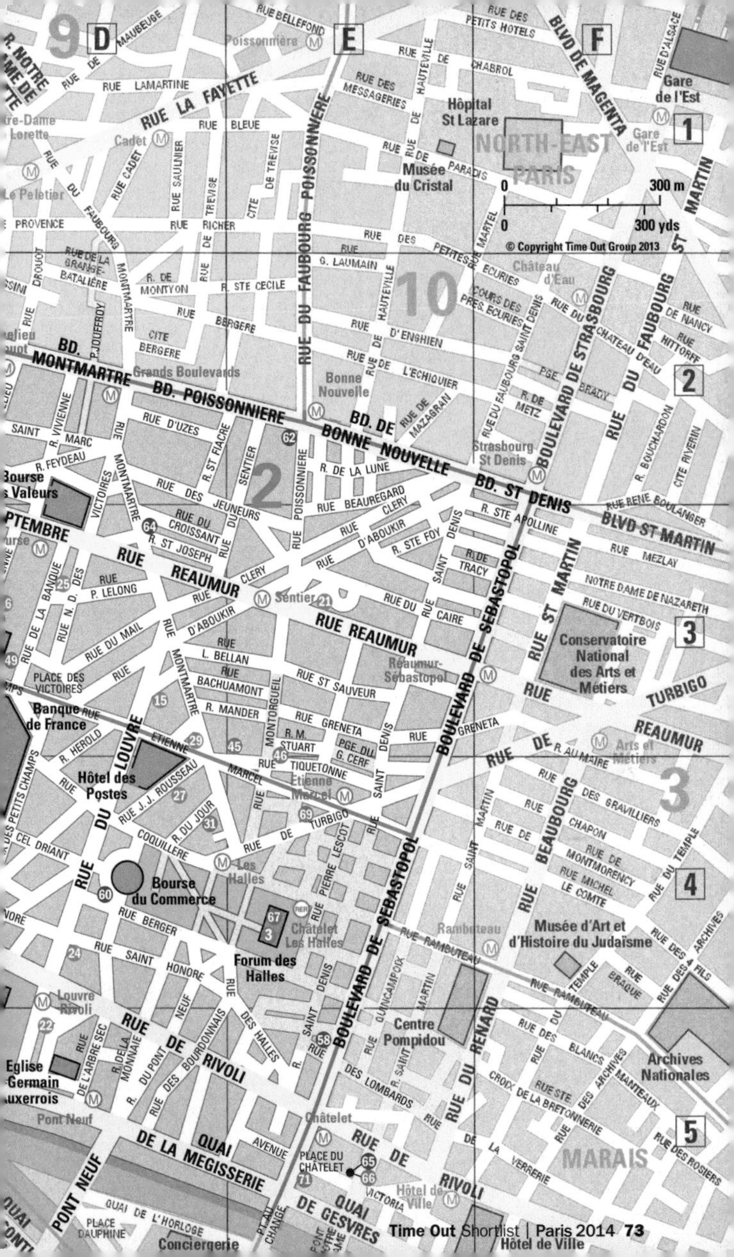
9
D
E
F
1
2
3
4
5
10
2
3
RUE BELLEFOND
Poissonnière
RUE DE MAUBEUGE
RUE LAMARTINE
RUE LA FAYETTE
RUE BLEUE
Cadet
RUE CADET
RUE SAULNIER
RUE DE TREVISE
CITE DE TREVISE
RUE DU FAUBOURG POISSONNIERE
RUE DES PETITS HOTELS
BLVD DE MAGENTA
RUE D'ALSACE
Gare de l'Est
RUE DE CHABROL
RUE DE HAUTEVILLE
RUE DES MESSAGERIES
Hôpital St Lazare
NORTH-EAST PARIS
RUE DE PARADIS
Musée du Cristal
0
300 m
300 yds
© Copyright Time Out Group 2013
RUE ST MARTIN
Le Peletier
PROVENCE
RUE RICHER
RUE DU FAUBOURG MONTMARTRE
RUE DES PETITES ECURIES
RUE MARTEL
Château d'Eau
RUE DE LA GRANGE-BATALIÈRE
RUE DROUOT
R. DE MONTYON
R. STE CECILE
RUE G. LAUMAIN
COURS DES PRES. ECURIES
RUE DU CHATEAU D'EAU
BOULEVARD DE STRASBOURG
RUE DU FAUBOURG ST MARTIN
RUE DE NANCY
RUE HITTORFF
P. JOUFFROY
CITE BERGERE
RUE BERGERE
RUE D'ENGHIEN
RUE DE L'ECHIQUIER
RUE DU FAUBOURG SAINT DENIS
PGE. BRADY
R. DE METZ
BD. MONTMARTRE
Grands Boulevards
BD. POISSONNIERE
Bonne Nouvelle
RUE DE MAZAGRAN
BD. DE BONNE NOUVELLE
Strasbourg St Denis
RUE BOUCHARDON
CITE RIVERIN
RUE VIVIENNE
SAINT MARC
RUE D'UZES
R. ST FIACRE
RUE DU SENTIER
RUE POISSONNIERE
R. DE LA LUNE
62
R. FEYDEAU
Bourse des Valeurs
RUE MONTMARTRE
RUE DES JEUNEURS
RUE BEAUREGARD
RUE CLERY
BD. ST DENIS
RUE RENE BOULANGER
BLVD ST MARTIN
RUE DU CROISSANT
64
R. ST JOSEPH
RUE D'ABOUKIR
R. STE FOY
R. STE APOLLINE
RUE MEZLAY
RUE REAUMUR
RUE SAINT DENIS
R. DE TRACY
BOULEVARD DE SEBASTOPOL
RUE DES VICTOIRES
RUE DE LA BANQUE
RUE N. D. DES VICTOIRES
25
P. LELONG
Sentier
21
RUE DU CAIRE
NOTRE DAME DE NAZARETH
RUE DU VERTBOIS
Conservatoire National des Arts et Métiers
RUE DU MAIL
RUE L. BELLAN
RUE BACHUAMONT
RUE ST SAUVEUR
Réaumur-Sébastopol
RUE TURBIGO
49
PLACE DES VICTOIRES
R. MANDER
RUE MONTORGUEIL
RUE GRENETA
Banque de France
15
R. M. STUART
PGE. DU G. CERF
RUE DE REAUMUR
Arts et Métiers
R. AU MAIRE
R. HEROLD
RUE DU LOUVRE
29
45
46
RUE ETIENNE MARCEL
RUE TIQUETONNE
Etienne Marcel
RUE DES GRAVILLIERS
RUE CHAPON
Hôtel des Postes
RUE J.J. ROUSSEAU
27
RUE DES PETITS CHAMPS
R. DU JOUR
31
69
RUE DE TURBIGO
RUE PIERRE LESCOT
RUE DE MONTMORENCY
RUE MICHEL LE COMTE
RUE DU TEMPLE
CEL DRIANT
COQUILLERE
Les Halles
RUE BEAUBOURG
Bourse du Commerce
60
RER
RUE BERGER
67
3
Châtelet Les Halles
Rambuteau
RUE RAMBUTEAU
Musée d'Art et d'Histoire du Judaïsme
RUE DES ARCHIVES
RUE DES 4 FILS
RUE SAINT HONORE
24
Forum des Halles
RUE QUINCAMPOIX
RUE BRAQUE
RUE DU RENARD
Louvre Rivoli
22
RUE DE RIVOLI
RUE DE L'ARBRE SEC
R. DE LA MONNAIE
RUE DU PONT NEUF
RUE DES BOURDONNAIS
RUE DES HALLES
58
Centre Pompidou
RUE DES BLANCS MANTEAUX
Archives Nationales
Eglise St Germain l'Auxerrois
DES LOMBARDS
R. SAINT MARTIN
RUE STE CROIX DE LA BRETONNERIE
Pont Neuf
Châtelet
RUE DE LA VERRERIE
QUAI DE LA MEGISSERIE
AVENUE VICTORIA
PLACE DU CHÂTELET
65
66
71
MARAIS
RUE DES ROSIERS
PONT NEUF
QUAI DE GESVRES
Hôtel de Ville
QUAI DE L'HORLOGE
PLACE DAUPHINE
PT. AU CHANGE
PONT NOTRE DAME
Conciergerie

Admission (with Musée de la Mode & Musée de la Publicité) €9.50; free-€8 reductions. **Map** p72 C4 ❻

Taken as a whole along with the Musée de la Mode et du Textile and Musée de la Publicité, this is one of the world's major collections of design and the decorative arts. The major focus here is French furniture and tableware, from extravagant carpets to delicate crystal and porcelain. Of most obvious attraction to the layman are the reconstructed period rooms, ten in all, showing how the other half lived from the late 1400s to the early 20th century.

Musée du Louvre

Rue de Rivoli, 1st (01.40.20.50.50, www.louvre.fr). M° Palais Royal Musée du Louvre. **Open** 9am-6pm Mon, Thur, Sat, Sun; 9am-9.45pm Wed, Fri. **Admission** *Permanent collections* €11; free-€6 reductions. **Map** p72 C5 ❼

The world's largest museum is also its most visited, with a remarkable 8.5 million visitors in 2011. It is a city within the city, a vast, multi-level maze of galleries, passageways, staircases and escalators. It's famous for the artistic glories within, but the very fabric of the museum is a masterpiece in itself – or rather, a collection of masterpieces modified and added to from one century to another. And the additions and modifications continue into the present day, with the opening of a wonderful new two-storey Islamic Arts department beneath the Cour Visconti in late 2012 (see p78), and the franchising of the Louvre 'brand' via new outposts in Lens in northern France (www.louvre-lens.fr) and Abu Dhabi. If any place demonstrates the central importance of culture in French life, this is it.

Musée de la Mode et du Textile

107 rue de Rivoli, 1st (01.44.55.57.50, www.lesartsdecoratifs.fr). M° Palais Royal Musée du Louvre or Pyramides. **Open** 11am-6pm Tue, Wed, Fri-Sun; 11am-9pm Thur (late opening during exhibitions only). **Admission** (with Musée des Arts Décoratifs & Musée de la Publicité) €9.50; free-€8 reductions. **Map** p72 C4 ❽

This municipal fashion museum holds Elsa Schiaparelli's entire archive and hosts exciting themed exhibitions. Dramatic black-walled rooms make a fine background to the clothes, and video screens and a cinema space show how the clothes move, as well as interviews with the creators.

Event highlights Behind the Seams: An Indiscreet Look at the Mechanics of Fashion (until 24 Nov 2013)

Musée de l'Orangerie

Jardin des Tuileries, 1st (01.44.77.80.07, www.musee-orangerie.fr). M° Concorde. **Open** 9am-6pm Mon, Wed-Sun. **Admission** €7.50; free-€5 reductions. **Map** p72 A4 ❾

The look of this Monet showcase is utilitarian and fuss-free, with the museum's eight, tapestry-sized *Nymphéas* (water lilies) paintings housed in two plain oval rooms. They provide a simple backdrop for the ethereal romanticism of Monet's works, which he painted late in his life. Downstairs, the Jean Walter and Paul Guillaume collection of Impressionism and the Ecole de Paris is a mixed bag of sweet-toothed Cézanne and Renoir portraits, with works by Modigliani, Rousseau, Matisse, Picasso and Derain.

Palais-Royal

Pl du Palais-Royal, 1st. M° Palais Royal Musée du Louvre. **Open** *Gardens* 7.30am-8.30pm daily. **Admission** free. **Map** p72 C4 ❿

Built for Cardinal Richelieu by Jacques Lemercier, the building was once known as Palais Cardinal. Richelieu left it to Louis XIII, whose widow Anne d'Autriche preferred it to the Louvre and rechristened it when she moved in with her son, the young Louis XIV. In the 1780s, the Duc d'Orléans enclosed the gardens in a three-storey peristyle and filled it with cafés, shops, theatres, sideshows and accommodation to raise

PARIS BY AREA

Liza p79

money for rebuilding the burned-down opera. Daniel Buren's striped columns grace the main courtyard.

Place de la Concorde

1st/8th. Mº Concorde. **Map** p72 A3 ⓫

This is the city's largest square, its grand east–west perspectives stretching from the Louvre to the Arc de Triomphe, and north–south from the Madeleine to the Assemblée Nationale across the Seine. In 1792, the centre statue of Louis XV was replaced with the guillotine for Louis XVI, Marie-Antoinette and many more.

Place Vendôme

1st. Mº Opéra or Tuileries. **Map** p72 B3 ⓬

Elegant place Vendôme got its name from a *hôtel particulier* built by the Duc de Vendôme that stood on the site. Opened in 1699, the eight-sided square was conceived by Hardouin-Mansart to show off an equestrian statue of the Sun King, torn down in 1792 and replaced in 1806 by the Colonne de la Grande Armée. During the 1871 Commune, this symbol of 'brute force and false glory' was pulled down; the present column is a replica. At no.12, you can visit the Grand Salon where Chopin died in 1849.

PARIS BY AREA

Eating & drinking

L'Ardoise

28 rue du Mont-Thabor, 1st (01.42.96.28.18, www.lardoise-paris.com). Mº Concorde or Tuileries. **Open** noon-3pm, 6.30-11pm Mon-Sat; 6.30-11pm Sun. Closed mid July-mid Aug. **€€. Bistro. Map** p72 B3 ⓭

One of the city's finest modern bistros, L'Ardoise is regularly packed with gourmets eager to sample Pierre Jay's delicious cooking. A wise choice might be six oysters with warm chipolatas and pungent shallot dressing; equally attractive is a hare pie with an escalope of foie gras nestling in its centre. Unusually, it's open on Sundays.

Bistro Volnay

8 rue Volney, 2nd (01.42.61.06.65). Mº Opéra or Madeleine. **Open** noon-2.30pm, 7-10.30pm Mon-Fri. **€€€. Bistro. Map** p72 B2 ⓮

The art deco-inspired Bistro Volnay has been so successful that owners Delphine Alcover and Magali Marian have opened another, Les Jalles, at the end of the road. And it does seem as if Volnay has everything to please: a welcoming dining room with big mirrors, glowing lamps and a gorgeous 1930s bar, smiling efficient waiters, a well-stocked cellar and a menu which beautifully manages the balance between nostalgic tradition and ambitious modernity.

Blend

NEW *44 rue d'Argout, 2nd (01.40.26.84.57, www.blendhamburger.com). Mº Bourse or Sentier.* **Open** noon-3pm, 7.30-11pm Mon-Sat; noon-4pm Sun. **€. Burgers. Map** p73 D3 ⓯

Parisians have officially gone burger bonkers: after the Camion qui Fume (a mobile gourmet burger van) and Big Fernand (an über-trendy take-away burger joint in the 10th), Blend has opened its doors in the bobo quarters of Etienne Marcel. The secret is in the ingredients: made with hand-cut veal and beef mince, provided by star butcher Yves-Marie le Bourdonnec, burgers are succulent and flavoursome, and marry wonderfully with the fresh toppings (think bacon, bleu d'Auvergne cheese, spinach leaves, chorizo, mint and cheddar). The bread and fries (both potato and sweet-potato) are also home-made, lending the whole affair a rather gourmet feel.

La Bourse ou la Vie

12 rue Vivienne, 2nd (01.42.60.08.83). Mº Bourse. **Open** noon-10pm Mon-Fri; 6-10pm Sat. Closed 1wk Aug & 1wk Dec. **€€. Bistro. Map** p73 D3 ⓰

After a career as an architect, the owner of La Bourse ou la Vie has a new mission in life: to revive the dying art of the perfect *steak-frites*. The only decision you'll need to make is which cut of beef to order with your chips, unless you pick the cod. Choose between ultra-tender *coeur de filet* or a huge, tender *bavette*. Rich, creamy pepper sauce is the speciality here, but the real surprise is the chips, which gain a distinctly animal flavour from the suet in which they are cooked.

Café Marly

93 rue de Rivoli, cour Napoléon, 1st (01.49.26.06.60). M° Palais Royal Musée du Louvre. **Open** 8am-2am daily. **€€. Café. Map** p72 C4 17

A class act, this, as you might expect of a Costes café whose lofty, arcaded terrace overlooks the Louvre's glass pyramid. It's reached through passage Richelieu (the entrance for advance Louvre ticket holders), and the prime location comes at a price: it's €6 for a Heineken – so you might as well splash out €12 on a chocolate martini or a Shark of vodka, lemonade and grenadine. Most wines are under €10 a glass, and everything is impeccably served by razor-sharp staff.

Café de la Paix

12 bd des Capucines, 9th (01.40.07.36.36, www.cafedelapaix.fr). M° Opéra. **Open** 7am-midnight daily. **€€. Café. Map** p72 B2 18

Lap up every detail – this is once-in-a-holiday stuff. Whether you're out on the historic terrace or looking up at the ornate stucco ceiling, you'll be sipping in the footsteps of the likes of Oscar Wilde, Josephine Baker, Emile Zola, and Bartholdi and the Franco-American Union (as they sketched out the Statue of Liberty). Let the immaculate staff bring you a kir (€12) or, for an afternoon treat, the vanilla millefeuille – possibly the best in Paris.

De la Ville Café

34 bd de Bonne-Nouvelle, 10th (01.48.24.48.09, www.delavillecafe.com). M° Bonne Nouvelle. **Open** 11am-2am daily. **Bar. Map** p73 E2 19

De la Ville has brought good news to Bonne-Nouvelle. A major expansion and refurbishment have upped the ante. Inside, the distressed walls remain, but the curvy club section at the back has become very cool. A grand staircase leads to a first-floor lounge and exhibition space.

Drouant

18 pl Gaillon, 2nd (01.42.65.15.16, www.drouant.com). M° Pyramides or Quatre Septembre. **Open** noon-2.30pm, 7pm-midnight daily. **€€€. Brasserie. Map** p72 C3 20

Star chef Antoine Westermann has whisked this landmark brasserie into the 21st century with bronze-coloured banquettes and butter-yellow fabrics. Westermann has dedicated this restaurant to the art of the hors d'oeuvre, in themed sets of four ranging from global (Thai beef salad with brightly coloured vegetables) to nostalgic (silky leeks in vinaigrette).

Frenchie

5 rue du Nil, 2nd (01.40.39.96.19, www.frenchie-restaurant.com). M° Sentier. **Open** 7-10.30pm Mon-Fri. **€€. Bistro. Map** p73 E3 21

Grégory Lemarchand honed his craft with Jamie Oliver in London before opening this loft-style bistro. It has been a huge hit, thanks to the bold flavours of dishes such as gazpacho with calamari, squash blossoms and plenty of herbs; braised lamb with roasted aubergine and spinach; and coconut tapioca with strawberry sorbet. It requires an almost superhuman effort to secure a table in the tiny dining room, but luckily there's Frenchie Bar à Vins across the street, where you can sample his Anglo-influenced take on bistro cooking without reservations.

Le Fumoir

6 rue de l'Amiral-de-Coligny, 1st (01.42.92.00.24, www.lefumoir.fr). M° Louvre Rivoli. **Open** 11am-2am daily. **Bar. Map** p73 D5 22

Unseen treasures

Take a stroll through 1,200 years of Islamic art.

What do you picture if you think of the Musée du Louvre (see p74)? The *Mona Lisa*? IM Pei's dramatic pyramid? Egyptian mummies? Or perhaps the *Winged Victory of Samothrace* or Géricault's haunting *Radeau de la Méduse*? What almost certainly doesn't spring to mind is Islamic art, despite the fact that this former royal palace has been amassing the largest collection of its kind in the Western world since the 19th century, with a cache of more than 18,000 objects gathered from three continents and covering 1,200 years of history.

The reason the collection has never made the headlines before has been because the Louvre, despite its illustrious proportions, has simply lacked the space to display it properly. But now, after a nine-year, €100 million makeover, the stunning Département des Arts de l'Islam has opened its doors.

Set in the Visconti wing, the two-storey, 3,000sq m gallery lies beneath the courtyard (architects Rudy Ricciotti and Mario Bellini couldn't change the Louvre's structure, so they had to dig down), beneath a floating golden roof of 2,350 triangles designed to look like a dragonfly wing. The two floors are linked by a remarkable staircase cast from a monumental block of black concrete.

As for the collection within, you can feast on some 3,000 works, including gold treasures from Syria, ivories, miniatures, Ottoman ceramics and textiles, all displayed in chronological order. Aside from finally giving a home to some of its most fabulous and hitherto hidden artefacts, the Louvre is sending out a clear message: despite today's political and religious tensions, the history and culture of the Arab and Western worlds are forever intertwined.

This elegant bar facing the Louvre has become a local institution: neo-colonial fans whirr lazily and oil paintings adorn the walls. A sleek crowd sips martinis or reads papers at the mahogany bar (originally from a Chicago speakeasy), giving way to young professionals in the restaurant and pretty things in the library. It can feel a touch try-hard, but expertly mixed cocktails should take the edge off any evening.

Harry's New York Bar

5 rue Daunou, 2nd (01.42.61.71.14, www.harrys-bar.fr). M° Opéra. **Open** noon-2am Mon-Thur, Sun; noon-3am Fri, Sat. **Bar**. **Map** p72 B2 (23)

The city's most stylish American bar is beloved of expats, visitors and hard-drinking Parisians. The bartenders mix some of the most sophisticated cocktails in town, from the trademark bloody mary (invented here, so they say) to the Pétrifiant, an elixir of half a dozen spirits splashed into a beer mug. Gershwin composed *An American in Paris* in the piano bar here.

Kaï

18 rue du Louvre, 1st (01.40.15.01.99). M° Louvre Rivoli. **Open** 12.30-2.15pm, 7.30-10.30pm Tue-Sat. Closed 1wk Apr & 3wks Aug. **€€€**. **Japanese**. **Map** p73 D4 (24)

This restaurant has developed a following among fashionable diners. The 'Kaï-style' sushi is a zesty take on a classic: marinated and lightly grilled yellowtail is pressed on to a roll of shiso-scented rice. Not to be outdone, grilled aubergine with miso, seemingly simple, turns out to be a smoky, luscious experience. A main of breaded pork lacks the finesse of the starters, but is still satisfying.

Liza

14 rue de la Banque, 2nd (01.55.35.00.66, www.restaurant-liza.com). M° Bourse. **Open** noon-2.15pm, 8-10pm Mon-Thur; noon-2.15pm, 8-11pm Fri; 8-11pm Sat; noon-3.30pm Sun. **€€**. **Lebanese**. **Map** p73 D3 (25)

Liza Soughayar's eaterie showcases the style and superb food of Beirut. Lentil, fried onion and orange salad is delicious, as are the *kebbe* (minced seasoned raw lamb) and grilled halloumi cheese with home-made apricot preserve. Main courses such as minced lamb with coriander-spiced spinach and rice are light, flavoursome and well presented.

Le Meurice

Hôtel Meurice, 228 rue de Rivoli, 1st (01.44.58.10.55, www.lemeurice.com). M° Tuileries. **Open** 7-10.30am, 12.30-2pm, 7.30-10pm Mon-Fri; 7-11am Sat, Sun. Closed 2wks Mar & Aug. **€€€€**. **Haute cuisine**. **Map** p72 B3 (26)

Chef Yannick Alléno produces some glorious, if rather understated, dishes, teasing flavour out of every leaf, frond, fin or fillet. A fine cheese tray comes from Quatrehomme, and the pastry chef amazes with his signature millefeuille.

Ô Château

68 rue Jean-Jacques Rousseau, 1st (01.44.73.97.80, www.o-chateau.com). M° Les Halles. **Open** 4pm-midnight daily. **Wine bar**. **Map** p73 D4 (27)

Sommelier Olivier Magny's spacious, convivial wine bar has been a great success since opening in 2011. There are no fewer than 40 wines available by the glass here, with the chance to taste some very rare bottles in *soupçon*-sized quantities. Thrice-daily tastings take place in the intimate tasting rooms.

Senderens

9 pl de la Madeleine, 8th (01.42.65.22.90, www.senderens.fr). M° Madeleine. **Open** noon-2.45pm, 7.30-11pm daily. Closed 1st 3wks Aug. **€€€€**. **Haute cuisine**. **Map** p72 A3 (28)

Alain Senderens reinvented his art nouveau institution a few years ago with a *Star Trek* interior and a mind-boggling fusion menu. You might find dishes such as roast duck foie gras with a warm salad of black figs and liquorice powder. Each dish comes with a suggested wine, whisky, sherry or punch.

Le Tambour

41 rue Montmartre, 2nd (01.42.33.06.90). M° Sentier. **Open** 7.30am-3.30am daily. **Bar. Map** p73 D3 29

The Tambour is a classic nighthawk's bar decked with vintage public transport paraphernalia, its wooden banquettes and bus stop-sign bar stools occupied by chatty regulars who give the 24-hour clock their best shot. There's a long dining room memorable for its métro map from Stalingrad station.

Thaïm

46 rue de Richelieu, 1st (01.42.96.54.67). M° Bourse or Palais Royal. **Open** noon-3pm, 7-11.30pm Mon-Fri; 7-11pm Sat. **€. Thai. Map** p72 C3 30

Thaïm has an elegant decor of dark wood and plum fabrics. Particularly good value is the three-course lunch menu, which might bring crisp fried parcels filled with spiced vegetables, an aromatic green fish curry (there is a choice of fish, meat or poultry every day), and coconut-pumpkin soup. There is a vast choice of teas, including an iced ginger-coconut version.

PARIS BY AREA

Shopping

Agnès b

2, 3, 4 & 6 rue du Jour, 1st (men 01.42.33.04.13, women 01.45.08.56.56, www.agnesb.com). M° Les Halles. **Open** *Oct-Apr* 10am-7pm Mon-Sat. *May-Sept* 10.30am-7.30pm Mon-Sat. **Map** p73 D4 31

Agnès b rarely wavers from her design vision: pure lines in fine quality cotton, merino wool and silk. Best buys are shirts, pullovers and cardigans. Her mini-empire of men's, women's, children's, travel and sportswear shops is compact; see the website for details.

Alice Cadolle

4 rue Cambon, 1st (01.42.60.94.22, www.cadolle.com). M° Concorde or Madeleine. **Open** 10.30am-6.30pm Mon, Tue; 10am-7pm Wed-Sat. Closed Aug. **Map** p72 B3 32

Five generations of lingerie-makers are behind this boutique, founded by Hermine Cadolle, who claimed to be the inventor of the bra. Poupie Cadolle continues the tradition in a cosy space devoted to a luxury ready-to-wear line of bras, panties and corsets. For a special treat, Cadolle Couture (255 rue St-Honoré, 1st, 01.42.60.94.94) will create bespoke lingerie (by appointment only).

Apple Store

12 rue Halévy, 9th (01.44.83.42.00, www.apple.com). M° Opéra. **Open** 9am-8pm Mon-Wed; 9am-9pm Thur-Sat. **Map** p72 C2 33

Apple's second Paris store opened in 2010 in a stunning belle époque former bank facing the Opéra Garnier. To fit in with such hallowed surroundings, Apple strayed from its standard model, retaining the original carved wooden staircase, wrought-iron railings, marble columns and mosaic tile floor.

Boucheron

26 pl Vendôme, 1st (01.42.61.58.16, www.boucheron.com). M° Opéra. **Open** 10.30am-7pm Mon-Sat. **Map** p72 B3 34

Boucheron was the first to set up shop on place Vendôme, attracting celebrity custom from the nearby Ritz hotel. Owned by Gucci, the grand jeweller produces stunning pieces, using traditional motifs with new accents: take, for example, its chocolate-coloured gold watch.

Chanel

31 rue Cambon, 1st (01.42.86.26.00, www.chanel.com). M° Concorde or Madeleine. **Open** 10am-7pm Mon-Sat. **Map** p72 B3 35

Fashion legend Chanel has managed to stay relevant, thanks to Karl Lagerfeld. Coco opened her first boutique in this street, at no.21, in 1910, and the tradition continues in this elegant interior. Lagerfeld has been designing for Chanel since 1983, and keeps on revamping the classics – the little black dress and the Chanel suit – with great success.

Colette

213 rue St-Honoré, 1st (01.55.35.33.90, www.colette.fr). Mº Pyramides or Tuileries. **Open** 11am-7pm Mon-Sat. **Map** p72 B3 36

The renowned one-stop concept and lifestyle store features a highly eclectic selection of accessories, fashion, books, media, gadgets, and hair and beauty brands, all in a swanky space.

Comme des Garçons

54 rue du Fbg-St-Honoré, 8th (01.53.30.27.27, www.comme-des-garcons.com). Mº Concorde or Madeleine. **Open** 11am-7pm Mon-Sat. **Map** p72 A2 37

Rei Kawakubo's design ideas and revolutionary mix of materials have influenced fashions of the past two decades, and are showcased in this fibreglass store. Comme des Garçons Parfums (23 pl du Marché-St-Honoré, 1st, 01.47.03.15.03) provides a futuristic setting for the brand's fragrances.

Didier Ludot

24 galerie de Montpensier, 1st (01.42.96.06.56, www.didierludot.fr). Mº Palais Royal Musée du Louvre. **Open** 10.30am-7pm Mon-Sat. **Map** p72 C3 38

Didier Ludot's temples to vintage haute couture appear in Printemps, Harrods and New York's Barneys. The pieces are stunning: Dior, Molyneux, Balenciaga, Pucci, Féraud and Chanel, from the 1920s onwards. Ludot also curates exhibitions, using the shop windows around the Palais-Royal as a gallery. La Petite Robe Noire (125 galerie de Valois, 1st, 01.40.15.01.04) stocks Ludot's own line of vintage little black dresses.

Erès

2 rue Tronchet, 8th (01.47.42.28.82, www.eres.fr). Mº Madeleine. **Open** 10am-7pm Mon-Sat. **Map** p72 B2 39

Erès's beautifully cut swimwear has embraced a sexy '60s look, with buttons on low-cut briefs. The top and bottom can be purchased in different sizes, or you can buy one piece of a bikini.

La Galerie du Carrousel du Louvre

99 rue de Rivoli, 1st (01.43.16.47.10, www.carrouseldulouvre.com). Mº Palais Royal Musée du Louvre. **Open** 10am-8pm daily. **Map** p72 C4 40

This massive underground centre – which is open every day of the year – is home to more than 35 shops, mostly big-name chains vying for your attention and cash. Options include an Apple Store, Swatch Store and L'Occitane en Provence.

Galeries Lafayette

40 bd Haussmann, 9th (01.42.82.34.56, fashion shows 01.42.82.30.25, fashion advice 01.42.82.35.50, www.galerieslafayette.com). Mº Chaussée d'Antin/RER Auber. **Open** 9.30am-8pm Mon-Wed, Fri, Sat; 9.30am-9pm Thur. **Map** p72 C2 41

Espace Luxe on the first floor features luxury prêt-à-porter and accessories and nine avant-garde designers, and a vast shoe department is home to some 150 brands. The men's fashion space on the third floor, Lafayette Homme, has natty designer corners and a 'Club' area with internet access. On the first floor, Lafayette Gourmet has exotic foods galore, and a wine cellar. Lafayette Maison over the road has five floors of home furnishings and design.

Hédiard

21 pl de la Madeleine, 8th (01.43.12.88.88, www.hediard.fr). Mº Madeleine. **Open** 9am-8.30pm Mon-Sat. **Map** p72 A2 42

Hédiard's charming shop dates back to 1880, when it was the first to introduce exotic foods to Paris, specialising in rare teas and coffees, spices, jams and candied fruits. Pop upstairs for a cuppa in the shop's posh tearoom.

Hervé Léger

24 rue Cambon, 1st (01.42.60.02.00, www.herveleger.com). Mº Concorde. **Open** 10am-7pm Mon-Sat. **Map** p72 B3 43

PARIS BY AREA

Lanvin

LANVIN
PARIS

A couple of decades ago, Hervé Léger's silhouette-cinching bandage dresses were as evocative of the era as supermodels Linda, Christy, Naomi and Cindy. But somewhere in the mid-'90s women lost their love of Lycra. In the past few seasons, however, updated reinterpretations of Léger's style, by the likes of Christopher Kane and Marios Schwab, have been nothing short of a fashion phenomenon. Less modified versions, sold by the Léger label itself (now owned and designed by Max Azria of BCBG fame), have been less critically acclaimed.

Jean-Paul Gaultier

6 rue Vivienne, 2nd (01.42.86. 05.05, www.jeanpaulgaultier.com). M° Bourse. **Open** 11am-7pm daily. **Map** p73 D3 44

Having celebrated his 30th year in the fashion business, Gaultier is still going strong. His boudoir boutique stocks men's and women's ready-to-wear and the reasonably priced JPG Jeans lines. The haute couture department is by appointment only.

Kiliwatch

64 rue Tiquetonne, 2nd (01.42.21. 17.37, www.espacekiliwatch.fr). M° Etienne Marcel. **Open** 2-7pm Mon; 11am-7.30pm Tue-Sat. **Map** p73 E3 45

The trailblazer of the rue Etienne-Marcel revival is filled with hoodies, casual shirts and jeans. Brands include Gas, Edwin and Pepe Jeans.

Kokon To Zai

48 rue Tiquetonne, 2nd (01.42.36. 92.41, www.kokontozai.co.uk). M° Etienne Marcel. **Open** 11.30am-7.30pm Mon-Sat. **Map** p73 E4 46

This tiny style emporium is sister to the Kokon To Zai in London. The neon-lit club feel of the mirrored interior matches the dark glamour of the designs. Unique pieces straight off the catwalk share space with creations by Marjan Peijoski, Noki, Raf Simons, Ziad Ghanem and new Norwegian designers.

Lanvin

22 rue du Fbg St-Honoré, 8th (01.44.71. 31.73, www.lanvin.com). M° Concorde or Madeleine. **Open** 10.30am-7pm daily. **Map** p72 A3 47

The couture house that began in the 1920s with Jeanne Lanvin has been reinvented by the indefatigable Albert Elbaz. In October 2007, he unveiled this revamped showroom that set new aesthetic standards for luxury fashion retailing. Lanvin has an exhibition room devoted to her in the Musée des Arts Décoratifs, and this apartment-boutique also incorporates original furniture from the Lanvin archive. All this would be nothing, of course, if the clothes themselves were not exquisite.

Lavinia

3 bd de la Madeleine, 1st (01.42.97. 20.20, www.lavinia.fr). M° Madeleine. **Open** 10am-8pm Mon-Fri; 9am-8pm Sat. **Map** p72 B2 48

Lavinia stocks a broad selection of French and non-French wines; its *cave* has everything from a 1945 Mouton-Rothschild at €22,000 to trendy and 'fragile' wines for under €10. Have fun tasting wine with the *dégustation* machines on the ground floor, which allow customers to taste a sip of up to ten different wines each week for €10.

Legrand Filles et Fils

1 rue de la Banque, 2nd (01.42.60. 07.12, www.caves-legrand.com). M° Bourse. **Open** 11am-7pm Mon; 10am-7.30pm Tue-Fri; 10am-7pm Sat. Closed Mon in July & Aug. **Map** p73 D3 49

Fine wines, teas and *bonbons*, and a showroom for regular wine tastings.

Marc by Marc Jacobs

19 pl du Marché-Saint-Honoré, 1st (01.40.20.11.30, www.marcjacobs.com). M° Tuileries. **Open** 11am-7pm Mon-Sat. **Map** p72 B3 50

The store for Jacobs' casual, punky line has fashionistas clustering like bees round a honeypot, not least for the fabulously inexpensive accessories that add spice to a tired outfit. A skateboard table and giant pedalo in the form of a swan are the centrepieces of the store, which stocks men's and women's prêt-à-porter, shoes and special editions.

Marc Jacobs

34 galerie de Montpensier, 1st (01.55. 35.02.60, www.marcjacobs.com). M° Palais Royal Musée du Louvre. **Open** 11am-7pm Mon-Sat. **Map** p72 C3 51

Marc Jacobs brought new life and verve – and an influx of fashionistas – to these elegant cloisters. Stocking womenswear, menswear, accessories and shoes, the shop has become a place of pilgrimage for the designer's legion of admirers.

Martin Margiela

23 & 25bis rue de Montpensier, 1st (womenswear 01.40.15.07.55, menswear 01.40.15.06.44, www. maisonmartinmargiela.com). M° Palais Royal Musée du Louvre. **Open** 11am-7pm Mon-Sat. **Map** p72 C4 52

This Paris outlet is a pristine, white, unlabelled space. Martin Margiela's collection for women (Line 1) has a blank label but is recognisable by external white stitching. You'll also find Line 6 (women's basics) and Line 10 (menswear), plus accessories for men and women and shoes.

Printemps

64 bd Haussmann, 9th (01.42.82. 50.00, www.printemps.com). M° Havre Caumartin/RER Auber. **Open** 9.35am-8pm Mon-Wed, Fri, Sat; 9.35am-10pm Thur. **Map** p72 B1 53

Fashion is where Printemps excels; an entire floor is devoted to shoes, and the beauty department stocks more than 200 brands. In Printemps de la Mode, French designers sit alongside the big international designers. The Fashion Loft offers a younger take on current trends. Printemps de la Maison stocks everything from everyday tableware to design classics. For refuelling, there's a tearoom, sushi bar and Café Be, an Alain Ducasse bakery.

Repetto

22 rue de la Paix, 2nd (01.44.71. 83.12, www.repetto.com). M° Opéra. **Open** 9.30am-7.30pm Mon-Sat. **Map** p72 B2 54

This ballet shoe-maker struck gold when it decided to reissue its dance shoes with pavement soles several years ago. The prowly *ballerines* and showbiz dance boots in black, metallic and spangly finishes are fun, timelessly stylish and exceptionally comfortable. The shoes are sold alongside the full range of real balletwear; what's more you can try out your *pointes* on a red carpet with a *barre* if you want to show off.

Salons du Palais-Royal Shiseido

142 galerie de Valois, Jardins du Palais-Royal, 1st (01.49.27.09.09, www.sergelutens.com). M° Palais Royal Musée du Louvre. **Open** 10am-7pm Mon-Sat. **Map** p72 C3 55

Under the arcades of the Palais-Royal, Shiseido's perfumier Serge Lutens practises his aromatic arts. A former photographer at Paris *Vogue* and artistic director of make-up at Christian Dior, Lutens is a maestro of rare taste. Bottles of his concoctions – Tubéreuse Criminelle, Rahat Loukoum and Ambre Sultan – can be sampled by visitors. Look out for Fleurs d'Oranger, which the great man defines as the smell of happiness itself. Many of the perfumes are exclusive to the Salons; prices start at around €100.

Stella McCartney

114-121 galerie de Valois, Jardins du Palais-Royal, 1st (01.47.03.03.80, www.stellamccartney.com). M° Palais Royal Musée du Louvre. **Open** 10.30am-7pm Mon-Sat. **Map** p72 C3 56

Stella McCartney is crazy about the 'clash of history, fashion and contemporary art' at the Palais-Royal, where she opened her sumptuous boutique. Thick carpets, maplewood and metal sculptures create a rarefied setting for women's prêt-à-porter, bags, shoes, sunglasses and her range of simple but stylish lingerie, as well as the perfume and skincare lines.

Yohji Yamamoto

4 rue Cambon, 1st (01.40.20.00.71, www.yohjiyamamoto.co.jp). M° Concorde. **Open** 10.30am-7pm Mon-Sat. **Map** p72 B3 57

Yamamoto has achieved his dream of having a flagship store on rue Cambon. This temple to the creator is as impressive as those in New York and Antwerp, a pristine white gallery space. Behind an origami-screen window mannequins clothed in his showpieces seem to float in the air. A grand staircase leads to womenswear on the first floor, while menswear is on the lower ground.

Nightlife

Au Duc des Lombards

42 rue des Lombards, 1st (01.42.33.22.88, www.ducdeslombards.com). M° Châtelet. **Open** *Concerts* 8pm, 10pm Mon-Sat. **Admission** €18-€25. **Map** p73 E5 58

Some of the capital's venerated jazz spots have lost the fight for survival in recent years. But this one has endured, and attracts a high class of performer and a savvy crowd.

Le Cab

2 pl du Palais-Royal, 1st (01.58.62.56.25, www.cabaret.fr). M° Palais Royal Musée du Louvre. **Open** 11.30pm-5am Thur-Sat. *Restaurant* 8-11.30pm Tue-Sat. **Admission** free Tue, Wed; €20 Thur-Sat. **Map** p72 C4 59

Le Cab is owned by the management behind Club Mix and Queen, and R&B and commercial house dominate the playlist. The doormen are tough, and if they don't like you, you won't get in (unless you've booked for dinner).

Chacha Club

47 rue Berger, 1st (01.40.13.12.12, www.chachaclub.fr). M° Châtelet. **Open** 8pm-6am Tue-Sat. **Admission** varies. **Map** p73 D4 60

Paris's fetishistic obsession with the cigarette has produced a new nightlife phenomenon: the fumoir. The Chacha Club was the first high-profile establishment to open one, and it forms just one of the sexy attributes of this hot haunt near Les Halles. It combines restaurant, bar and club in a suite of rooms with 1930s-inspired decor.

Olympia

28 bd des Capucines, 9th (08.92.68.33.68, www.olympiahall.com). M° Opéra. **Open** *Box office* noon-7pm daily. *Concerts* times vary. **Map** p72 B2 61

The Beatles, Frank Sinatra, Jimi Hendrix and Edith Piaf all performed here over the years. Now it's mostly home to nostalgia and *variété*, although big names still drop by – Crystal Castles performed in 2013.

Rex

5 bd Poissonnière, 2nd (01.42.36.10.96, www.rexclub.com). M° Bonne Nouvelle. **Open** 11.30pm-6am Wed-Sat. **Admission** free-€15. **Map** p73 E2 62

The Rex's sound system puts over 40 different sound configurations at the DJ's fingertips. Once associated with techno pioneer Laurent Garnier, the Rex still occupies an unassailable position as the city's serious club music venue.

Le Scop'Club

5 av de l'Opéra, 8th (01.42.60.64.45, www.lescopclub.com). M° Pyramides. **Open** 8-11pm Tue-Thur; 11pm-5am Fri, Sat. **Admission** €10-€15. **Map** p72 C3 63

This small club is all about electro-rock, with black-painted walls and live acts taking to the stage at weekends. Gigs aren't free, but DJ sets by the likes of MGMT and 'music label battles' are interesting alternatives on other nights. The crowd is young and dressed to impress, but the Scop'Club is easier to get into than when it was Paris Paris.

Silencio

142 rue de Montmartre, 2nd (www.silencio-club.com). M° Bourse or Grands Boulevards. **Open** 6pm-6am Tue-Sun. **Admission** varies. **Map** p73 D3 64

David Lynch's first Paris joint, named after the cult setting in his 2001 movie *Mulholland Drive*, is mainly for private members. If you're not up for full-blown membership, access is after midnight. The director designed every aspect of the decor, from the gold-leaf walls to the 1950s-style furniture.

Théâtre du Châtelet

1 pl du Châtelet, 1st (01.40.28.28.40, www.chatelet-theatre.com). M° Châtelet. **Open** times vary. **Admission** varies. **Map** p73 E5 65

This venerable theatre and classic music hall has another life as a jazz and *chanson* venue, with performances by top-notch international musicians.

Arts & leisure

Châtelet – Théâtre Musical de Paris

1 pl du Châtelet, 1st (01.40.28.28.40, www.chatelet-theatre.com). M° Châtelet. **Box office** 11am-7pm Mon-Sat; 1hr before performance Sun. **Admission** €28.50-€100.50. **Map** p73 E5 66

The Châtelet is fast becoming Paris's main venue for musicals hailing from Broadway and the West End – such as *West Side Story* and *Carousel* – which are usually performed in the original language by visiting companies.

Forum des Images

2 rue du Cinéma, Forum des Halles, 1st (01.44.76.63.00, www.forumdesimages.net). M° Les Halles. **Admission** (per day) €4-€5. **Map** p73 E4 67

The Forum was conceived partly as a screening venue for old and little-known movies, and partly as an archive centre for every kind of moving picture featuring Paris; today, the collection numbers over 6,500 documentaries, adverts, newsreels and films.

Opéra National de Paris, Palais Garnier

Pl de l'Opéra, 9th (08.92.89.90.90, www.operadeparis.fr). M° Opéra. **Box office** 11.30am-6.30pm Mon-Sat. *By phone* 9am-6pm Mon-Fri; 9am-1pm Sat. **Admission** €10-€180. **Map** p72 B2 68

The Palais Garnier is the jewel in the crown of Paris music-making. The Opéra National often favours the high-tech Bastille for new productions, but the matchless acoustics of the Palais Garnier are superior to the new house.

Spa Nuxe

NEW *32 rue Montorgueil, 1st (01.42.36.65.65, www.nuxe.com). M° Les Halles.* **Open** 10am-9pm Mon-Fri; 9.30am-7.30pm Sat. **Map** p73 E4 69

This luxurious day spa housed in stone vaults with wooden cabins and safari-style tents offers massages and skin treatments using Nuxe's gentle, plant-based products. The facials begin with a short foot, tummy and neck message.

Théâtre National de l'Opéra Comique

Pl Boieldieu, 2nd (01.42.44.45.40, www.opera-comique.com). M° Richelieu Drouot. **Box office** 11am-7pm Mon-Sat; 11am-5pm Sun. **Admission** €5-€120. **Map** p72 C2 70

Its promotion to national theatre status has brought this jewel box of a theatre back to life, exploring a specifically French repertoire often ignored by larger houses.

Event highlights Claude Debussy's Pelléas et Mélisande (Feb 2014)

Théâtre de la Ville

2 pl du Châtelet, 4th (01.42.74.22.77, www.theatredelaville-paris.com). M° Châtelet. **Box office** 11am-7pm Mon; 11am-8pm Tue-Sat. **Admission** €15-€30. **Map** p73 E5 71

Features hip chamber music outfits such as the Kronos and Takács Quartets, Early Music pioneer Fabio Biondi, and pianist Aleksandar Madzar.

Montmartre & Pigalle

Perched up on a hill (or *butte*), Montmartre is the highest point in Paris, its tightly packed houses spiralling round the mound below the dome of **Sacré-Coeur**. Despite the many tourists (chiefly around place du Tertre), it's surprisingly easy to fall under the spell of this romantic district. Climb stairways, peer down alleys and into ivy-covered houses and quiet squares, and explore streets such as rue des Abbesses, rue des Trois-Frères and rue des Martyrs, with their cafés, boutiques and bohemian residents.

At the bottom of the hill, in once-notorious Pigalle, the seediness of yesteryear's sex clubs and brothels is steadily being replaced by hip music venues and clubs.

Sights & museums

Cimetière de Montmartre

20 av Rachel, access by staircase from rue Caulaincourt, 18th (01.53.42.36.30). M° Blanche or Place de Clichy. **Open** *6 Nov-15 Mar* 8am-5.30pm Mon-Fri; 8.30am-5.30pm Sat; 9am-5.30pm Sun, public hols. *16 Mar-5 Nov* 8am-6pm Mon-Fri; 8.30am-6pm Sat; 9am-6pm Sun, public hols. **Admission** free. **Map** p89 A1 ❶

Truffaut, Nijinsky, Berlioz, Degas, Offenbach and German poet Heine are all buried here. So, too, are La Goulue, the first great cancan star, and consumptive heroine Alphonsine Plessis, inspiration for *La Traviata*. Flowers are still left on the grave of diva Dalida.

Musée d'Art Halle St-Pierre

2 rue Ronsard, 18th (01.42.58.72.89, www.hallesaintpierre.org). M° Anvers. **Open** *Jan-July, Sept-Dec* 10am-6pm Mon-Fri; 10am-7pm Sat; 11am-6pm Sun. *Aug* noon-6pm Mon-Fri. **Admission** prices vary. **Map** p89 C2 ❷

The former market in the shadow of Sacré-Coeur specialises in *art brut*, *art outsider* and *art singulier* from its own and other collections.

Brilliance in a bun

Where to tuck into the best burgers in Paris.

Parisians have gone burger bonkers over the past couple of years. This fast-food trend has been most in evidence in the arrival of mobile gourmet burger van **Le Camion qui Fume** (01.84.16.33.75, www.lecamionquifume.com), which began hitting the streets in December 2011. Run by young Californian chef Kristin Frederick, who worked at Spago in LA and later trained at Paris's Ecole Ferrandi, the van brings the Californian food truck trend to all corners of Paris. Visit the website to see where it will be parked, and when. And expect to queue.

Le Camion was followed by **Big Fernand** (see p91), an über-trendy takeaway burger joint dubbed 'L'atelier du hamburger' – 'the hamburger workshop'. The concept is for customers to build their own burgers, selecting a combination of meat (beef, chicken, lamb or veal), cheese (goat's cheese, Saint Nectaire, Tomme de Savoie), grilled vegetables, spices and sauces.

The latest opening to jump on the bandwagon is **Blend** (see p76), in Etienne Marcel. And if the queues are anything to go by, this modern 24-seater burger bar is going to be relished for a long time. Expect hand-cut veal and beef mince, own-made brioche buns, sweet-potato fries and house tomato sauce. Artisan beers and cool decor round off the experience.

Musée de l'Erotisme

72 bd de Clichy, 18th (01.42.58.28.73, www.musee-erotisme.com). M° Blanche. **Open** 10am-2am daily. **Admission** €10; €8 reductions. **Map** p89 A2 ❸

Seven floors of erotic art and artefacts. The first three run from first-century Peruvian phallic pottery through Etruscan fertility symbols to Yoni sculptures from Nepal; the fourth gives a history of Paris brothels; the top floors host exhibitions of erotic art.

Musée de Montmartre

12 rue Cortot, 18th (01.49.25.89.37, www.museedemontmartre.fr). M° Lamarck-Caulaincourt. **Open** 10am-6pm daily. **Admission** €8; free-€6 reductions. **Map** p89 B1 ❹

This 17th-century manor house displays the history of the hilltop, with rooms devoted to composer Gustave Charpentier and a tribute to the Lapin Agile cabaret. The delightful gardens have just been renovated.

Musée National Gustave Moreau

14 rue de la Rochefoucauld, 9th (01.48.74.38.50, www.musee-moreau.fr). M° Trinité. **Open** 10am-12.45pm, 2-5.15pm Mon, Wed, Thur; 10am-5.15pm Fri-Sun. **Admission** €5; free-€3 reductions. **Map** p89 A4 ❺

This wonderful museum combines the private apartment of Symbolist painter Gustave Moreau (1825-98) with the vast gallery he built to display his work. Don't miss the trippy *Jupiter et Sémélé* on the second floor. The museum is set to close for renovations during late 2013.

Musée de la Vie Romantique

Hôtel Scheffer-Renan, 16 rue Chaptal, 9th (01.55.31.95.67, www.vie-romantique.paris.fr). M° Blanche or St-Georges. **Open** 10am-6pm Tue-Sun. **Admission** free. *Exhibitions* prices vary. **Map** p89 A3 ❻

When Dutch artist Ary Scheffer lived in this small villa, the area teemed with

Montmartre & Pigalle

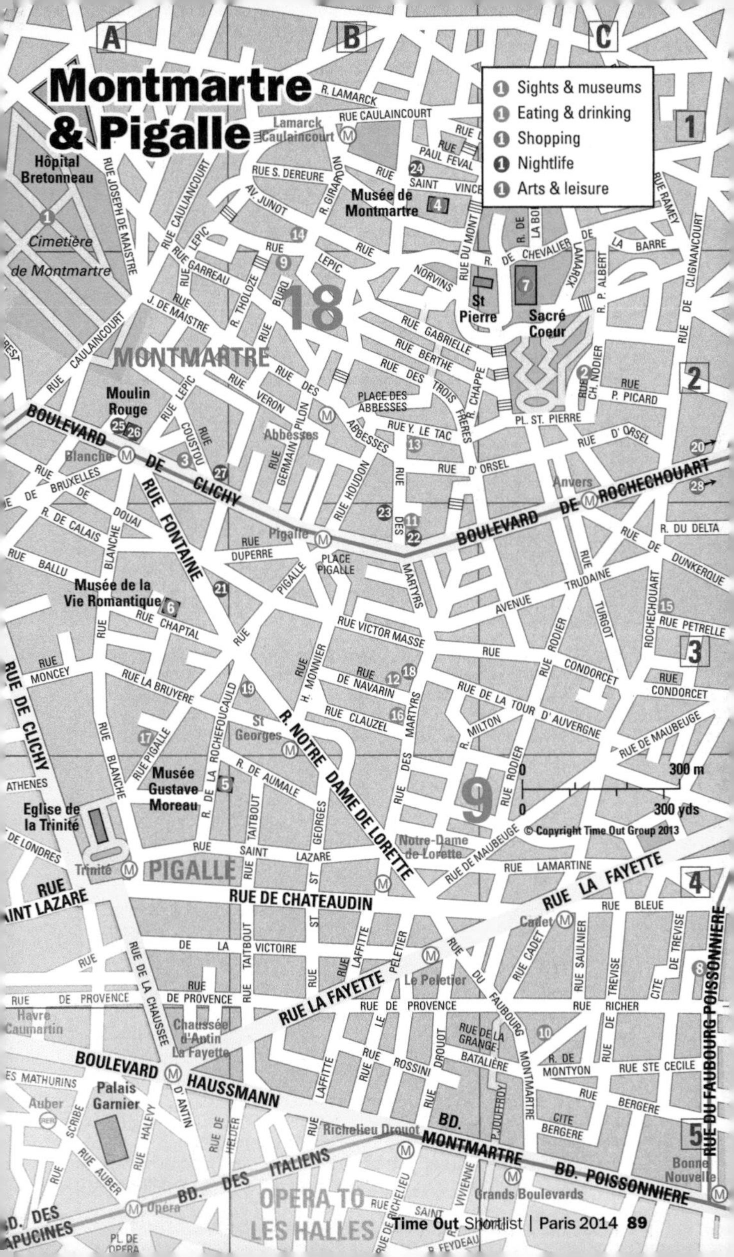

La Maison Mère

composers, writers and artists. Aurore Dupin, Baronne Dudevant (George Sand) was a guest at Scheffer's soirées and the museum is devoted to Sand, although the watercolours, jewels and plastercast of her right arm that she left behind show little of her ideas or affairs.

Sacré-Coeur

35 rue du Chevalier-de-la-Barre, 18th (01.53.41.89.00, www.sacre-coeur-montmartre.com). M° Abbesses or Anvers. **Open** *Basilica* 6am-11pm daily. *Crypt & dome* Winter 10am-5.45pm daily. Summer 9am-6.45pm daily. **Admission** free. *Crypt & dome* €5. **Map** p89 C2 ⑦

Work on this enormous mock Romano-Byzantine edifice began in 1877. It was commissioned after the nation's defeat by Prussia in 1870, voted for by the Assemblée Nationale and built from public subscription. Finally completed in 1914, it was consecrated in 1919. The interior boasts lavish mosaics.

Eating & drinking

Big Fernand

NEW *55 rue du Faubourg Poissonnière, 9th (01.47.70.54.72, www.bigfernand.com). M° Cadet or Poissonnière.* **Open** noon-2.30pm, 7.30-10.30pm Mon-Sat. **€€. Burgers. Map** p89 C4 ⑧

See box p88.

Le Coq Rico

NEW *98 rue Lepic, 18th (01.42.59.82.89, www.lecoqrico.com). M° Abbesses or Lamarck-Caulincourt.* **Open** noon-2.30pm, 7.30-11pm daily. **€€€. Bistro. Map** p89 B1 ⑨

Antoine Westermann's new venture is a classy 'bistrotisserie' where comfort food is transformed into gourmet treats – gooey boiled egg comes with crunchy soldiers and truffle-infused butter. There's a list of poultry suppliers at the bottom of the menu, a transparency that will appeal to health-conscious locals – even if prices are high (€95 for a whole chicken serving two to four).

Les Fils à Maman

7 bis Rue Geoffroy-Marie, 9th (01.48.24.59.39, www.lesfilsamaman.com). M° Grands Boulevards. **Open** 11.30am-2.30pm, 7-11pm Mon-Fri; 7-11pm Sat. **€€. Bistro. Map** p89 C5 ⑩

In the area near the Folies Bergère a band of five 'mothers' boys' has created a restaurant evoking their mums' home cooking. Even the mums get into the kitchen on the first Tuesday of the month to turn out *blanquette de veau*, chicken cordon bleu and Nutella-flavoured puddings.

La Fourmi

74 rue des Martyrs, 18th (01.42.64.70.35). M° Pigalle. **Open** 8am-2am Mon-Thur; 8am-4am Fri, Sat; 10am-2am Sun. **Bar. Map** p89 B3 ⑪

La Fourmi is an old bistro that has been converted for today's tastes, with picture windows lighting the spacious interior. The classic zinc bar counter is crowned by industrial lights, and an excellent music policy and cool clientele ensure a pile of flyers.

La Maison Mère

4 rue de Navarin, 9th (01.42.81.11.00, www.lamaisonmere.fr). M° Saint-Georges or Pigalle. **Open** noon-3pm, 7pm-2am Tue-Sat; noon-3pm Sun. **€€€. Bistro. Map** p89 B3 ⑫

Forget any ideas of a traditional French kitchen: this place is more Mom than Mère. Embrace, instead, the New York-style decor and menu, with crab cake, Brooklyn platters, Long Island platters and so on. The five burgers will delight enthusiasts. The house fries could be better and the whole doesn't come cheap, but nobody's perfect. Friendly service, a good wine selection and top cheesecake all go a long way towards sweetening the bill.

Le Miroir

94 rue des Martyrs, 18th (01.46.06.50.73). M° Abbesses. **Open** noon-2pm, 7.30-10pm Tue-Sat. **€€. Bistro. Map** p89 B2 ⑬

This friendly bistro is a welcome addition to the neighbourhood. Big mirrors, red banquettes and a glass ceiling at the back give it character, while the professional food and service reflect the owners' haute cuisine training. Expect dishes such as salad of whelks with white beans, crisp-skinned duck and chanterelle mushrooms.

Le Moulin de la Galette

83 rue Lepic, 18th (01.46.06.84.77, www.lemoulindelagalette.fr). M° Notre-Dame-de-Lorette. **Open** noon-11pm daily. Closed Aug. **€€€**. **Bistro**. **Map** p89 B1 ⓮

The Butte Montmartre was once dotted with windmills, and this survivor houses a chic restaurant. It's hard to imagine a more picturesque setting in Montmartre. The kitchen makes an effort with dishes such as foie gras with melting beetroot cooked in lemon balm and juniper or suckling pig.

Pétrelle

34 rue Pétrelle, 9th (01.42.82.11.02, www.petrelle.fr). M° Anvers. **Open** 8-10pm Tue-Sat. Closed 4wks July/Aug & 1wk Dec. **€€**. **Bistro**. **Map** p89 C3 ⓯

Jean-Luc André is as inspired a decorator as he is a cook, and the quirky charm of his dining room has made it popular with fashion designers and film stars. The €29 no-choice menu is huge value (marinated sardines with tomato relish, rabbit with roasted vegetables, deep purple poached figs).

Rose Bakery

46 rue des Martyrs, 9th (01.42.82.12.80). M° Notre-Dame-de-Lorette. **Open** 9am-6pm Tue-Sun. Closed 2wks Aug & 1wk Dec. **€**. **Café**. **Map** p89 B3 ⓰

This English-themed café run by a Franco-British couple stands out for the quality of its ingredients, as well as the too-good-to-be-true puddings. The DIY salad plate is crunchily satisfying, but the *pizzettes*, daily soups and occasional risottos are equally good.

Rouge Passion

14 rue Jean-Baptiste Pigalle, 9th (01.42.85.07.62, www.rouge-passion.fr). M° Pigalle or St Georges. **Open** noon-3pm, 7pm-midnight Mon-Fri; 7pm-midnight Sat; 11.30am-4pm Sun. Closed 3wks Aug. **Wine bar**. **Map** p89 A3 ⓱

Two bright upstarts are behind this venture. Offering a long list of wines, a small but mouthwatering selection of hot dishes, salads, cheese and saucisson platters and decor that's satisfyingly vintage, the formula is spot on.

Shopping

Arnaud Delmontel

39 rue des Martyrs, 9th (01.48.78.29.33, www.arnaud-delmontel.com). M° St-Georges. **Open** 7am-8.30pm Mon, Wed-Sun. No credit cards. **Map** p89 B3 ⓲

With its crisp crust and chewy crumb shot through with irregular holes, Delmontel's Renaissance bread is one of the finest in Paris. He puts the same skill into his almond croissants and *tarte au citron à l'ancienne*.

Causses

NEW *55 rue Notre-Dame de Lorette, 9th (01.53.16.10.10, www.causses.org). M° Pigalle or Saint Georges.* **Open** 10am-9.30pm Mon-Sat.**Map** p89 B3 ⓳

SoPi's (SouthPigalle) new *alimentation générale extraordinaire* feels like an urban farm shop, offering a winning formula of quality seasonal produce, gourmet preserves, breads, sandwiches and salads. For expats in need of a taste of home, Tyrrell's crisps, Covent Garden soups, HP sauce and quality English biscuits abound.

Tati

4 bd de Rochechouart, 18th (01.55.29.52.20, www.tati.fr). M° Barbès Rochechouart. **Open** 10am-7pm Mon-Fri; 9.30am-7pm Sat. **Map** p89 C2 ⓴

Expect to find anything from T-shirts to wedding dresses, as well as household goods, at this discount heaven.

CAUSSES
Causses

CAUSSES
SAIN | SAVOUREUX | SIMPLE
CHARTE D'ENGAGEMENTS
SANS GLUTEN • GLUTEN FREE

Nightlife

Le Bus Palladium

6 rue Pierre Fontaine, 9th (01.45.26. 80.35, www.lebuspalladium.com). M° St-Georges, Pigalle or Blanche. **Open** *Concerts* 9pm-midnight. *Club* midnight-5am Thur-Sat. **Map** p89 A3 ㉑

This legendary rock venue is back on the map with a vintage house vibe somewhere between retro rockabilly and punk psychedelia.

La Cigale/La Boule Noire

120 bd de Rochechouart, 18th (01.49.25.81.75, www.lacigale.fr). M° Anvers or Pigalle. **Open** times vary. **Map** p89 B3 ㉒

One of Paris's finest venues, the horse-shoe shaped theatre La Cigale is linked to more cosy venue La Boule Noire, good for catching cult-ish visiting acts.

Le Divan du Monde

75 rue des Martyrs, 18th (01.40.05. 06.99, www.divandumonde.com). M° Abbesses or Pigalle. **Open** times vary. **Admission** €5-€30. **Map** p89 B3 ㉓

After a drink in the Fourmi opposite, pop over to the Divan for one-off parties and events. Upstairs specialises in VJ events, and downstairs holds dub, reggae, funk and world club nights.

Au Lapin Agile

22 rue des Saules, 18th (01.46.06. 85.87, www.au-lapin-agile.com). M° Lamarck Caulaincourt. **Shows** 9pm-1am Tue-Sun. **Admission** Show (incl 1 drink) €24; €17 reductions (except Sat & public hols). No credit cards. **Map** p89 B1 ㉔

The prices have gone up, tourists outnumber the locals and they sell their own compilation CDs these days, but that's all that seems to have changed since this bar first opened in 1860.

La Machine du Moulin Rouge

90 bd de Clichy, 18th (01.53.41.88.89, www.lamachinedumoulinrouge.com). M° Blanche. **Open** times vary. **Admission** varies. **Map** p89 A2 ㉕

This three-floor bar/club/live venue has had a substantial makeover and is now reborn with a dash of decadence. The main dancefloor, La Chaufferie, used to be the Moulin Rouge's boiler room, but the *Alice in Wonderland*-style decor is a breath of fresh air.

Moulin Rouge

82 bd de Clichy, 18th (01.53.09.82.82, www.moulin-rouge.com). M° Blanche. **Dinner** 7pm. **Shows** 9pm, 11pm daily. **Admission** *Show* (incl champagne) €105. *Dinner & show* €175-€200. *Show only* €95. **Map** p89 A2 ㉖

Toulouse-Lautrec posters, glittery lamp-posts and fake trees lend tacky charm to this revue, while 60 Doriss dancers cavort with faultless synchronisation. Costumes are flamboyant and the *entr'acte* acts funny.

Les Trois Baudets

64 bd de Clichy, 18th (01.42.62.33.33, www.lestroisbaudets.com). M° Pigalle. **Open** times vary. **Admission** €5-€20. **Map** p89 A2 ㉗

With a 250-seater theatre, an enviable sound system, two bars and a restaurant, this new concert hall encourages *chanson française* and other musical genres (rock, electro, folk and slam).

Arts & leisure

Le Louxor

NEW *170 bd Magenta, 10th (08.92. 68.05.79, www.cinemalouxor.fr). M° Barbès Rochechouart.* **Open** times vary. **Admission** varies. **Map** p89 C2 ㉘

Opened in 1921 and once a temple of silent cinema, the art deco Louxor fell on hard times after World War II and became a drug den, 1980s club and gay disco before being abandoned for 25 years. It reopened triumphantly as a cinema in April 2013, with a new brief to promote cultural, artistic and educational projects. Admire the fabulous architecture from the third-floor bar.

PARIS BY AREA

Canal St-Martin

North-east Paris

In the city's folklore, north-east Paris is working-class Paris – and although patches are gentrifying and little actual industry remains, the area still has a rough and ready vibe. Many of the streets here are somewhat on the tatty side, but others are artsy and fashionable, especially those close to the Canal St-Martin; and large swathes of the north-east are excitingly multi-ethnic, with thriving North African, Turkish and Caribbean enclaves.

Sights & museums

Canauxrama

13 quai de la Loire, 19th (01.42. 39.15.00, www.canauxrama.fr).
Tickets €16; free-€8.50 reductions. **Map** p97 C1 ❶
Take a trip up the city's second waterway, the Canal St-Martin. The tree-lined canal is a pretty sight, and the trip even goes underground, where the tunnel walls are enlivened by a light show.

Gare du Nord

Rue de Dunkerque, 10th (08.91. 36.20.20). M° Gare du Nord.
Map p97 A2 ❷
The grandest of the great 19th-century train stations (and Eurostar terminal since 1994) was designed by Hittorff between 1861 and 1864. The stone façade, with Ionic capitals and statues representing towns served by the station, hides a vast iron-and-glass vault.

Musée de la Musique

Cité de la Musique, 221 av Jean-Jaurès, 19th (01.44.84.44.84, www.cite-musique.fr). M° Porte de Pantin.
Open noon-6pm Tue-Sat; 10am-6pm Sun. **Admission** €8; free-€6.40 reductions. **Map** p97 E1 ❸
This innovative museum houses a collection of instruments from the old Conservatoire, interactive computers and scale models of opera houses and concert halls. Visitors are supplied with an audio guide in a choice of languages, and the musical commentary is a joy,

playing the appropriate instrument as you approach each exhibit.
Event highlights Europunk: Une Révolution Artistique (15 Oct 2013-19 Jan 2014).

Parc des Buttes-Chaumont

Rue Botzaris, rue Manin, rue de Crimée, 19th. M° Buttes Chaumont. **Open** *Oct-Apr* 7am-8pm daily. *May-Sept* 7am-10pm daily. **Map** p97 E2 ❹
See box p98.

Eating & drinking

Le 9b

NEW *68 bd de la Villette, 19th (01.40.18.08.10, www.le9b.com). M° Colonel Fabien.* **Open** 10am-2am daily. **Map** p97 C3 ❺
Does the name remind you of anything? It's old favourite Le 9 Billards. This bar – which preceded Les Disquaires on rue Jean-Pierre Timbaud – has just been reborn on boulevard de la Villette, not far from Café Chéri(e) (see p99). It's already full to bursting each night with a blend of electro, hip hop, funk and rock on the crammed dancefloor, and cocktails and couscous on the menu.

Bar Ourcq

68 quai de la Loire, 19th (01.42.40.12.26). M° Laumière .**Open** 3pm-midnight Wed, Thur; 3pm-2am Fri, Sat; 3-10pm Sun. No credit cards. **Bar**. **Map** p97 D1 ❻
This was one of the first hip joints to hit the Canal de l'Ourcq, with an embankment broad enough to accommodate *pétanque* games (ask at the bar) and a cluster of deckchairs. The cabin-like interior is pretty cosy, and drinks are listed in a hit parade of prices, starting with €2.50 for a *demi*.

Chez Jeanette

47 rue du Fbg-St Denis, 10th (01.47.70.30.89). M° Château d'Eau or Strasbourg St-Denis. **Open** 8am-2am Mon-Sat; 9am-2am Sun. **€**. **Café**. **Map** p97 A3 ❼
When she sold her café a few years ago, Jeanette handed over to the young team from Chez Justine. Now the awful 1940s lights, tobacco-stained wallpaper depicting the Moulin Rouge and PVC-covered banquettes have been rewarded with a Fooding prize for decor, and the café is one of Paris's hippest spots for an aperitif.

Chez Prune

36 rue Beaurepaire, 10th (01.42.41.30.47). M° Jacques Bonsergent. **Open** 8am-2am Mon-Sat; 10am-2am Sun. **Bar**. **Map** p97 B3 ❽
This supremely hip retro café, with high ceilings and low lighting, sticks to a simple formula: groups of friends crowd around the banquettes, picking at cheese or meat platters. Mostly, though, they come for a few leisurely drinks or an *apéro* before heading to one of the late-night venues in the area.

La Fidélité

12 rue de la Fidélité, 10th (01.47.70.19.34, www.lafidelite.com). M° Gare de L'Est. **Open** 8pm-1am Mon-Sat. **€€**. **Brasserie**. **Map** p97 A3 ❾
There was a huge buzz when La Clique took this place over, and so far the brasserie is setting a high standard with its elegant styling and good, well-priced food – the lunchtime prix fixe is a bargain and the *joue de boeuf* is sublime. On Thursdays and Fridays, the basement morphs into the Cave de la Fidélité, a jukebox bar.

Le Verre Volé

67 rue de Lancry, 10th (01.48.03.17.34). M° Jacques Bonsergent. **Open** 9.30am-1am daily. Closed Aug. **€€**. **Bistro**. **Map** p97 B3 ❿
This organic-only *cave à vins* doubles up as a minuscule wine bar and restaurant. Although wine is the focus, you're obliged to eat; a hearty sausage and mash will set you back around €15. Purists who would prefer a simple snack with their *bon vin* should opt for a plate of charcuterie and cheese.

North-east Paris

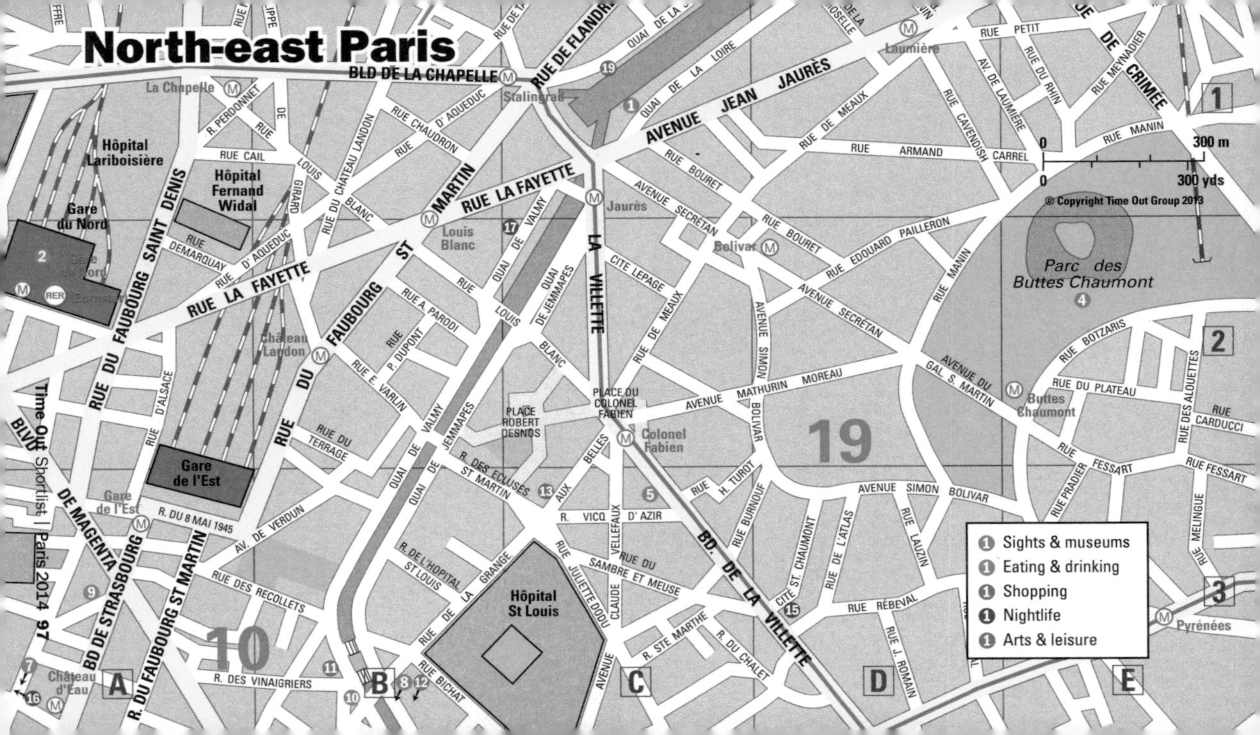

Bonheur in Belleville

Skip the Tuileries and head for the 19th instead.

Rosa Bonheur

There are plenty of handsomely ordered opportunities to indulge in a bit of park life in Paris, from the gravelled pathways of the Jardin des Tuileries to the ornamental ponds of the Jardin du Luxembourg. But if you're looking for something a little less formal, one patch of greenery that's definitely worth a stroll is the **Parc des Buttes-Chaumont** (see p96). Set high up in Belleville and too often overlooked by weekenders keen not to stray too far from the tourist loop, this 19th arrondissement gem is one of the city's most magical spots. When the city's boundaries were expanded in 1860, Belleville – once a village that provided Paris with fruit, wine and weekend escapes – was absorbed and the Buttes-Chaumont was created on the site of a former gypsum and limestone quarry. The park, with its meandering paths, waterfalls, temples and vertical cliffs, was designed by Adolphe Alphand for Haussmann, and was opened as part of the celebrations for the Universal Exhibition in 1867.

After lounging with the locals for a few hours, head for the park's hugely hip hangout, the wonderfully jolly Rosa Bonheur *guinguette* (www.rosabonheur.fr). Open until midnight, it makes the perfect place to sip an *apéro* and take in the stunning views of the city stretching out below.

Shopping

Antoine et Lili

95 quai de Valmy, 10th (01.40.37.41.55, www.antoineetlili.com). M° Jacques Bonsergent. **Open** 11am-7pm Mon, Sun; 11am-8pm Tue-Sat. **Map** p97 B3 ⓫
Antoine et Lili's fuchsia-pink, custard-yellow and apple-green shopfronts are a new raver's dream. The Canal St-Martin 'village' comprises womenswear, a kitsch home decoration boutique and childrenswear.

Culture(s)

46 rue de Lancry, 10th (01.48.03.58.71). M° Jacques Bonsergent or République. **Open** 11am-2pm, 3-7pm Tue-Sat. **Map** p97 B3 ⓬
Located in a loft-style studio, this unusual, quirky florist combines exotic flowers, trees and garden-themed items, such as floral printed rain hats. Truly original.

Viveka Bergström

23 rue de la Grange aux Belles, 10th (01.40.03.04.92, www.viveka-bergstrom.com). M° Colonel Fabien. **Open** noon-7pm Tue-Sat. **Map** p97 B3 ⓭
The daughter of Saab's aeroplane designer in the 1950s, Viveka Bergström makes slinky tassel necklaces, oversized beaten gold rings and brooches, and conversation starters such as the angel-wing bracelet and a necklace featuring a map of Paris.

Nightlife

Le Cabaret Sauvage

59 Bd Macdonald, 19th (01.42.09.03.09, www.cabaretsauvage.com). M° Porte de la Villette. **Open** 9pm-dawn, days vary. **Admission** €10-€20. **Map** p97 E1 (off map) ⓮
A stylish venue that's taken over by outside promoters for occasional club nights. The world music focus has recently been superseded by electronic and drum 'n' bass nights.

Café Chéri(e)

44 bd de la Villette, 19th (01.42.02.02.05). M° Belleville. **Open** noon-2am daily. **Admission** free. **Map** p97 D3 ⓯
A popular DJ bar, especially in summer when people flock to the terrace. Expect anything from DJ Jet Boy's electro punk to rock, funk, hip hop, rare groove, indie, dance, jazz, and '80s classics.

New Morning

7-9 rue des Petites-Ecuries, 10th (01.45.23.51.41, www.newmorning.com). **Admission** approx €20. **Map** p97 A3 ⓰
One of the best places for the latest cutting-edge jazz exponents, with a policy that also embraces *chanson*, blues, world and sophisticated pop.

Point Ephémère

200 quai de Valmy, 10th (01.40.34.02.48, www.pointephemere.org). M° Jaurès or Louis Blanc. **Open** noon-2am Mon-Sat; noon-9pm Sun. **Admission** varies. **Map** p97 C2 ⓱
This is a classy affair, bringing together local rock, jazz and world gigs with a decent restaurant, dance and recording studios and exhibitions.

Arts & leisure

Hammam Med Centre

43-45 rue Petit, 19th (01.42.02.31.05, www.hammammed.com). M° Ourcq. **Open** *Women* 11am-10pm Mon-Fri; 9am-7pm Sun. *Mixed (swimwear required)* 10am-9pm Sat. **Map** p97 E1 ⓲
This hammam is hard to beat – spotless mosaic-tiled surroundings, flowered sarongs and a relaxing pool.

MK2 Bibliothèque

14 quai de la Seine, 19th (08.92.69.84.84, www.mk2.fr). M° Stalingrad. **Open** times vary. **Admission** €10.50; €5-€7 reductions. **Map** p97 C1 ⓳
MK2's mini multiplex on the quai de la Loire was seen as a key factor in the social rise of this part of town. Now the chain has opened a multiplex across the water, with a boat from one to the other.

PARIS BY AREA

Centre Pompidou

The Marais & Eastern Paris

Whereas historic *quartiers* like Montmartre and St-Germain-des-Prés are well past their heyday, the Marais has been luckier, and for the last two decades has been one of the hippest parts of the city, stuffed with modish hotels, boutiques and restaurants – in no small part due to its popularity with the gay crowd. It's also prime territory for arts-lovers, thanks to its generous quotient of museums, and its tightly knit street plan – largely untouched by Haussmann – makes it a charming place in which to get lost for a few hours. The Marais' neighbour to the west is Beaubourg, whose focal point is the iconic Centre Pompidou, with the city's all-important Hôtel de Ville a stone's throw to the south.

A little further east is the Oberkampf district, home to some of the city's best bars and a nightlife hub for the last decade.

Sights & museums

Atelier Brancusi

Piazza Beaubourg, 4th (01.44.78.12.33, www.centrepompidou.fr). M° Hôtel de Ville or Rambuteau. **Open** 2-6pm Mon, Wed-Sun. **Admission** free. **Map** p102 A2 ❶

When Constantin Brancusi died in 1957, he left his studio and its contents to the state, and it was later rebuilt by the Centre Pompidou. His fragile works in wood and plaster, the endless columns and streamlined bird forms show how he revolutionised sculpture.

Centre Pompidou (Musée National d'Art Moderne)

Rue St-Martin, 4th (01.44.78.12.33, www.centrepompidou.fr). M° Hôtel de Ville or Rambuteau. **Open** 11am-9pm (last entry 8pm) Mon, Wed-Sun (until 11pm some exhibitions). **Admission** *Museum & exhibitions* €11-€13; free-€10 reductions. **Map** p102 A2 ❷

The Centre Pompidou (or 'Beaubourg') holds the largest collection of modern art in Europe. For the main collection, buy tickets on the ground floor and take the escalators to level four for post-1960s art. Level five spans 1905 to 1960. Masterful ensembles let you see the span of Matisse's career on canvas and in bronze, the variety of Picasso's invention, and the development of cubic orphism by Sonia and Robert Delaunay. Others on the hits list include Braque, Duchamp, Mondrian, Malevich, Kandinsky, Dalí, Giacometti, Ernst, Miró, Calder, Magritte, Rothko and Pollock. Video art and installations by the likes of Mathieu Mercier and Dominique Gonzalez-Foerster are in a room given over to *nouvelle création*. The Centre Pompidou's Metz outpost opened a couple of years ago.

Event highlights Claude Simon: L'Inépuisable Chaos du Monde (until 6 Jan 2014)

Cimetière du Père-Lachaise

Bd de Ménilmontant, 20th (01.55. 25.82.10). M° Père-Lachaise. **Open** *6 Nov-15 Mar* 8am-5.30pm Mon-Fri; 8.30am-5.30pm Sat; 9am-5.30pm Sun. *16 Mar-5 Nov* 8am-6pm Mon-Fri; 8.30am-6pm Sat; 9am-6pm Sun & public hols. **Map** p103 F2 ❸

Père-Lachaise is the celebrity cemetery – it has the mortal remains of almost anyone French, talented and dead that you care to mention. Not even French, for that matter. Creed and nationality have never prevented entry: you just had to have lived or died in Paris or have an allotted space in a family tomb. Finding a particular grave can be tricky, so buy a map from the hawkers at the Père-Lachaise métro or from one of the shops nearby. Highlights include Chopin's medallion portrait and the muse of Music, Jim Morrison's grave, plus famous neighbours La Fontaine and Molière, who knew each other in real life and now share the same fenced-off plot.

Hôtel de Ville

29 rue de Rivoli, 4th (01.42.76.40.40, www.paris.fr). M° Hôtel de Ville.
Open 10am-7pm Mon-Sat. Tours by appointment only. **Map** p102 A3 ❹

The palatial, multi-purpose Hôtel de Ville is the heart of the city administration. Free exhibitions are held in the Salon d'Accueil (10am-6pm Mon-Fri). The rest of the building, accessible by weekly tours (book in advance), has parquet floors, marble statues and painted ceilings.

Maison Européenne de la Photographie

5-7 rue de Fourcy, 4th (01.44.78.75.00, www.mep-fr.org). M° St-Paul. **Open** 11am-8pm Wed-Sun. **Admission** €7; free-€4 reductions. **Map** p102 B4 ❺

Probably the capital's best photography exhibition space, hosting retrospectives by Larry Clark and Martine Barrat, along with work by emerging photographers. The building, an airy mansion with a modern extension, contains a huge permanent collection.

Maison de Victor Hugo

Hôtel de Rohan-Guéménée, 6 pl des Vosges, 4th (01.42.72.10.16, www.musee-hugo.paris.fr). M° Bastille or St-Paul. **Open** 10am-6pm Tue-Sun. **Admission** free. *Exhibitions* prices vary. **Map** p102 C4 ❻

Victor Hugo lived here from 1833 to 1848, and today the house is a museum devoted to the great man. On display are his first editions, nearly 500 drawings and Hugo's home-made furniture.

Le Mémorial de la Shoah

17 rue Geoffroy-l'Asnier, 4th (01.42.77. 44.72, www.memorialdelashoah.org). M° Pont Marie or St-Paul. **Open** 10am-6pm Mon-Wed, Fri, Sun; 10am-10pm Thur. *Research centre* 10am-5.30pm Mon-Wed, Fri, Sun; 10am-7.30pm Thur. **Admission** free. **Map** p102 A4 ❼

Airport-style security checks mean queues are likely, but don't let that put you off: the Mémorial de la Shoah is an

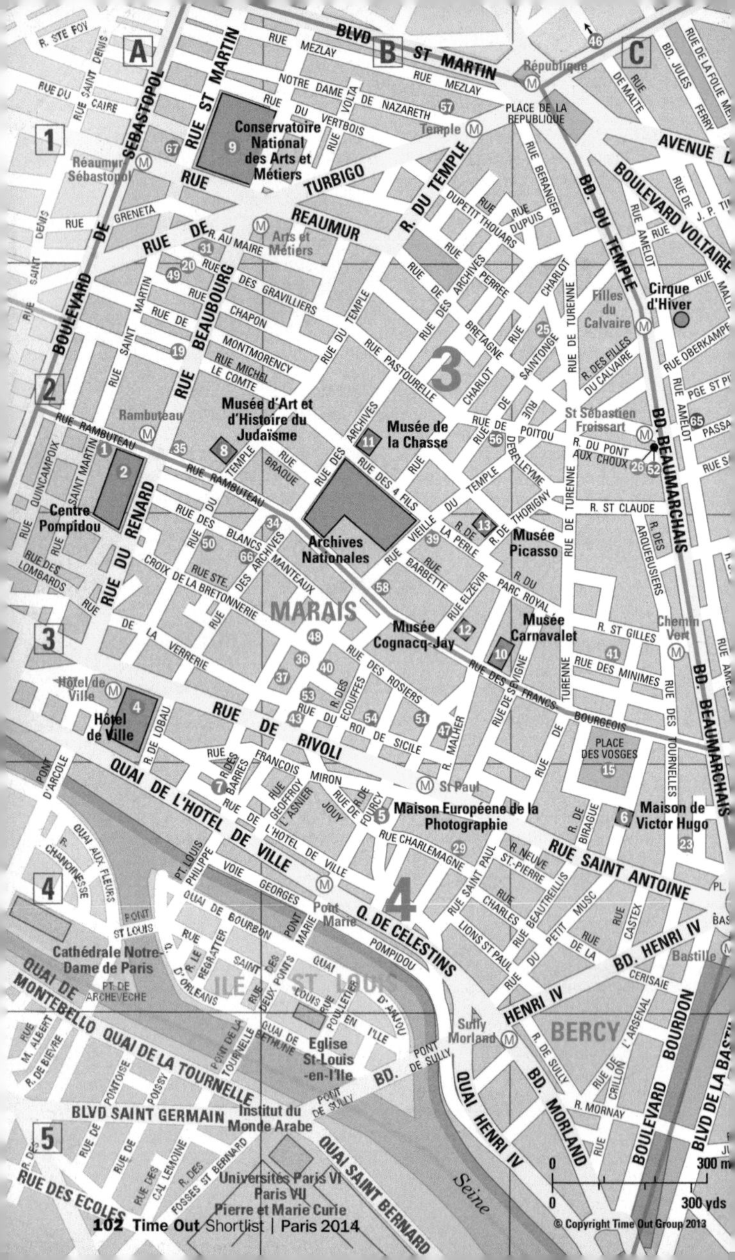
A
B
C
1
2
3
4
5
BLVD ST MARTIN
RUE MEZLAY
République
PLACE DE LA REPUBLIQUE
Temple
R. STE FOY
RUE SAINT DENIS
RUE DU CAIRE
BOULEVARD DE SEBASTOPOL
RUE ST MARTIN
Conservatoire National des Arts et Métiers
RUE NOTRE DAME DE NAZARETH
RUE DU VERTBOIS
RUE VOLTA
RUE TURBIGO
Réaumur-Sébastopol
RUE GRENETA
RUE REAUMUR
Arts et Métiers
R. AU MAIRE
R. DU TEMPLE
RUE DUPETIT THOUARS
RUE DUPUIS
RUE BERANGER
BD. DU TEMPLE
RUE DE MALTE
BD. JULES FERRY
RUE DE LA FOLIE MERICOURT
AVENUE
BOULEVARD VOLTAIRE
RUE AMELOT
RUE J. P. TIMBAUD
Cirque d'Hiver
Filles du Calvaire
RUE DE BEAUBOURG
RUE DES GRAVILLIERS
RUE CHAPON
RUE MONTMORENCY
RUE MICHEL LE COMTE
RUE RAMBUTEAU
Rambuteau
Musée d'Art et d'Histoire du Judaïsme
Musée de la Chasse
RUE DES ARCHIVES
RUE PASTOURELLE
RUE DE BRETAGNE
RUE CHARLOT
RUE DE SAINTONGE
RUE DE TURENNE
R. DES FILLES DU CALVAIRE
RUE OBERKAMPF
RUE DE POITOU
St Sébastien Froissart
R. DU PONT AUX CHOUX
BD. BEAUMARCHAIS
R. ST CLAUDE
RUE DES 4 FILS
RUE DEBELLEYME
RUE DE THORIGNY
R. DE LA PERLE
Musée Picasso
Archives Nationales
Centre Pompidou
RUE DU RENARD
RUE QUINCAMPOIX
RUE DES LOMBARDS
RUE VIEILLE DU TEMPLE
RUE BARBETTE
RUE ELZEVIR
R. DU PARC ROYAL
RUE DES BLANCS MANTEAUX
RUE STE. CROIX DE LA BRETONNERIE
MARAIS
Musée Cognacq-Jay
Musée Carnavalet
R. ST GILLES
Chemin Vert
RUE DES MINIMES
RUE DE LA VERRERIE
RUE DES FRANCS-BOURGEOIS
RUE DE SEVIGNE
RUE DES ROSIERS
RUE DES ECOUFFES
RUE DU ROI DE SICILE
RUE MALHER
PLACE DES VOSGES
RUE DES TOURNELLES
Hôtel de Ville
RUE DE LOBAU
RUE DE RIVOLI
RUE FRANCOIS MIRON
St Paul
QUAI DE L'HOTEL DE VILLE
Maison Européene de la Photographie
Maison de Victor Hugo
RUE CHARLEMAGNE
R. NEUVE ST.-PIERRE
RUE SAINT ANTOINE
RUE SAINT PAUL
RUE CHARLES
RUE BEAUTREILLIS
RUE DU PETIT MUSC
RUE CASTEX
BD. HENRI IV
Bastille
PONT D'ARCOLE
QUAI AUX FLEURS
R. CHANOINESSE
PT. LOUIS PHILIPPE
VOIE GEORGES POMPIDOU
Pont Marie
Q. DE CELESTINS
QUAI DE BOURBON
PONT ST LOUIS
Cathédrale Notre-Dame de Paris
PT. DE ARCHEVECHE
ILE ST LOUIS
QUAI D'ORLEANS
RUE SAINT LOUIS EN L'ILE
QUAI D'ANJOU
QUAI DE BETHUNE
Eglise St-Louis-en-l'Ile
HENRI IV
Sully Morland
BERCY
BD. MORLAND
QUAI HENRI IV
BOULEVARD BOURDON
BLVD DE LA BASTILLE
QUAI DE MONTEBELLO
QUAI DE LA TOURNELLE
PONT DE LA TOURNELLE
PONT DE SULLY
BLVD SAINT GERMAIN
Institut du Monde Arabe
QUAI SAINT BERNARD
Universités Paris VI Paris VII Pierre et Marie Curie
RUE DES ECOLES
R. DES FOSSES ST BERNARD
RUE DU CAL LEMOINE
RUE DE PONTOISE
RUE DE POISSY
R. DE BIEVRE
Seine
R. MORNAY
300 m
300 yds
© Copyright Time Out Group 2013

The Marais & Eastern Paris

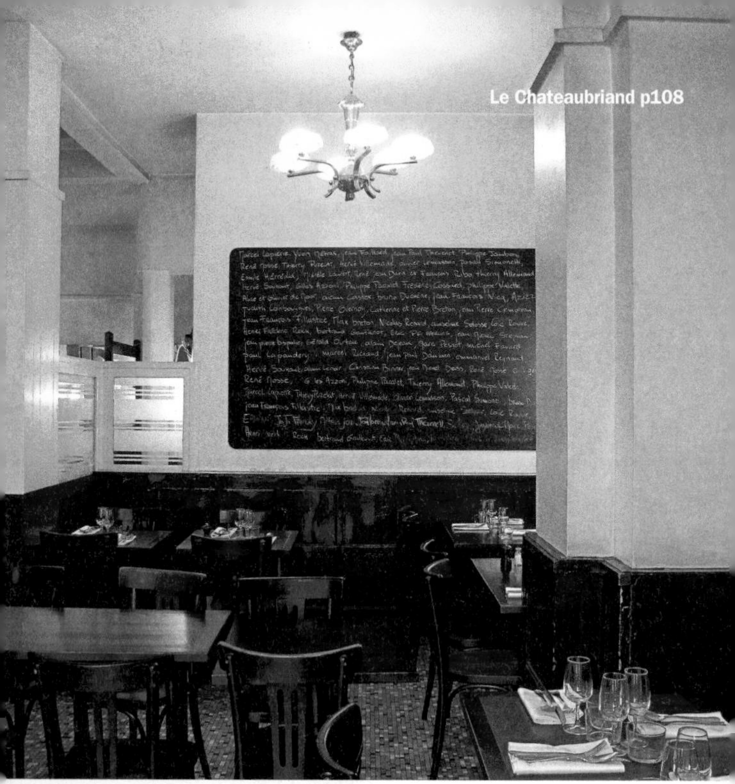

Le Chateaubriand p108

impressively presented and moving memorial to the Holocaust. Enter via the Wall of Names, where limestone slabs are engraved with the first and last names of each of the 76,000 Jews deported from France from 1942 to 1944 with, as an inscription reminds the visitor, the say-so of the Vichy government. The basement-level exhibition documents the plight of French and European Jews.

Musée d'Art et d'Histoire du Judaïsme

Hôtel de St-Aignan, 71 rue du Temple, 3rd (01.53.01.86.53, www.mahj.org). M° Rambuteau. **Open** 11am-6pm Mon-Fri; 10am-6pm Sun. Closed Jewish hols. **Admission** €6.80; free-€4.50 reductions. **Map** p102 A2 ❽

This museum sprang from the collection of a private association formed in 1948 to safeguard Jewish heritage after the Holocaust. Displays illustrate ceremonies, rites and learning, and show how styles were adapted around the globe through examples of Jewish decorative arts. Photographic portraits of modern French Jews, with audio soundtrack, bring a contemporary edge. The Holocaust is marked by Boris Taslitzky's stark sketches from Buchenwald and Christian Boltanski's courtyard memorial to the Jews who lived in the building in 1939, 13 of whom died in the camps.

Musée des Arts et Métiers

60 rue Réaumur, 3rd (01.53.01.82.00, www.arts-et-metiers.net). M° Arts et Métiers. **Open** 10am-6pm Tue, Wed, Fri-Sun; 10am-9.30pm Thur. **Admission** €6.50; free-€4.50 reductions. **Map** p102 A1 ❾

Europe's oldest science museum is a fascinating, well laid out and vast collection of treasures. Here are beautiful astrolabes, celestial spheres, barometers, clocks, some of Pascal's calculating devices, the Lumière brothers' cinematograph, an enormous 1938 TV set, and still larger exhibits like Cugnot's 1770 'Fardier' (the first ever powered vehicle) and Clément Ader's steam-powered Avion 3. The visit concludes in the chapel, which contains old cars, a scale model of the Statue of Liberty and the monoplane in which Blériot crossed the Channel in 1909.

Musée Carnavalet

23 rue de Sévigné, 3rd (01.44.59.58.58, www.carnavalet.paris.fr). M° St-Paul. **Open** 10am-6pm Tue-Sun. **Admission** free. *Exhibitions* prices vary. **Map** p102 B3 ❿

Here, 140 rooms depict the history of Paris, from pre-Roman Gaul to the 20th century. Original 16th-century rooms house Renaissance collections, with portraits by Clouet and furniture and pictures relating to the Wars of Religion. The first floor covers the period up to 1789 and neighbouring Hôtel Le Peletier de St-Fargeau covers the period from 1789 onwards. Displays relating to 1789 detail that year's convoluted politics and bloodshed, with prints and memorabilia, including a chunk of the Bastille. There are items belonging to Napoleon, a cradle given by the city to Napoleon III, and a reconstruction of Proust's bedroom.

Musée de la Chasse et de la Nature

Hôtel Guénégaud, 62 rue des Archives, 3rd (01.53.01.92.40, www.chassenature.org). M° Rambuteau. **Open** 11am-6pm Tue-Sun. **Admission** €6; free-€4.50 reductions. **Map** p102 B2 ⓫

A two-year overhaul turned the three-floor hunting museum from a musty old-timer into something really rather special. The history of hunting and man's larger relationship with the natural world are examined in such things as a series of wooden cabinets devoted to the owl, wolf, boar and stag, each equipped with a bleached skull, small drawers you can open to reveal droppings and footprint casts, and a binocular eyepiece you can peer into for footage of the animal in the wild.

Musée Cognacq-Jay

Hôtel Donon, 8 rue Elzévir, 3rd (01.40.27.07.21, www.paris.fr/musees). M° St-Paul. **Open** 10am-6pm Tue-Sun. **Admission** free. **Map** p102 B3 ⓬

This museum houses a collection put together in the early 1900s by La Samaritaine founder Ernest Cognacq and his wife Marie-Louise Jay. They stuck mainly to 18th-century French works (Watteau, Fragonard, Boucher, Greuze and pastellist Quentin de la Tour), though some English artists (Reynolds, Romney, Lawrence) and Dutch and Flemish names (an early Rembrandt, Ruysdael, Rubens), plus Canalettos and Guardis, have managed to slip in. Pictures are displayed in panelled rooms with furniture, porcelain, tapestries and sculpture of the period.

Musée National Picasso

Hôtel Salé, 5 rue de Thorigny, 3rd (01.42.71.25.21, www.musee-picasso.fr). M° Chemin Vert or St-Paul. **Map** p102 B3 ⓭

The Musée Picasso is currently closed for restoration, and is due to reopen in late 2013. Check the website for details. In the meantime, the Centre Pompidou and Musée de l'Orangerie both contain Picasso collections.

Place de la Bastille

4th/11th/12th. M° Bastille. **Map** p102 C4 ⓮

Nothing remains of the prison that, on 14 July 1789, was stormed by revolutionary forces. Parts of the foundations can be seen in the métro. The Colonne de Juillet, topped by a gilded *génie* of Liberty, is a monument to Parisians who fell during the revolutions of July 1830 and 1848.

Place des Vosges

4th. M° St-Paul. **Map** p102 C4 ⓯

Paris's first planned square was commissioned in 1605 by Henri IV and inaugurated by his son Louis XIII in 1612. With harmonious red-brick and stone arcaded façades and pitched slate roofs, it differs from the later pomp of the Bourbons. Mme de Sévigné, salon hostess and letter-writer, was born at no.1bis in 1626. At that time the garden hosted duels and trysts.

La Promenade Plantée

Av Daumesnil, 12th. M° Gare de Lyon or Ledru-Rollin. **Map** p103 D5 ⓰

The railway tracks atop the Viaduc des Arts were replaced in the late 1980s by a promenade planted with roses, shrubs and rosemary. It continues at ground level through the Jardin de Reuilly and the Jardin Charles Péguy on to the Bois de Vincennes.

Le Viaduc des Arts

15-121 av Daumesnil, 12th (www.viaduc-des-arts.com). M° Gare de Lyon or Ledru-Rollin. **Map** p103 D5 ⓱

Glass-fronted workshops in the arches beneath the Promenade Plantée provide showrooms for furniture and fashion designers, picture-frame gilders, tapestry restorers, porcelain decorators, and chandelier, violin and flute makers.

Eating & drinking

L'Alimentation Générale

64 rue Jean-Pierre-Timbaud, 11th (01.43.55.42.50, www.alimentation-generale.net). M° Parmentier. **Open** 7pm-2am Wed, Sun; 7pm-4am Thur-Sat. **Bar**. **Map** p103 D1 ⓲

The 'Grocery Store' is rue Jean-Pierre-Timbaud's answer to La Mercerie (see p111): it, too, is a big old space filled with junk. Cupboards of kitsch china and lampshades made from kitchen sponges are an inspired touch. The beer is equally well chosen – Flag, Sagres, Picon and Orval – and the house cocktail involves basil and figs.

L'Ambassade d'Auvergne

22 rue du Grenier-St-Lazare, 3rd (01.42.72.31.22, www.ambassade-auvergne.com). M° Arts et Métiers. **Open** noon-2pm, 7.30-10pm daily. **€€**. **Bistro**. **Map** p102 A2 ⓳

This rustic *auberge* is a fitting embassy for the hearty fare of central France. An order of cured ham comes as two hefty, plate-filling slices, and the salad bowl is chock-full of green lentils cooked in goose fat, studded with bacon and shallots. The *rôti d'agneau* arrives as a pot of melting chunks of lamb in a rich, meaty sauce with a helping of tender white beans. Dishes arrive with the flagship *aligot*, the creamy, elastic mash-and-cheese concoction.

Andy Whaloo

69 rue des Gravilliers, 3rd (01.42.71.20.38). M° Arts et Métiers. **Open** 6pm-2am Tue-Sat. **Bar. Map** p102 A2 ⑳

Andy Whaloo, created by the people behind its neighbour 404 and London's Momo and Sketch, is Arabic for 'I have nothing'. Bijou? This place brings new meaning to the word. The formidably fashionable crowd fights for coveted 'seats' on upturned paint cans; it's a beautifully designed venue, crammed with Moroccan artefacts and a spice rack of colours. It's quiet early on, with a surge around 9pm.

Le Baron Rouge

1 rue Théophile-Roussel, 12th (01.43.43.14.32). M° Ledru-Rollin. **Open** 10am-3pm, 5-10pm Tue-Fri; 10am-10pm Sat; 10am-4pm Sun. **Bar. Map** p103 E5 ㉑

It sells wine, certainly – great barrels of the stuff are piled high and sold by the glass at very reasonable prices. But the Red Baron is not just a wine bar – more a local chat room, where regulars congregate to yak over their *vin*, along with a few draught beers and perhaps a snack of sausages or oysters. Despite its lack of seating (there are only four tables), it's a popular pre-dinner spot.

Le Bistrot Paul Bert

18 rue Paul-Bert, 11th (01.43.72.24.01). M° Charonne or Faidherbe Chaligny. **Open** noon-2pm, 7.30-11pm Tue-Sat. Closed Aug. **€€. Bistro. Map** p103 F4 ㉒

This heart-warming bistro gets it right almost down to the last crumb. A starter salad of *ris de veau* illustrates the point, with lightly browned veal sweetbreads perched on a bed of green beans and baby carrots with a sauce of sherry vinegar and deglazed cooking juices. A roast shoulder of suckling pig and a thick steak with a raft of golden, thick-cut *frites* look inviting indeed. Desserts are superb too, including what may well be the best *île flottante* in Paris. If you happen to be in the area at lunchtime, bear in mind that the prix fixe menu is remarkable value.

Bofinger

5-7 rue de la Bastille, 4th (01.42.72.87.82, www.bofingerparis.com). M° Bastille. **Open** noon-3pm, 6.30pm-midnight daily. **€€. Brasserie. Map** p102 C4 ㉓

Bofinger draws big crowds for its art nouveau setting and brasserie atmosphere. Downstairs is the prettiest place in which to eat, but the upstairs room is air-conditioned. An à la carte selection might start with garlicky snails or a well-made langoustine terrine, followed by an intensely seasoned salmon tartare, a generous (if unremarkable) cod steak, or calf's liver accompanied by cooked melon. Alternatively, you could have the foolproof brasserie meal of oysters and fillet steak, washed down by the fine Gigondas.

Café Charbon

109 rue Oberkampf, 11th (01.43.57.55.13, www.lecafecharbon.com). M° Ménilmontant or Parmentier. **Open** 9am-2am Mon, Tue, Sun; 9am-3am Thur; 9am-4am Fri, Sat. Closed Aug. **Bar. Map** p103 E1 ㉔

The bar in this restored belle époque building sparked the Oberkampf nightlife boom. Its booths, mirrors and adventurous music policy put trendy locals at ease, capturing the essence of café culture spanning each end of the 20th century. After more than 15 years, the formula still works.

Candelaria

52 rue de Saintonge, 3rd (01.42.74. 41.28, www.candelariaparis.com). M° Filles du Calvaire or République. **Open** noon-11pm Mon-Wed, Sun; noon-midnight Thur-Sat. **Bar. Map** p102 C2 ㉕

Has Paris woken up to the temptations of the taco? Apparently so, thanks to this taqueria, where local hipsters come to sip margaritas or house specials such as the *guêpe verte* (tequila, lime, pepper, cucumber, spices and agave syrup). On the food front, you have the choice between tacos and tostadas (€3 for one, €5.50 for two).

Cantine Merci

111 bd Beaumarchais, 3rd (01.42. 77.78.92). M° St-Sébastien Froissart. **Open** noon-3pm Mon-Sat (until 6pm for tea). €. **Café. Map** p102 C2 ㉖

Concept store Merci is all about feeling virtuous even as you indulge, and its basement canteen is a perfect example. Salads, soup and risotto of the day, an organic salmon plate, and the *assiette merci* (perhaps chicken kefta with two salads) make up the brief menu, complete with invigorating teas and juices.

Le Chateaubriand

129 av Parmentier, 11th (01.43.57. 45.95, www.lechateaubriand.net). M° Goncourt. **Open** 7.30-11pm Tue-Sat. Closed 2wks Dec. €€€. **Bistro. Map** p103 D1 ㉗

Basque chef Iñaki Aizpitarte runs this stylish bistro. Dishes have been deconstructed down to their very essence and put back together again. You'll understand if you try starters such as steak tartare garnished with a quail's egg or asparagus with tahini foam and little splinters of sesame-seed brittle. The cooking's not always so cerebral – goat's cheese with stewed apple jam is brilliant.

China

50 rue de Charenton, 12th (01.43.46. 08.09, www.lechina.eu). M° Bastille or Ledru Rollin. **Open** noon-2am Mon-Fri; 5pm-2am Sat, Sun. Closed Aug. **Bar. Map** p103 D5 ㉘

This sexy take on a 1930s Shanghai gentleman's club, with red walls, leather chesterfields and the longest bar in Paris, serves some of the finest cocktails in town (including its signature singapore sling). The Cantonese cuisine is pricey, so skip dinner and head upstairs to the cigar bar (if you're romantically inclined) or downstairs to the cellar for weekly jazz, pop and world music concerts.

Cru

7 rue Charlemagne, 4th (01.40.27. 81.84, www.restaurantcru.fr). M° St-Paul. **Open** 12.30-2.30pm, 7-11pm Tue-Sat; 12.30-3pm Sun. €€. **Bistro. Map** p102 B4 ㉙

Opening a raw-food restaurant is a gamble, so the owners of Cru cheat here and there, offering root vegetable 'chips' and a few *plancha* dishes. Still, the menu has plenty for the crudivore, such as some unusual carpaccios (the veal with preserved lemon is particularly good) and intriguing 'red' and 'green' plates, variations on the tomato and cucumber.

Le Dauphin

131 av Parmentier, 11th (01.55.28. 78.88, www.restaurantledauphin.net). M° Goncourt. **Open** noon-2pm, 7-11pm Tue-Fri; 7-11pm Sat. Closed 24 Dec-1 Jan. €. **Wine bar. Map** p103 D1 ㉚

Iñaki Aizpitarte's Le Dauphin, a Rem Koolhaus-designed tapas-style place a few doors from Le Chateaubriand, offers dishes such as *magret séché*, *tempura de gambas* and *tarte au citron meringuée*. As at Le Chateaubriand, sourcing is all-important – bread comes from Du Pain et des Idées.

Derrière

69 rue des Gravilliers, 3rd (01.44.61. 91.95, www.derriere-resto.com). M° Arts et Métiers. **Open** noon-2.30pm, 8-11.30pm Mon-Sat; noon-4pm, 8-11.30pm Sun. €€. **Bistro. Map** p102 A1 ㉛

PARIS BY AREA

Mourad Mazouz, the man behind Momo and Sketch in London, has hit on another winning formula with this apartment-restaurant in the same street as his restaurant 404 and bar Andy Wahloo. The cluttered-chic look mixes contemporary fixtures and antique furniture. It attracts a young, hip crowd that appreciates the high-calorie comfort food, such as roast chicken with buttery mashed potatoes.

L'Encrier

55 rue Traversière, 12th (01.44.68. 08.16). M° Gare de Lyon or Ledru-Rollin. **Open** noon-2.30pm, 7.30-11pm Mon-Fri; 7.30-11pm Sat. Closed Aug & Christmas wk. **€**. **Bistro**. **Map** p103 D5 32

Through the door and past the velvet curtain, you find yourself face to face with the kitchen – and a crowd of locals, many of whom seem to know the charming boss personally. Start with fried rabbit kidneys on a bed of salad dressed with raspberry vinegar, an original and wholly successful combination, and follow with goose *magret* with honey served with sautéed potatoes. To end, share a chocolate cake or try the popular profiteroles.

Le Floréal

73 rue du Fbg-du-Temple, 10th (01.40.18.46.79). M° Goncourt. **Open** 8am-2am daily. **€**. **Diner**. **Map** p103 D1 33

The proprietors of Chez Jeanette (see p96) and Chez Justine have chosen a prime site opposite Le Chateaubriand and Le Dauphin for their new venture, Le Floréal – an American-style diner serving hamburgers and cupcakes (and favourite of Matthieu Almeric, Daniel Craig's good-looking nemesis in *Quantum of Solace*).

Le Gaigne

12 rue Pecquay, 4th (01.44.59. 86.72, www.restaurantlegaigne.fr). M° Rambuteau. **Open** 12.15-2pm, 7.30-10.30pm Tue-Sat. **€€**. **Bistro**. **Map** p102 B3 34

It's a familiar story: young chef with haute cuisine credentials opens a small bistro in an out-of-the-way street. Here, the restaurant is even tinier than usual, with only 20 seats, and the cooking is unusually inventive. Chef Mickaël Gaignon worked with Pierre Gagnaire, and it shows in dishes such as *l'oeuf bio* – three open eggshells filled with creamed spinach, carrot and celeriac – or roast monkfish with broccoli purée and a redcurrant emulsion. The dining room is pleasantly modern.

Le Hangar

12 impasse Berthaud, 3rd (01.42.74. 55.44). M° Rambuteau. **Open** noon-2.30pm, 7.30-11pm Tue-Sat. Closed Aug. **€**. No credit cards. **Bistro**. **Map** p102 A2 35

It's worth making the effort to find this bistro by the Centre Pompidou, with its terrace tucked away in a hidden alley and its excellent cooking. A bowl of tapenade and toast are supplied to keep you going while choosing from the comprehensive *carte*. It yields, for starters, tasty and grease-free *rillettes de lapereau* (rabbit) alongside perfectly balanced pumpkin and chestnut soup. Main courses include pan-fried foie gras on a smooth potato purée made with olive oil.

Jaja

NEW *3 rue Sainte-Croix-de-la-Bretonnerie, 4th (01.42.74.71.52, www.jaja-resto.com). M° Hôtel de Ville.* **Open** noon-2.30pm, 8-11pm daily. **€€**. **Bistro**. **Map** p102 B3 36

Natural wines figure heavily on the list at Jaja. Founded by former wine journalist Julien Fouin in a small *hôtel particulier*, the look is stylish with wood floors and 1950s chairs. Much of the menu is organic – Poujauran bread, Aubrac beef – and most of the wines are organic or even biodynamic. You'll find some classy Bordeaux grands crus, plus a few interesting foreign wines, on a list arranged not by appellation but by mood.

PARIS BY AREA

Gaîté Lyrique p115

Lizard Lounge

18 rue du Bourg-Tibourg, 4th (01.42.72.81.34, www.cheapblonde.com). M° Hôtel de Ville. **Open** noon-2am daily. **Bar. Map** p102 B3 37

An anglophone favourite deep in the Marais, this loud and lively joint provides lager in pints (€6), plus cocktails (€7) and a viewing platform for beer-goggled oglers. Bargain boozing (cocktails €5) kicks off at 5pm; from 8pm to 10pm there's another happy hour in the cellar bar; on Mondays, it lasts all day.

La Mercerie

98 rue Oberkampf, 11th (01.56.98.14.10). M° Parmentier. **Open** 5pm-2am Mon-Fri; 3pm-2am Sat, Sun. **Bar. Map** p103 E1 38

The spacious Mercerie has bare walls (bare everything, in fact) and room for the usual Oberkampf shenanigans of death-wish drinking against a backdrop of loud, eclectic music. A DJ programme is lipsticked on the back bar mirror. Happy hour is from 7pm to 9pm, so you can cane the house vodkas and still have enough euros to finish the job. The back area provides intimacy.

La Perle

78 rue Vieille-du-Temple, 3rd (01.42.72.69.93). M° Chemin Vert or St-Paul. **Open** 6.30am-2am Mon-Fri; 8am-2am Sat, Sun. **Bar. Map** p102 B3 39

The Pearl achieves a rare balance between all-day and late-night venue, and has a good hetero/homo mix. It feels like a neighbourhood bar; labourers and screenwriters rub elbows with young dandies, keeping one eye on the mirror and an ear on the electro-rock.

Le Petit Fer à Cheval

30 rue Vieille-du-Temple, 4th (01.42.72.47.47, www.cafeine.com). M° St-Paul. **Open** 9am-2am daily. **Bar. Map** p102 B3 40

Even a miniature Shetland pony would be pushed to squeeze his hoof into this *fer à cheval* (horseshoe) – this adorable little café has one of France's smallest bars. Tucked in behind the glassy façade is a friendly dining room lined with reclaimed métro benches; if you want scenery, the tables out front overlook the bustle of rue Vieille-du-Temple. In business for more than 100 years, the café enjoyed a retro makeover by Xavier Denamur in the 1990s, and today sports vintage film posters.

Le Petit Marché

9 rue de Béarn, 3rd (01.42.72.06.67). M° Chemin Vert. **Open** noon-3pm, 7.45pm-midnight daily. **€€. Bistro. Map** p102 C3 41

Petit Marché's menu is short and modern with Asian touches. Raw tuna is flash-fried in sesame seeds and served with a Thai sauce, making for a refreshing starter; crispy-coated deep-fried king prawns have a similar oriental lightness. The main vegetarian risotto is rich in basil, coriander, cream and green beans. Pan-fried scallops with lime are precision-cooked and accompanied by a good purée and more beans. There's a short wine list.

Quatre Fois Cinq

83 rue de la Roquette, 11th (01.40.09.80.46). M° Chemin Vert. **Open** 6-11pm Mon, Sun; 11.30am-2.30pm, 6-11pm Tue-Sat. **Wine bar. Map** p103 E3 42

Quatre Fois Cinq, the sum of which wittily equals *vin*, was opened in 2010 by Vincent Delages, who trained as an *oenologue* but decided he wanted a city life and contact with customers 'to help people discover wine' instead. All the bottles, many natural or organic, can be bought to take away or drunk on the spot for a small mark-up. There are also 15 or so wines available by the glass – perhaps a red Tramontane from Languedoc-Roussillon to accompany a plate of excellent Spanish pata negra and chorizo.

Stolly's

16 rue Cloche-Perce, 4th (01.42.76.06.76, www.cheapblonde.com). M° Hôtel de Ville or St-Paul. **Open** 4pm-2am daily. **Bar. Map** p102 B3 43

PARIS BY AREA

This seen-it-all drinking den has been serving a mainly anglophone crowd for nights immemorial. The staff make the place what it is, and a summer terrace eases libation, as do the long happy hours; but don't expect anyone at Stolly's to faff about with food.

Le Train Bleu

Gare de Lyon, pl Louis-Armand, 12th (01.43.43.09.06, www.le-train-bleu.com). M° Gare de Lyon. **Open** 11.30am-3pm, 7-11pm daily. **€€€. Brasserie. Map** p103 D5 44

This listed dining room – with vintage frescoes and big oak benches – exudes a pleasant air of anticipation. Don't expect cutting-edge cooking, but rather fine renderings of French classics. Lobster served on walnut oil-dressed salad leaves is a generous, beautifully prepared starter. Mains of veal chop topped with a cap of cheese, and *sandre* (pike-perch) coupled with a 'risotto' of *crozettes* are also pleasant. A few reasonably priced wines would be a welcome addition.

PARIS BY AREA

Shopping

L'Autre Boulange

43 rue de Montreuil, 11th (01.43.72.86.04, www.lautreboulange.com). M° Faidherbe Chaligny or Nation. **Open** 7.30am-1.30pm, 3-7.30pm Mon-Fri; 7.30am-1pm Sat. Closed Aug. **Map** p103 F5 45

Michel Cousin bakes up to 23 types of organic loaf in his wood-fired oven – varieties include the *flutiot* (rye bread with raisins, walnuts and hazelnuts), the *sarment de Bourgogne* (sourdough and a little rye) and a spiced cornmeal bread.

Du Pain et des Idées

34 rue Yves Toudic, 10th (01.42.40.44.52, www.dupainetdesidees.com). M° Jacques Bonsergent. **Open** 6.45am-8pm Mon-Fri. **Map** p102 C1 46

Christophe Vasseur is a previous winner of the Gault-Millau prize for Best Bakery. Among his specialities are Le Rabelais – *pain brioché* with saffron, honey and nuts; and Le Pagnol aux Pommes, a bread studded with royal gala apple (with its skin on), raisins and orange flower water.

L'Eclaireur

40 rue de Sévigné, 4th (01.48.87.10.22, www.leclaireur.com). M° St-Paul. **Open** 11am-7pm Mon-Sat. **Map** p102 B3 47

Sophisticated, avant-garde L'Eclaireur stocks designs by Comme des Garçons, Martin Margiela and Dries van Noten. Among its finds, check out smocks by Finnish designer Jasmin Santanen.

Free 'P' Star

8 rue Ste-Croix-de-la-Bretonnerie, 4th (01.42.76.03.72, www.freepstar.com). M° St-Paul. **Open** 11am-9pm Mon-Sat; noon-9pm Sun. **Map** p102 B3 48

Late-night shopping is fun at this Aladdin's cave of retro glitz, ex-army wear and glad rags that has provided fancy dress for many a Paris party.

Galerie Fatiha Selam

NEW *58 rue Chapon, 3rd (09.83.33.65.69, www.fatihaselam.com). M° Rambuteau or Arts et Métiers.* **Open** 11am-7pm Mon-Sat. **Map** p102 A2 49

This new addition to a burgeoning gallery street opened in late 2012 with an exhibition of US artist Stephen Schultz's dreamlike canvases. Fatiha Selam brings a fresh eye to the NoMa art scene and promises to explore figurative and abstract contemporary artists both known and emerging.

I Love My Blender

36 rue du Temple, 3rd (01.42.77.50.32, www.ilovemyblender.fr). M° Hôtel de Ville. **Open** 10am-7pm Tue-Sat; 10am-5pm Sun. **Map** p102 A3 50

Christophe Persouyre left a career in advertising to share his passion for English and American literature: all the books he stocks were penned in English, and here you can find their mother-tongue and translated versions.

K Jacques

16 rue Pavée, 4th (01.40.27.03.57, www.kjacques.fr). M° St-Paul. **Open** 10am-7.15pm Mon-Sat; 1-7.15pm Sun. **Map** p102 B3 51

Set up in Saint-Tropez in 1933 by Jacques Keklikian and his wife, the K Jacques workshop started life stitching together basic leather sandals for visitors to the Med resort. The Homère (or Homer) was, and still is, the signature piece – Picasso loved them, and over the years they've counted Colette and Brigitte Bardot among their fans.

Merci

111 bd Beaumarchais, 3rd (01.42.77.00.33, www.merci-merci.com). M° St-Sébastien Froissart. **Open** 10am-7pm Mon-Sat. **Map** p102 C2 52

Concept store Merci is housed in an elaborately reconfigured 19th-century fabric factory. Inside, three loft-like floors heave with furniture, jewellery, stationery, fashion, household products, kidswear and a haberdashery.

Nodus

22 rue Vieille-du-Temple, 4th (01.42.77.07.96, www.nodus.fr). M° Hôtel de Ville or St-Paul. **Open** 10.45am-2pm, 3-7.30pm Mon-Sat; 1-7.30pm Sun. **Map** p102 B3 53

Under the wooden beams of this cosy men's shirt specialist are rows of striped, checked and plain dress shirts, stylish silk ties with subtle designs, and silver-plated crystal cufflinks.

Noir Kennedy

22 rue du Roi de Sicile, 4th (01.44.61.79.71). M° Saint-Paul. **Open** 1-8pm Mon; 11am-8pm Tue-Sat; 2-8pm Sun. **Map** p102 B3 54

This vintage clothes store maintains a strong sense of style. Classic pieces by Cheap Monday mingle with British rockabilly-style items, and traditional red phone booths serve as changing rooms. With not a sequinned top in sight, Noir Kennedy is totally and deliciously rock 'n' roll.

Première Pression Provence

3 rue Antoine Vollon, 12th (01.53.33.03.59, www.premiere-pression-provence.com). M° Ledru Rollin. **Open** 10.30am-2.30pm, 3.30-7.30pm Tue-Sat; 10am-5pm Sun. **Map** p103 E5 55

This is L'Occitane creator Olivier Baussan's latest project, where you are encouraged to taste spoonfuls of single-producer olive oil to educate your palate about the nuances of *vert*, *mûr* and *noir* (known as the '*fruités*') before buying.

Shine

15 rue de Poitou, 3rd (01.48.05.80.10). M° Filles du Calvaire. **Open** 11am-7.30pm Mon-Sat; 1-7pm Sun. **Map** p102 B2 56

See by Chloé, Marc by Marc Jacobs and Acne Jeans are among the goodies in this glossy showcase.

WAIT

NEW *9 rue Notre-Dame de Nazareth, 3rd (09.82.52.84.34, www.wait-paris-com). M° République.* **Open** 11am-7pm Mon-Sat. **Map** p102 B1 57

See box p114.

Zadig & Voltaire

42 rue des Francs-Bourgeois, 3rd (01.44.54.00.60, www.zadig-et-voltaire.com). M° Hôtel de Ville or St-Paul. **Open** 10.30am-7.30pm Mon-Sat; noon-7.30pm Sun. **Map** p102 B3 58

Zadig & Voltaire's relaxed collection is a winner. Popular separates include cotton tops, shirts and faded jeans.

Nightlife

Ateliers de Charonne

21 rue de Charonne, 11th (01.40.21.83.35, www.ateliercharonne.com). M° Charonne or Ledru-Rollin. **Open** 8pm-1am daily. *Concerts* 9pm Mon-Sat; 7pm Sun. **Admission** free. **Map** p103 D4 59

This club is the place to see the rising stars of gypsy jazz (*jazz manouche*). If you want a spot near the front of the stage, reserve for dinner and the show.

Bachelor bliss

All the modern man needs at WAIT.

Imagine a man's ultimate fantasy living room and you have **WAIT** (see p113), a shop filled with everything from retro video game consoles, surfboards, skateboards and shades to a reconditioned racing bike, vintage furniture, cool shirts, T-shirts and baseball caps. Plus the crucial accessory for the modern man – scented candles.

'It's not just a concept shop, but it's our office, showroom and ideas lab,' says Antoine Mocquard, one half of the duo behind the store. He and Julien Tual, both from Brittany, met in Rennes and started designing ultra-light glasses and sunglasses made from wood five years ago. Having outgrown their premises in the St-Paul area, the pair moved to this up-and-coming district and decided to fill the space with 'everything we like', which ranges from Thomas Bexon Australian surfboards to Fabrice Houdry art. Brands sourced from all over the world include Australian fashion label TCSS, La Paz checked shirts, Moupia baseball caps, Good Guys vegan shoes and delightful Papier Tigre notebooks. The bike is on *dépôt-vente* from La Bicyclette, which repairs and customises vintage racers, and the 1970s sideboard was originally bought to display their sunglasses in Merci.

Antoine and Julien have also designed a trio of white steel tables, and in early 2013 launched their own fashion brand. Also called WAIT, it offers a unique take on traditional Breton togs, such as a densely knitted navy jumper with three different-coloured wooden buttons on the shoulder. 'It's 90 per cent Breton and ten per cent Parisian,' says Antoine. A little like these guys, who have brought a touch of Atlantic surf to the city.

Le Bataclan

50 bd Voltaire, 11th (01.43.14.00.30, www.le-bataclan.com). M° Oberkampf. **Open** times vary. **Map** p103 D2 60
Established in 1864, this highly distinctive venue remains admirably discerning in its booking of rock, world, jazz and hip hop acts.

L'International

5-7 rue Moret, 11th (01.49.29.76.45, www.linternational.fr). M° Ménilmontant. **Open** 6pm-2am daily. **Map** p103 E1 61
This concert-bar is a breath of fresh air, with free entry and a string of on-the-up bands playing to hip indie crowds every night of the week.

La Mécanique Ondulatoire

8 passage Thière, 11th (01.43.55.69.14, www.myspace.com/lamecanique). M° Bastille or Ledru Rollin. **Open** 6pm-2am Mon-Sat. *Concerts* times vary. **Admission** €4-€7. **Map** p103 D4 62
Cementing Bastille's status as Paris's prime hangout for rockers, this exciting venue has three levels and alternates eclectic DJs with live acts in the cellar, plus there's jazz on Tuesday nights.

Le Motel

8 passage Josset, 11th (01.58.30.88.52, www.myspace.com/lemotel). M° Ledru Rollin. **Open** 6pm-1.45am Tue-Sun. Closed Aug. **Map** p103 E4 63
This most Anglophile of Paris bars, with Stone Roses and Smiths posters adorning the walls, manages to fit plenty of live bands, including some of the best local talent, on to its tiny stage.

Nouveau Casino

109 rue Oberkampf, 11th (01.43.57.57.40, www.nouveaucasino.net). M° Parmentier. **Open** *Concerts* times vary. **Map** p103 E1 64
Nouveau Casino is a gig venue that also hosts some of the city's liveliest club nights. Local collectives, international names and record labels, such as Versatile, regularly host nights here.

Panic Room

101 rue Amelot, 11th (01.58.30.93.43, www.panicroomparis.com). M° St-Sébastien Froissart. **Open** 6.30pm-2am Mon-Sat. Closed 2wks Aug. **Admission** free. **Map** p102 C2 65
The excellent Goldrush collective has live acts and DJs blasting the sound system in the basement, while upstairs friendly barmen serve affordable cocktails behind a concrete counter.

Arts & leisure

Les Bains du Marais

31-33 rue des Blancs-Manteaux, 4th (01.44.61.02.02, www.lesbainsdumarais.com). M° St-Paul. **Open** times vary. **Map** p102 A3 66
This hammam and spa mixes the modern and traditional (lounging beds and mint tea). Facials, waxing and essential oil massages (€70) are also available. The hammam is €35.

Gaîté Lyrique

3bis rue Papin, 3rd (01.53.01.51.51, www.gaite-lyrique.net). M° Réaumur Sébastapol. **Box office** 2-8pm Tue-Sat; 2-6pm Sun. **Map** p102 A1 67
The belle époque Gaîté Lyrique theatre has been turned into Paris's first digital cultural centre; a seven-floor, multidisciplinary concert hall-cum-gallery that thrusts visitors deep into the realms of digital art, music, graphics, film, fashion, design and video games.

Opéra National de Paris, Bastille

Pl de la Bastille, 12th (08.92.89.90.90, www.operadeparis.fr). M° Bastille. **Box office** (130 rue de Lyon, 12th) 2.30-6.30pm Mon-Sat. *By phone* 9am-6pm Mon-Fri; 9am-1pm Sat. **Admission** €5-€180. **Map** p103 D4 68
Despite the unflattering acoustics, the standard of performance here is high and there are some exciting evenings planned under director Nicolas Joel. **Event highlights** Verdi's La Traviata (2-20 June 2014).

PARIS BY AREA

La Conciergerie p120

The Seine & Islands

The Seine

It's perhaps surprising that it took so long for the Seine to become a tourist magnet. For much of the 19th and 20th centuries, the Seine was barely given a second thought by anyone who wasn't working on it or driving along its quayside roads. But in 1994, UNESCO added 12 kilometres (7.5 miles) of Paris riverbank to its World Heritage register. Floating venues such as Batofar became super-trendy; and in the last 15 years, it's been one new attraction after another.

It's at its best in summer. Port de Javel and Jardin Tino-Rossi become open-air dancehalls; and there's the jamboree of Paris-Plages, Mayor Delanoë's hugely successful city beach that brings sand, palm trees, loungers and free entertainment to both sides of the Seine. And, of course, there's a wealth of boat tours on offer.

In 2013, Delanoë's ambitious redesign plans for the traffic-choked *berges* saw a stretch of Left Bank road running from Pont de l'Alma to Pont Royal – from just east of Musée du Quai Branly up to and including the Musée d'Orsay – converted into a pedestrian promenade dotted with gardens, cafés and even a floating cinema screen. Forget the Côte d'Azur next August – and head for the banks of the Seine instead.

Sights & museums

Vedettes du Pont-Neuf
Square du Vert-Galant, 1st (01.46.33. 98.38, www.vedettesdupontneuf.com). M° Pont Neuf. **Tickets** €13; free-€7 reductions. **Map** p117 B1 ❶
The hour-long cruise takes in all the major sights, from the Eiffel Tower to Notre-Dame. You can sit inside just a foot or two above water level or outside on the top deck.

The Seine & Islands

The bridges

From the honeyed arches of the oldest, the Pont Neuf (1607), to the swooping lines of the newest, the Passerelle Simone-de-Beauvoir (2006), the 37 bridges are among the best-known landmarks in the city, and enjoy some of its best views.

Over the years, the city's *ponts* have been bombed, bashed by buses and boats, weather-beaten and even trampled to destruction: in 1634, the Pont St-Louis collapsed under the weight of a religious procession.

The 19th century was boom time for bridge-building: 21 were built in all, including the city's first steel, iron and suspension bridges. The Pont de la Concorde used up what was left of the Bastille after the storming of 1789; the romantic Pont des Arts was the capital's first solely pedestrian crossing (built in 1803 and rebuilt in the 1980s). The most glitteringly exuberant bridge is the Pont Alexandre III, with its bronze and glass, garlanding and gilded embellishments.

More practical is the Pont de l'Alma, with its Zouave statue that has long been a flood monitor: when the statue's toes get wet, the state raises the flood alert and starts to close the quayside roads; when he's up to his ankles in Seine, it's no longer possible to navigate the river by boat. This offers some indication of how devastating the 1910 flood was, when the plucky Zouave disappeared up to his neck – as did parts of central Paris.

The 20th century brought some spectacular additions. Pont Charles-de-Gaulle, for example, stretches like the wing of a huge aeroplane, and iron Viaduc d'Austerlitz (1905) is striking yet elegant as it cradles métro line 5. The city's newest crossing, the Passerelle Simone-de-Beauvoir, links the Bibliothèque Nationale to the Parc de Bercy.

Ile de la Cité

The Ile de la Cité is where Paris was born around 250 BC, when the Parisii, a tribe of Celtic Gauls, founded a settlement on this convenient bridging point of the Seine. Romans, Merovingians and Capetians followed, in what became a centre of political and religious power right into the Middle Ages: royal authority at one end, around the Capetian palace; the Church at the other, by **Notre-Dame**.

Perhaps the most charming spot on the island is the western tip, where Pont Neuf spans the Seine. Despite its name, it is the oldest bridge in Paris. Its arches are lined with grimacing faces, said to be modelled on some of the courtiers of Henri III. Down the steps is leafy square du Vert-Galant. In the centre of the bridge is an equestrian statue of Henri IV; the original went up in 1635, was melted down to make cannons during the Revolution, and replaced in 1818.

Sights & museums

Cathédrale Notre-Dame de Paris

Pl du Parvis-Notre-Dame, 4th (01.42. 34.56.10, www.cathedraledeparis.com). M° Cité/RER St-Michel Notre-Dame. **Open** 8am-6.45pm Mon-Fri; 8am-7.15pm Sat, Sun. *Towers* Apr-Sept 10am-6.30pm daily (June-Aug until 11pm Sat, Sun). Oct-Mar 10am-5.30pm daily. **Admission** free. *Towers* €8.50; free-€5.50 reductions. **Map** p117 C2 ❷

Notre-Dame was constructed between 1163 and 1334, and the amount of time and money spent on it reflected the city's growing prestige. The west front remains a high point of Gothic art for the balanced proportions of its twin towers and rose window, and the three doorways with their rows of saints and sculpted tympanums: the *Last Judgement* (centre), *Life of the Virgin*

Cathédrale Notre-Dame de Paris

(left) and *Life of St Anne* (right). Inside, take a moment to admire the long nave with its solid foliate capitals and high altar with a marble *Pietà* by Coustou.

Climb up the towers to appreciate the masonry. The route runs up the north tower and down the south. Between the two you get a close-up view of the gallery of chimeras – the fantastic birds and hybrid beasts designed by Viollet-le-Duc along the balustrade. After a detour to see the massive bell, a staircase leads to the top of the south tower.

As of February 2013, Notre-Dame has eight new bells, forged to try to reproduce the sound of pre-Revolutionary Paris as part of the cathedral's 850th anniversary year.

La Conciergerie

2 bd du Palais, 1st (01.53.40.60.80). M° Cité/RER St-Michel Notre-Dame. **Open** 9.30am-6pm daily. **Admission** €8.50; free-€5.50 reductions. *With Sainte-Chapelle* €12.50; €8.50 reductions. **Map** p117 B1 ❸

The Conciergerie looks every inch the medieval fortress. However, much of the façade was added in the 1850s. The visit takes you through the Salle des Gardes, the medieval kitchens with their four huge chimneys, and the Salle des Gens d'Armes, a vaulted Gothic hall built between 1301 and 1315. After the royals moved to the Louvre, the fortress became a prison under the watch of the Concierge. The wealthy had private cells with their own furniture, which they paid for; others had to make do with straw beds. A list of Revolutionary prisoners, including a hairdresser, shows that not all victims were nobles. In Marie-Antoinette's cell, the Chapelle des Girondins, are her crucifix, some portraits and a guillotine blade.

La Crypte Archéologique

Pl Jean-Paul II, 4th (01.55.42.50.10, www.crypte.paris.fr). M° Cité/RER St-Michel Notre-Dame. **Open** 10am-6pm Tue-Sun. **Admission** €4; free-€3 reductions. **Map** p117 C2 ❹

Hidden under the forecourt in front of the cathedral is a large void containing pieces of Roman quaysides, ramparts and hypocausts, medieval cellars, shops and pavements, the foundations of the Eglise Ste-Geneviève-des-Ardens, an 18th-century foundling hospital and a 19th-century sewer. You get a vivid sense of the layers of history piled one atop another during 16 centuries.

Mémorial des Martyrs de la Déportation

Sq de l'Ile de France, 4th (01.46.33.87.56). M° Cité/RER St-Michel Notre-Dame. **Open** *Oct-Mar* 10am-noon, 2-5pm daily. *Apr-Sept* 10am-noon, 2-7pm daily. **Admission** free. **Map** p117 C2 ❺

This tribute to the 200,000 Jews, Communists, homosexuals and *résistants* deported to concentration camps from France in World War II stands on the eastern tip of the island. A blind staircase descends to river level, where chambers are lined with tiny lights and the walls are inscribed with verse. A barred window looks on to the Seine.

Sainte-Chapelle

6 bd du Palais, 1st (01.53.40.60.80). M° Cité/RER St-Michel Notre-Dame. **Open** *Mar-Oct* 9.30am-6pm daily. *Nov-Feb* 9am-5pm daily. **Admission** €8.50; free-€5.50 reductions. *With Conciergerie* €12.50; €8.50 reductions. **Map** p117 B2 ❻

Devout King Louis IX (St Louis, 1226-70) had a hobby of accumulating holy relics (and children: he fathered 11). In the 1240s, he bought what was advertised as the Crown of Thorns, and ordered Pierre de Montreuil to design a shrine. The result was the exquisite Flamboyant Gothic Sainte-Chapelle. With 15m (49ft) windows, the upper level, intended for the royal family and the canons, appears to consist almost entirely of stained glass. The windows depict hundreds of scenes from the Old and New Testaments, culminating with the Apocalypse in the rose window.

Shopping

L'Occitane en Provence

1 rue d'Arcole, 4th (01.55.42.06.11, www.loccitane.com). M° Cité. **Open** 10.30am-7pm daily. **Map** p117 C2 ❼

The many branches of this popular Provençal chain offer natural beauty products in neat packaging.

Ile St-Louis

The Ile St-Louis is one of the most exclusive residential addresses in the city. Delightfully unspoiled, it has fine architecture, narrow streets and pretty views from the tree-lined quays, and still retains the air of a tranquil backwater.

Rue St-Louis-en-l'Ile – lined with fine historic buildings that now house gift shops and gourmet food stores (many open on Sunday), quaint tearooms, stone-walled bars, restaurants and hotels – runs the length of the island. The grandiose Hôtel Lambert at no.2 was built by Le Vau in 1641 for Louis XIII's secretary, and has sumptuous interiors by Le Sueur, Perrier and Le Brun. At no.51 – Hôtel Chenizot – look out for the bearded faun adorning the doorway, flanked by dragons supporting the balcony.

At the western end there are great views of the buttresses of Notre-Dame from the terrace of the Brasserie de l'Ile St-Louis.

Sights & museums

Eglise St-Louis-en-l'Ile

19bis rue St-Louis-en-l'Ile, 4th (01.46.34.11.60, www.saintlouisenlile.catholique.fr). M° Pont Marie. **Open** 9.30am-1pm, 2-7.30pm Mon-Sat; 9am-1pm, 2-7pm Sun. **Admission** free. **Map** p117 D3 ❽

The island's church was built between 1664 and 1765, following plans by Louis Le Vau and later completed by Gabriel Le Duc. The interior boasts Corinthian columns and a sunburst over the altar, and the church hosts occasional classical music concerts.

Eating & drinking

Berthillon

29-31 rue St-Louis en l'Ile, 4th (01.43.54.31.61, www.berthillon.fr). M° Pont Marie. **Open** 10am-8pm Wed-Sun. **€€. Ice-cream. Map** p117 D2 ❾

The flavours here change throughout the season, but if it's available don't miss the bitter chocolate sorbet. In winter Berthillon serves delicious hot chocolate and – even naughtier – a chocolate '*affogato*' (a ball of vanilla ice-cream served in a white porcelain mug with hot chocolate poured over and topped with praline cream).

Mon Vieil Ami

69 rue St-Louis-en-l'Ile, 4th (01.40.46.01.35, www.mon-vieil-ami.com). M° Pont Marie. **Open** noon-2.30pm, 6.30-11pm Wed-Sun. Closed 3wks Jan & 1st 3wks Aug. **€€. Bistro. Map** p117 D2 ❿

Antoine Westermann has created a true foodie destination here. Starters such as tartare of diced raw vegetables with sautéed baby squid arranged on top impress with deft seasoning. Typical of the main courses is a casserole of roast duck with caramelised turnips and couscous.

Le Sergent Recruteur

NEW *41 rue St-Louis-en-l'Ile, 4th (01.43.54.75.42, www.lesergentrecruteur.fr). M° Pont Marie or Sully-Morland.* **Open** noon-2pm, 7-10pm Tue-Sat. **€€€. Haute cuisine.** Map p117 D2 ⓫

Avant-garde Spanish designer Jaime Hayón and chef Antonin Bonnet have turned this former pub into a handsome restaurant. The 'carte blanche' menus, where you're led by the whims of the chef (€65 or €95 at lunch, €95 or €145 at dinner), offer daring versions of classic French dishes: foie gras with rhubarb confit, wild duck with spelt, mango and herb ice cream. Service is adroit and professional.

PARIS BY AREA

The 7th & Western Paris

PARIS BY AREA

The seventh arrondissement is dotted with the machinery of state and diplomacy: it's home to France's parliament, a gaggle of foreign embassies and the HQ of UNESCO. Unsurprisingly, much of the district is formal and aloof as a result. Thankfully, though, two of its greatest attractions – an A-shaped assembly of 19th-century iron lattice and a gallery in an old Beaux Arts train station – have decided to embrace the future with thoroughly modern makeovers. The Eiffel Tower is installing a dramatic glass floor for 2014 and the Musée d'Orsay is gleaming after a stunning renovation.

For a view from a different angle, **Vedettes de Paris** (Port de Suffren, 7th, www.vedettesde paris.com) runs all manner of Seine cruises, from hour-long sightseeing to evening champagne-tasting trips complete with sommelier.

Sights & museums

Les Égouts de Paris

Opposite 93 quai d'Orsay, by Pont de l'Alma, 7th (01.53.68.27.81). M° Alma Marceau/RER Pont de l'Alma. **Open** 11am-4pm (until 5pm May-Sept) Mon-Wed, Sat, Sun. Closed 2wks Jan. **Admission** €4.30; free-€3.50 reductions. No credit cards. **Map** p123 B1 ❶

For centuries, the main source of drinking water in Paris was the Seine, which was also the main sewer. Construction of an underground sewerage system began at the time of Napoleon. Today, the Égouts de Paris constitutes a smelly museum; each sewer in the 2,100km (1,305-mile) system is marked with a replica of the street sign above.

Eiffel Tower

Champ de Mars, 7th (08.92.70.12.39, www.tour-eiffel.fr). M° Bir-Hakeim/RER Champ de Mars Tour Eiffel. **Open** *By lift* Mid June-Aug 9am-12.45am daily

The 7th & Western Paris

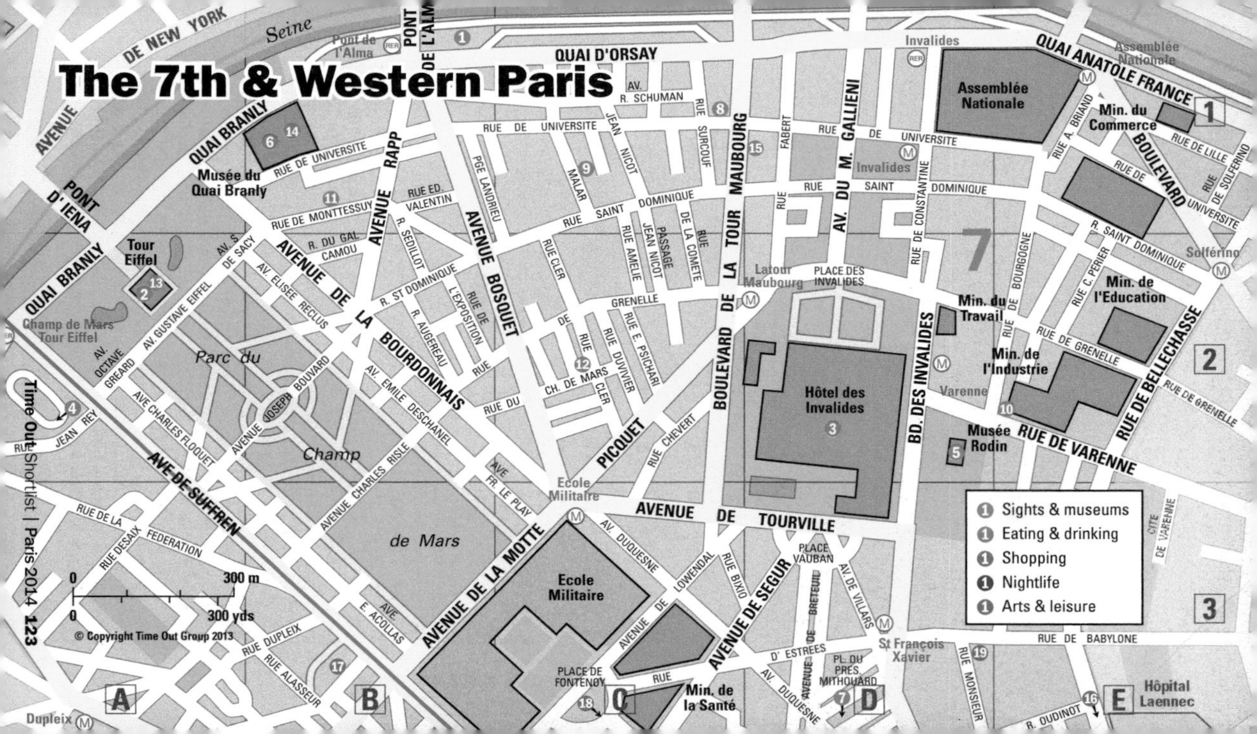

(last ascent 11pm). Sept-mid June 9.30am-11.45pm daily (last ascent 10.30pm). *By stairs* (1st & 2nd levels) Mid June-Aug 9am-12.45am daily (last ascent midnight). Sept-mid June 9.30am-6.30pm daily (last ascent 6pm). **Admission** *By stairs* €5; €3-€3.50 reductions; free under-4s. *By lift* (1st & 2nd levels) €8.50; €4-€7 reductions; (3rd level) €14; €9.50-€12.50 reductions; free under-4s. **Map** p123 A2 ❷

No building better symbolises Paris than the Eiffel Tower. Maupassant claimed he left Paris because of it, William Morris visited daily to avoid having to see it from afar – and it was originally meant to be a temporary structure. Construction took just over two years and used some 2,500,000 rivets. And not a great deal has changed since – until now. The Eiffel Tower is undergoing its third facelift since opening more than 120 years ago: the €25m revamp is radical, to say the least, with the first-floor central void being filled in with a solid glass floor surrounded by inclined safety barriers, so visitors with a head for heights will be able to eyeball the queues 57m below.

Les Invalides & Musée de l'Armée

Esplanade des Invalides, 7th (08.10. 11.33.99, www.invalides.org). M° La Tour-Maubourg or Les Invalides. **Open** *Apr-Sept* 10am-6pm Mon, Wed-Sun (Dôme until 7pm July, Aug); 10am-9pm Tue. *Oct-Mar* 10am-5pm daily. Closed 1st Mon of mth. **Admission** *Musée de l'Armée & Eglise du Dôme* €9; free-€7 reductions. **Map** p123 D2 ❸

Topped by its gilded dome, the Hôtel des Invalides was (and in part still is) a hospital. Commissioned by Louis XIV for wounded soldiers, it once housed up to 6,000 invalids. The complex contains two churches – the Eglise St-Louis was for the soldiers, the Eglise du Dôme for the king.

The Invalides complex also houses the enormous Musée de l'Armée. The Antique Armour wing is packed full of armour and weapons that look as good as new. The Plans-Reliefs section is a collection of 18th- and 19th-century scale models of French cities, used for military strategy. The World War I rooms are moving, with the conflict brought into focus by uniforms, paintings, a scale model of a trench on the western front and, most sobering of all, white plastercasts of the hideously mutilated faces of two soldiers. The World War II wing takes in not just the Resistance, but also the Battle of Britain and the war in the Pacific (there's a replica of Little Boy, the bomb dropped on Hiroshima). Included in the entry price is the Historial Charles de Gaulle.

Maison de la Culture du Japon

101bis quai Branly, 15th (01.44.37. 95.01, www.mcjp.asso.fr). M° Bir-Hakeim/RER Champ de Mars Tour Eiffel. **Open** noon-7pm Tue, Wed, Fri, Sat; noon-8pm Thur. Closed Aug. **Admission** free. **Map** p123 A2 ❹

This glass-fronted Japanese cultural centre screens films and puts on exhibitions and plays. It also contains a library, an authentic tea pavilion on the roof and a well-stocked shop.

Musée National Rodin

Hôtel Biron, 79 rue de Varenne, 7th (01.44.18.61.10, www.musee-rodin.fr). M° Varenne. **Open** 10am-5.45pm Tue, Thur-Sun; 10am-8.45pm Wed. **Admission** €9; free-€5 reductions. *Gardens* free-€1. **Map** p123 D2 ❺

The Rodin museum occupies the *hôtel particulier* where the sculptor lived in the final years of his life. The *Kiss*, the *Cathedral*, the *Walking Man*, portrait busts and early terracottas are exhibited indoors. Rodin's works are accompanied by pieces by his mistress and pupil, Camille Claudel. The walls are hung with paintings by Van Gogh, Monet, Renoir, Carrière and Rodin himself. Most visitors have greatest affection for the gardens: look out for the *Burghers of Calais*, the elaborate *Gates*

Quays to the city

The Berges de Seine are becoming blissfully car-free.

A Bateau-Mouche may not be the most original way to while away an hour in Paris, but you definitely get plenty of bang for your buck in terms of the sights you'll be able to tick off along the route. The Eiffel Tower, the Grand Palais, the Assemblée Nationale, the Musée d'Orsay, place de la Concorde, the Louvre, Notre-Dame, Ile St-Louis and the Jardin des Plantes all reveal themselves as you chug gently along the Seine.

And in 2014, there'll be even more to shout about as the city council forges ahead with plans to pedestrianise parts of the Seineside expressway, which will be given over to far more relaxing pursuits instead. Depriving car drivers of their riverside monopoly, the Berges de Seine plan involves the redevelopment of 2.3km of former Left Bank road running from the Pont de l'Alma to the Pont Royal – from just east of the Musée du Quai Branly up to the Musée d'Orsay.

The project isn't just about reclaiming the old expressway, but it's also about grabbing a large chunk of river at the same time, erecting floating platforms with a raft of new attractions on board. Cruising upstream from the Eiffel Tower, you'll pass several of the project's star attractions on your right, including the spectacular new '*emmarchement*', an apparently airborne flight of stairs connecting the upper and lower quays in front of the Musée d'Orsay that will double up as an open-air auditorium for cinema projected on to a floating screen; an 1,800sq m floating garden that stretches across five islands connected by bridges; and floating sports facilities moored in the Bibliothèque area *à la* Piscine Josephine Baker. In between, a cluster of new barges at the foot of Pont Alexandre III will play host to a new nightlife area.

It has all the ingredients of a Delanoë project: green, cultural, leftfield and celebratory. An obvious extension of Paris-Plages, which remains the mayor's most successful project, Berges de Seine is also a dramatic response to the fact that these riverbanks and the monuments along them were put on UNESCO's World Heritage register in 1991, but little was done to acknowledge that or redress the car-obsessed development of the 1960s.

As for the hyped 'trampoline bridge' over the Seine, this remains a fantasy. But with a new mayor at the helm from 2014, who knows what might be next?

Saxe-Breteuil p128

of Hell, and the *Thinker*. The museum is undergoing renovations until 2014, but will remain open with a series of rolling exhibitions.

Musée du Quai Branly

37-55 quai Branly, 7th (01.56.61.70.00, www.quaibranly.fr). RER Pont de l'Alma. **Open** 11am-7pm Tue, Wed, Sun; 11am-9pm Thur-Sat. **Admission** €8.50; free-€6 reductions. **Map** p123 B1 ❻

Surrounded by trees on the banks of the Seine, this museum is a showcase for non-European cultures. Treasures include a tenth-century anthropomorphic Dogon statue from Mali, Aztec statues, Gabonese masks, Vietnamese costumes and Peruvian feather tunics. **Event highlights** Karnak, l'Art est une Parole (15 Oct 2013-26 Jan 2014)

Musée Valentin Haüy

5 rue Duroc, 7th (01.44.49.27.27, www.avh.asso.fr). M° Duroc. **Open** 2.30-5pm Tue, Wed. Closed July-mid Sept. **Admission** free. **Map** p123 D3 ❼

This tiny museum is devoted to the history of braille. You can explore on your own with the aid of French, English or braille explanatory texts, or allow the curator, Noêle Roy, to show you round. She will give a tour in English if preferred. The first exhibit is a shocking print, depicting the fairground freak show that inspired Valentin Haüy to devote his life to educating not only the blind, but also the public who came to laugh at the likes of this blind orchestra forced to perform in dunce's hats.

Eating & drinking

Le 144 Petrossian

144 rue de l'Université, 7th (01.44. 11.32.32, www.petrossian.fr). M° La Tour Maubourg. **Open** 12.15-2.30pm, 7.30-10.30pm Tue-Sat. **€€€. Russian. Map** p123 C1 ❽

Senegalese-French chef Rougui Dia directs the kitchen of this famed caviar house. You'll find Russian specialities such as blinis, salmon and caviar from the Petrossian boutique downstairs, but Dia has added preparations and spices from all over the world. So you might start with carnaroli rice, codfish caviar and parmesan.

L'Ami Jean

27 rue Malar, 7th (01.47.05.86.89, www.amijean.eu). M° Ecole Militaire. **Open** noon-2pm, 7-10pm Tue-Sat. Closed Aug. **€€. Bistro. Map** p123 C1 ❾

This long-running Basque address is an ongoing hit thanks to chef Stéphane Jégo. Tender veal shank comes deboned with a side of baby onions and broad beans with tiny cubes of ham, and house-salted cod is soaked, sautéed and doused with an elegant vinaigrette.

L'Arpège

84 rue de Varenne, 7th (01.47.05. 09.06, www.alain-passard.com). M° Varenne. **Open** noon-2.30pm, 8-10.30pm Mon-Fri. **€€€€. Haute cuisine. Map** p123 E2 ❿

Assuming that you can swallow an exceptionally high bill, chances are you'll have a spectacular time at chef Alain Passard's Left Bank establishment. A main course of sautéed free-range chicken with a roasted shallot, an onion, potato *mousseline* and pan juices is the apotheosis of comfort food.

Au Bon Accueil

14 rue de Monttessuy, 7th (01.47.05. 46.11, www.aubonaccueilparis.com). M° Alma Marceau. **Open** noon-2.30pm, 7-10.30pm Mon-Fri. Closed 2wks Aug. **€€€. Bistro. Map** p123 B1 ⓫

Jacques Lacipière runs Au Bon Accueil, and Keita Kitamura turns out the beautiful food. Perhaps most impressive is the restaurant's use of little-known fish such as grey mullet and meagre (*maigre*), rather than the usual endangered species. The lunch menu might highlight such ingredients as *suprême de poulet noir du Cros de la Géline*, free-range chicken raised on a farm run by two former cabaret singers.

Le Café du Marché

38 rue Cler, 7th (01.47.05.51.27). M° Ecole Militaire. **Open** 7am-midnight Mon-Sat; 7am-5pm Sun. **€. Café.** **Map** p123 C2 ⓬

This address is frequented by trendy locals, shoppers hunting down a particular type of cheese and tourists who've managed to make it this far from the Eiffel Tower. Its *pichets* of decent house plonk go down a treat, and mention must be made of the food – such as the house salad with lashings of foie gras.

Jules Verne

Pilier Sud, Eiffel Tower, 7th (01.45.55.61.44, www.lejulesverne-paris.com). M° Bir Hakeim or RER Champ de Mars Tour Eiffel. **Open** 12.15-1.30pm, 7-9.30pm daily. **€€€€. Haute cuisine. Map** p123 A2 ⓭

You have to have courage to take on an icon like the Eiffel Tower, but Alain Ducasse has done just that. Ducasse protégé Pascal Féraud updates French classics, combining all the grand ingredients you'd expect with light, modern textures. Try dishes such as sea bass steamed with seaweed, chicken and crayfish fricassée, and a wonderfully delicate rhubarb tartlet. Book ahead.

Les Ombres

27 quai Branly, 7th (01.47.53.68.00, www.lesombres-restaurant.com). M° Alma-Marceau. **Open** noon-2.30pm, 7-11pm daily. **€€€. Bistro.** **Map** p123 B1 ⓮

The view of the Eiffel Tower at night would be reason enough to come to this restaurant on the top floor of the Musée du Quai Branly, but Auvergne-born chef Cyril Lenoir's food also demands you take notice. In summer, you can book a table on the delightful terrace.

Il Vino

13 bd de La Tour-Maubourg, 7th (01.44.11.72.00, www.ilvinobyenrico bernardo.com). M° La Tour-Maubourg. **Open** noon-2pm, 7pm-midnight daily. **€€€€. Italian. Map** p123 D1 ⓯

Enrico Bernardo, winner of the World's Best Sommelier award, runs this restaurant where you're given nothing more than a wine list. Each of 15 wines by the glass is matched with a surprise dish, or the chef can build a meal around the bottle of your choice. Food shows a strong Italian influence.

Shopping

Fromagerie Quatrehomme

62 rue de Sèvres, 7th (01.47.34.33.45). M° Duroc or Vaneau. **Open** 8.45am-1pm, 4-7.45pm Tue-Thur; 8.45am-7.45pm Fri, Sat. **Map** p123 E3 ⓰

Marie Quatrehomme runs this *fromagerie*. Justly famous for her comté fruité, beaufort and st-marcellin, she also sells specialities such as goat's cheese with pesto.

Marie-Anne Cantin

12 rue du Champ-de-Mars, 7th (01.45. 50.43.94, www.cantin.fr). M° Ecole Militaire or La Tour Maubourg. **Open** 2-7.30pm Mon; 8.30am-7.30pm Tue-Sat; 8.30am-1pm Sun. **Map** p123 B3 ⓱

Cantin, supplier to posh Paris restaurants, offers aged *chèvres* and amazing morbier, mont d'or and comté.

Saxe-Breteuil

Av de Saxe, 7th. M° Ségur. **Open** 7am-2.30pm Thur; 7am-3pm Sat. **Map** p123 C3 ⓲

This market has an unrivalled setting facing the Eiffel Tower, as well as the city's most chic produce. Look out for farmer's goat's cheese, abundant oysters and a handful of small producers.

Arts & leisure

La Pagode

57bis rue de Babylone, 7th (01.45.55. 48.48, www.allocine.fr). M° St-François-Xavier. **Admission** €9; €7.50 reductions. No credit cards. **Map** p123 D3 ⓳

This glorious edifice is a 19th-century replica of a pagoda. It's one of the loveliest cinemas in the world.

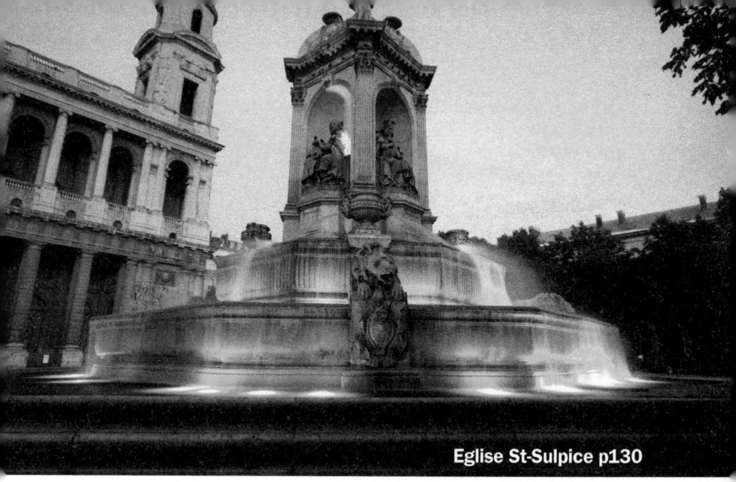

St-Germain-des-Prés & Odéon

St-Germain may be more Louis Vuitton than Boris Vian these days, but there are still enough small galleries and bookshops to ensure that it retains a whiff of its bohemian past. In the middle third of the 20th century, the area was prime arts and *intello* territory, a place known as much for its high jinks as for its lofty thinking: the haunt of Picasso, Giacometti, Camus, Prévert and, *bien sûr*, the Bonnie and Clyde of French philosophy, Jean-Paul Sartre and Simone de Beauvoir; the hotspot of the Paris jazz boom after World War II; and the heart of the Paris book trade. This is where the cliché of café terrace intellectualising was coined, but nowadays couturiers have largely replaced publishers. Never mind: it's a very smart and attractive part of the city to wander around in, and also has some very good restaurants.

St-Germain-des-Prés grew up around the medieval abbey, the oldest church in Paris and site of an annual fair that drew merchants from across Europe. There are traces of its cloister and part of the abbot's palace behind the church on rue de l'Abbaye. Constructed in 1586 in red brick with stone facing, the palace prefigured the architecture of place des Vosges. Charming place de Furstemberg (once the palace stables) is home to the house and studio where the elderly Delacroix lived when painting the murals in St-Sulpice; it now houses the **Musée National Delacroix**. Wagner, Ingres and Colette all lived on nearby rue Jacob; its elegant 17th-century *hôtels particuliers* now contain specialist book, design and antiques shops and a few pleasant hotels. Further east, rue de Buci hosts a market and upmarket food shops.

Ecole Nationale Supérieure des Beaux-Arts (Ensb-a)

14 rue Bonaparte, 6th (01.47.03.50.00, www.ensba.fr). M° St-Germain-des-Prés. **Open** 1-7pm Tue-Sun. **Admission** €4; €2 reductions. *Exhibitions* prices vary. **Map** p131 C1 ❶

The city's most prestigious fine arts school resides in what remains of the 17th-century Couvent des Petits-Augustins, the 18th-century Hôtel de Chimay, some 19th-century additions and chunks of various French châteaux moved here after the Revolution (when the buildings briefly served as a museum of French monuments).

Eglise St-Germain-des-Prés

3 pl St-Germain-des-Prés, 6th (01.55.42.81.33, www.eglise-sgp.org). M° St-Germain-des-Prés. **Open** 8am-7.45pm Mon-Sat; 9am-8pm Sun. **Admission** free. **Map** p131 C2 ❷

The oldest church in Paris. On the advice of Germain (later Bishop of Paris), Childebert, son of Clovis, had a basilica and monastery built here around 543. It was first dedicated to St Vincent, and came to be known as St-Germain-le-Doré because of its copper roof, then later as St-Germain-des-Prés ('of the fields'). During the Revolution the abbey was burned and a saltpetre refinery installed; the spire was added in a 19th-century restoration. Still, most of the present structure is 12th century, and ornate carved capitals and the tower remain from the 11th. Tombs include those of Jean-Casimir, deposed King of Poland who became Abbot of St-Germain in 1669, and Scots nobleman William Douglas.

Eglise St-Sulpice

Pl St-Sulpice, 6th (01.42.34.59.98, www.paroisse-saint-sulpice-paris.org). M° St-Sulpice. **Open** 7.30am-7.30pm daily. **Admission** free. **Map** p131 C3 ❸

It took 120 years (starting in 1646) and six architects to finish St-Sulpice. The grandiose Italianate façade, with its two-tier colonnade, was designed by Jean-Baptiste Servandoni. He died in 1766 before the second tower was finished, leaving one tower five metres shorter than the other. The trio of murals by Delacroix in the first chapel – *Jacob's Fight with the Angel, Heliodorus Chased from the Temple* and *St Michael Killing the Dragon* – create a suitably sombre atmosphere.

Jardin & Palais du Luxembourg

Pl André Honorat, pl Edmond-Rostand or rue de Vaugirard, 6th (01.44.54.19.49, www.senat.fr/visite). M° Odéon/RER Luxembourg. **Open** *Jardin* summer 7.30am-dusk daily; winter 8am-dusk daily. **Map** p131 C4 ❹

The palace itself was built in the 1620s for Marie de Médicis, widow of Henri IV, by Salomon de Brosse on the site of the former mansion of the Duke of Luxembourg. Its Italianate style was intended to remind her of the Pitti Palace in her native Florence. The palace now houses the French parliament's upper house, the Sénat.

The mansion next door (Le Petit Luxembourg) is the residence of the Sénat's president. The gardens, though, are the real draw: part formal (terraces and gravel paths), part 'English garden' (lawns and mature trees), they are the quintessential Paris park. The garden is crowded with sculptures: a looming Cyclops, queens of France, a miniature Statue of Liberty, wild animals, busts of Flaubert and Baudelaire, and a monument to Delacroix. There are orchards and an apiary. The Musée du Luxembourg hosts prestigious exhibitions. Most interesting, though, are the people: an international mixture of *flâneurs* and *dragueurs*, chess players and martial-arts practitioners, as well as children on ponies, in sandpits and playing with sailing boats on the pond.

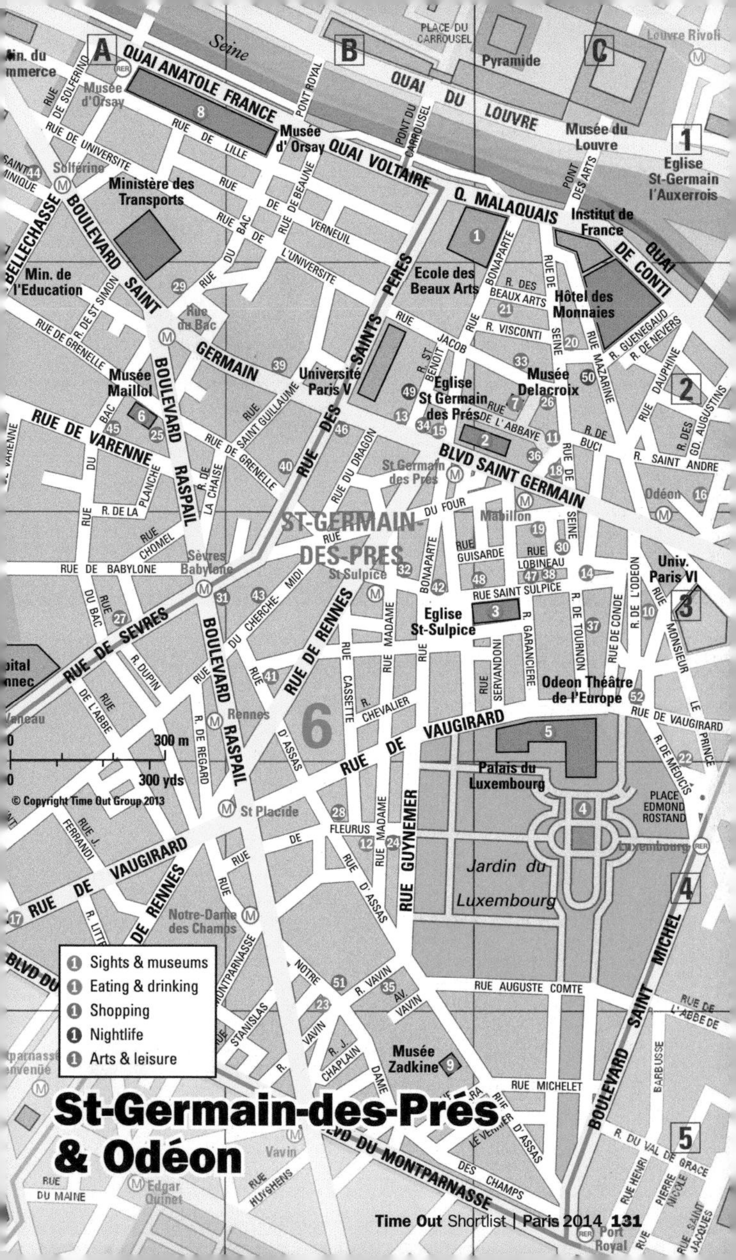

St-Germain-des-Prés & Odéon

La Palette p135

Musée du Luxembourg

19 rue de Vaugirard, 6th (01.40.13.62.00, www.museeduluxembourg.fr). M° Cluny La Sorbonne or Odéon/RER Luxembourg. **Open** 10am-10pm Mon, Fri; 10am-7.30pm Tue-Thur, Sat, Sun. **Admission** €11; free-€7.50 reductions. **Map** p131 C3 ❺

When it opened in 1750, this small museum was the first public gallery in France. After major renovations, the museum reopened its doors in early 2011. Book ahead to avoid queues.

Event highlights La Renaissance et le Rêve: Bosch, Veronese, Greco… (9 Oct 2013-26 Jan 2014)

Musée Maillol

59-61 rue de Grenelle, 7th (01.42.22.59.58, www.museemaillol.com). M° Rue du Bac. **Open** 10.30am-7pm (last admission 6.15pm) Mon-Thur, Sat, Sun; 10.30am-9.30pm (last admission 8.45pm) Fri. **Admission** €11; free-€9 reductions. **Map** p131 A2 ❻

Dina Vierny was 15 when she met Aristide Maillol (1861-1944) and became his principal model for the next decade, idealised in such sculptures as *Spring*, *Air* and *Harmony*. In 1995, she opened this museum, exhibiting Maillol's drawings, engravings, pastels, tapestry panels, ceramics and early Nabis-related paintings, as well as sculptures and terracottas that epitomise his calm classicism. The venue has works by Picasso, Rodin, Gauguin, Degas and Cézanne, a room of Matisse drawings, rare Surrealist documents and works by naïve artists. Vierny has also championed Kandinsky and Ilya Kabakov, whose *Communal Kitchen* installation recreates the atmosphere of Soviet domesticity.

Musée National Delacroix

6 rue de Furstenberg, 6th (01.44.41.86.50, www.musee-delacroix.fr). M° St-Germain-des-Prés. **Open** 9.30am-5pm Mon, Wed-Sun. **Admission** €5; free reductions. **Map** p131 C2 ❼

Eugène Delacroix moved to this apartment and studio in 1857 to be near the Eglise St-Sulpice, where he was painting murals. This collection includes small oil paintings, free pastel studies of skies, sketches and lithographs.

Musée d'Orsay

1 rue de la Légion-d'Honneur, 7th (01.40.49.48.14, www.musee-orsay.fr). M° Solférino/RER Musée d'Orsay. **Open** 9.30am-6pm Tue, Wed, Fri-Sun; 9.30am-9.45pm Thur. **Admission** €9; free-€6.50 reductions. **Map** p131 A1 ❽

See box p136.

Event highlights Gustave Doré: L'Imaginaire au Pouvoir (11 Feb-11 May 2014)

Musée Zadkine

100bis rue d'Assas, 6th (01.55.42.77.20, www.zadkine.paris.fr). M° Notre-Dame-des-Champs/RER Port-Royal. **Open** 10am-6pm Tue-Sun. **Admission** free. *Exhibitions* €4; free-€3 reductions. **Map** p131 B5 ❾

Works by the Russian-born Cubist sculptor Ossip Zadkine are displayed around this tiny house and garden near the Jardin du Luxembourg. Zadkine's works cover musical, mythological and religious subjects, and his style varies with his materials. There are drawings and poems by Zadkine and paintings by his wife, Valentine Prax. The museum reopened in late 2012 after a two-year revamp.

Eating & drinking

Le Bar Dix

10 rue de l'Odéon, 6th (01.43.26.66.83, www.lebar10.com). M° Odéon. **Open** 6pm-2am daily. No credit cards. **Bar. Map** p131 C3 ❿

Generations of students have glugged back jugs of the celebrated home-made sangría (€3 a glass in happy hour) while squeezed into the cramped upper bar, tattily authentic with its Jacques Brel record sleeves, Yves Montand handbills and pre-war light fittings.

Spelunkers and hopeless romantics negotiate the hazardous stone staircase to drink in the cellar bar, with its candlelight and old advertising murals. Can someone please come and slap a preservation order on the place?

Le Bar du Marché

75 rue de Seine, 6th (01.43.26.55.15). Mº Mabillon or Odéon. **Open** 8am-2am daily. **Bar. Map** p131 C2 ⓫

The market in question is the Cours des Halles, the bar a convivial corner café opening on to the pleasing bustle of St-Germain-des-Prés. Simple dishes such as a ham omelette or a plate of herring in the €7 range, and Brouilly or muscadet at €4-€5 a glass, are proffered by beret-topped waiters. Locals easily outnumber tourists, confirming Rod Stewart's astute observation that Paris gives the impression that no one is ever working.

Bread & Roses

7 rue de Fleurus, 6th (01.42.22.06.06, www.breadandroses.fr). Mº St-Placide. **Open** 8am-7.15pm Mon-Sat. **€€. Café. Map** p131 B4 ⓬

Giant wedges of cheesecake sit alongside French pastries, and huge savoury puff-pastry tarts are perched on the counter. Attention to detail shows even in the taramasalata, which is matched with buckwheat-and-seaweed bread. Prices reflect the quality of the often organic ingredients.

Café de Flore

172 bd St-Germain, 6th (01.45.48.55.26, www.cafedeflore.fr). Mº St-Germain-des-Prés. **Open** 7am-2am daily. **€€. Café. Map** p131 B2 ⓭

Bourgeois locals crowd the terrace tables at lunch, eating club sandwiches with knives and forks as anxious waiters frown at couples with pushchairs or single diners occupying tables for four. This historic café, former HQ of the Lost Generation intelligentsia, attracts tourists, and celebrities from time to time. But a *café crème* is €5.20, and the omelettes and *croques* are best eschewed in favour of the better dishes on the menu. There are play readings on Mondays and philosophy debates on the first Wednesday of the month.

Le Comptoir

Hôtel Le Relais Saint-Germain, 9 carrefour de l'Odéon, 6th (01.43.29.12.05). Mº Odéon. **Open** noon-6pm, 8.30-11pm (last orders 9pm) Mon-Fri; noon-11pm Sat, Sun. **€€. Brasserie. Map** p131 C3 ⓮

Yves Camdeborde runs the bijou 17th-century Hôtel Le Relais Saint-Germain, whose art deco dining room, modestly dubbed Le Comptoir, serves brasserie fare from noon to 6pm and on weekend nights, and a five-course prix fixe feast on weekday evenings. The single dinner sitting lets the chef take real pleasure in his work. On the daily menu, you might find dishes like rolled saddle of lamb with vegetable-stuffed 'Basque ravioli'. The catch? Dinner can be booked up six months in advance.

Les Deux Magots

6 pl St-Germain-des-Prés, 6th (01.45.48.55.25, www.lesdeuxmagots.com). Mº St-Germain-des-Prés. **Open** 7.30am-1am daily. **€€. Café. Map** p131 B2 ⓯

If you stand outside Les Deux Magots, you have to be prepared to photograph tourists wanting solid proof of their encounter with French philosophy. The former haunt of Sartre and de Beauvoir now draws a less pensive crowd that can be all too *m'as-tu vu*, particularly at weekends. The hot chocolate is still good, though. Visit on a weekday afternoon when the editors return, manuscripts in hand, to the inside tables, leaving enough elbow room to engage in some serious discussion.

L'Epigramme

9 rue de l'Eperon, 6th (01.44.41.00.09). Mº Odéon. **Open** noon-2.30pm, 7-10.30pm Tue-Sat. **€€. Bistro. Map** p131 C2 ⓰

L'Epigramme is a pleasantly bourgeois dining room with terracotta floor tiles, wood beams, a glassed-in kitchen and comfortable chairs. Like the decor, the food doesn't aim to innovate but sticks to tried and true classics with the occasional twist. Marinated mackerel in a mustardy dressing on toasted country bread gets things off to a promising start, but the chef's skill really comes through in main courses such as perfectly seared lamb with glazed root vegetables and intense *jus*. It's rare to find such a high standard of cooking at this price. Be sure to book.

La Ferrandaise

8 rue de Vaugirard, 6th (01.43.26.36.36, www.laferrandaise.com). Mº Odéon/RER Luxembourg. **Open** 7-10.30pm Mon; noon-2.30pm, 7-10.30pm Tue-Thur; noon-2.30pm, 7-11pm Fri; 7-11pm Sat. **€€**. **Bistro**. **Map** p131 A4 ⑰

This bistro has established a faithful following. A platter of excellent ham, sausage and terrine arrives as you study the blackboard menu, and the bread is crisp-crusted, thickly sliced sourdough. Two specialities are the potato stuffed with escargots in a camembert sauce, and a wonderfully flavoured, slightly rosé slice of veal. Desserts might include intense chocolate with rum-soaked bananas.

Germain

25-27 rue de Buci, 6th (01.43.26.02.93, www.beaumarly.com). Mº Mabillon or Odéon. **Open** 9am-2am daily. **€€**. **Brasserie**. **Map** p131 C2 ⑱

Quaint rue de Buci has been shaken up by the extravagance of Germain, a versatile brasserie halfway between *Alice in Wonderland* and London's Sketch. The heated terrace is great for people watching, and the main ground-floor room, which features the lower part of a vast yellow statue piercing through the ceiling above, is perfect for a quick lunch. There's also a cosy salon for cocktails, a more conservative dining room at the back, and a private room on the first floor with a snooker table and the top half of the yellow statue. The food is almost childishly classic, but always with a twist (ham and butter macaroni with truffle, perhaps).

J'Go

Rue Clément, 6th (01.43.26.19.02, www.lejgo.com). Mº Mabillon or Odéon. **Open** 11am-midnight daily. **€€**. **Wine bar**. **Map** p131 C3 ⑲

As its name suggests, J'Go (pronounced *gigot*) is all about lamb – well, meat of various kinds, actually: a buzzing wine bar by day, it becomes a *rôtisserie* at meal times, serving its speciality spit-roasted lamb from Quercy, black pig from Bigorre, and whole roasted chickens. The set menu is well worth it, offering perhaps a whole jar of pâté, a giant salad, and lamb with creamy stewed *haricots blancs*. If you'd rather stick to wine and tapas, sidle up to one of the wooden barrels, choose your poison and share a plate of charcuterie or foie gras *tartines*.

La Palette

43 rue de Seine, 6th (01.43.26.68.15). Mº Odéon. **Open** 9am-2am Mon-Sat. Closed Aug. **€€**. **Café**. **Map** p131 C2 ⑳

La Palette is the café-bar of choice for the Beaux-Arts students who study at the venerable institution around the corner, and young couples who steal kisses in the wonderfully preserved art deco back room decorated with illustrations. Grab a spot on the leafy terrace if you can.

Le Restaurant

L'Hôtel, 13 rue des Beaux-Arts, 6th (01.44.41.99.01, www.l-hotel.com). Mº St-Germain-des-Prés. **Open** 12.30-2.30pm, 7.30-10pm Tue-Sat. **€€€**. **Haute cuisine**. **Map** p131 C2 ㉑

L'Hôtel's restaurant is a wonderfully atmospheric spot for lunch or dinner. You can choose from a short seasonal menu with such dishes as pan-fried tuna, John Dory or suckling pig. But for the same price you can enjoy the marvellous four-course *menu dégustation*

Well hung

The Musée d'Orsay is gleaming after a revamp.

After partially closing for 18 months, the **Musée d'Orsay** (see p133) reopened fully in 2012 to gasps of admiration. On arriving at the fifth-floor Impressionist galleries one is confronted with a huge, wide space where the giant clockface window, previously hidden by corridors, floods the dark room with light.

The Impressionist galleries, previously a series of bland, skylit rooms that suffered from bottlenecks and overcrowding, have been utterly transformed with dark, moody colours such as anthracite, purple, vermillion and bottle-green. But it's not just the walls that make the paintings of Monet, Manet, Renoir and Cézanne sing out as if they had been painted yesterday. It is also the Solux lighting, which reveals every colour in the spectrum. The effect is extra-sensory: you can smell the surf of Monet's *Rough Sea at Etretat*, feel the heat of Renoir's surprising *Mosque in Algiers*, and taste the crispness of Pissarro's *White Freeze*, which hangs on a wall of winter paintings directly facing hot, southern scenes.

This is part of a dynamic approach to hanging that throws out the traditional chronological or artist-by-artist approach to juxtapose different visions of the same theme, even to the extent of bringing sculpture into the gallery. And the seating is a work of art too, with Tokujin Yoshioka's glass benches rippling in the centre of each room.

or, even better, the *menu surprise*. Past highlights have included smoked Somme eel with horseradish and lime.

Le Rostand

6 pl Edmond-Rostand, 6th (01.43.54.61.58). RER Luxembourg. **Open** 8am-midnight daily. **Bar**. **Map** p131 C3 ㉒

Le Rostand has a truly wonderful view of the Jardin du Luxembourg from its classy interior, decked out with oriental paintings, a mahogany bar and wall-length mirrors. Perfect for a civilised drink after a stroll round the gardens.

Le Timbre

3 rue Ste-Beuve, 6th (01.45.49.10.40, www.restaurantletimbre.com). M° Vavin. **Open** noon-2pm, 7-10.30pm Tue-Sat. Closed Aug & 1wk Dec. **€€**. **Bistro**. **Map** p131 B4 ㉓

Chris Wright's restaurant might be the size of the average student garret, but this Mancunian aims high. Typical of his cooking is a plate of fresh asparagus elegantly cut in half lengthways and served with dabs of anise-spiked sauce and balsamic vinegar. Mains are also pure in flavour – a slab of pork, pan-fried, comes with petals of red onion.

Shopping

APC

38 rue Madame, 6th (01.42.22.12.77, www.apc.fr). M° St-Placide. **Open** 11am-7.30pm Mon-Sat; 12.30-6.30pm Sun. **Map** p131 B4 ㉔

The look here is simple but stylish: think perfectly cut basics in muted tones. Hip without trying too hard, its jeans are a big hit.

L'Artisan Parfumeur

24 bd Raspail, 7th (01.42.22.23.32, www.artisanparfumeur.com). M° Rue du Bac. **Open** 10.30am-7.30pm Mon-Sat. **Map** p131 A2 ㉕

Among the scented candles, potpourri and charms, you'll find the best vanilla perfume that Paris can offer – Mûres et Musc, a bestseller for two decades.

Hermès p138

Arty Dandy

1 rue de Furstenberg, 6th (01.43.54.00.36, www.artydandy.com). M° Mabillon. **Open** 10am-7pm Mon-Fri; 11am-8pm Sat. **Map** p131 C2 ㉖

Arty Dandy is a concept shop that embraces the surreal, the tongue-in-cheek and the poetic – an R.MUTT sticker to create your own Duchampian loo, and the 'Karl who?' bag (which KL himself has been known to carry) are instant pleasers. More sublime offerings include Jaime Hayon's 'Lover' figurines.

Le Bon Marché

24 rue de Sèvres, 7th (01.44.39.80.00, www.bonmarche.fr). M° Sèvres Babylone. **Open** 10am-8pm Mon-Wed, Sat; 10am-9pm Thur, Fri. **Map** p131 A3 ㉗

Luxury boutiques take pride of place on the ground floor; escalators designed by Andrée Putman take you up to the fashion floor, which has an excellent selection of designer labels. Designer names also abound in Balthazar, the men's section. For top-notch nibbles, try the brand new Rose Bakery Tea Room on the second floor.

Christian Constant

37 rue d'Assas, 6th (01.53.63.15.15). M° Rennes or St-Placide. **Open** 9.30am-8.30pm Mon-Fri; 9am-8pm Sat, Sun. **Map** p131 B4 ㉘

A master chocolate-maker and *traiteur*, Constant scours the globe for ideas. His *ganaches* are subtly flavoured with verbena, jasmine or cardamom.

Deyrolle

46 rue du Bac, 7th (01.42.22.30.07, www.deyrolle.com). M° Rue du Bac. **Open** 10am-1pm, 2-7pm Mon; 10am-7pm Tue-Sat. **Map** p131 A2 ㉙

Famous taxidermy shop Deyrolle has a bizarre menagerie of lions, giraffes, polar bears, butterflies and bugs of all shapes and sizes. It remains a great place to buy a tiger for the living room, purchase creepy crawlies to scare friends and family or fire your children's imagination.

Gérard Mulot

76 rue de Seine, 6th (01.43.26.85.77, www.gerard-mulot.com). M° Odéon. **Open** 6.45am-8pm Mon, Tue, Thur-Sun. Closed Easter & Aug. **Map** p131 C3 ㉚

Gérard Mulot rustles up stunning pastries. Try the *mabillon*: caramel mousse with apricot jam.

Hermès

17 rue de Sèvres, 6th (01.42.22.80.83). M° Sèvres Babylone. **Open** 10.30am-7pm Mon-Sat. **Map** p131 A3 ㉛

If you thought that Hermès was about horsey scarves and little else, a visit to this shop should dispel the equestrian rumours forever. Designed by Denis Montel, the concept store is set in the Hôtel Lutetia's former indoor pool. The renovations have produced one of the best-looking retail spaces on the Left Bank. While the trademark scarves and ties are all present and correct, the three-floor store also focuses strongly on homewares, from wallpaper and carpets to sumptuous reproductions of 1930s-era furniture by renowned designer Jean-Michel Frank.

Hervé Chapelier

1bis rue du Vieux-Colombier, 6th (01.44.07.06.50, www.hervechapelier.fr). M° St-Germain-des-Prés or St-Sulpice. **Open** 10.15am-7pm Mon-Sat. **Map** p131 B3 ㉜

Pick up a classic two-tone bag. Sizes range from purses to weekend bags.

Huilerie Artisanale Leblanc

12 rue Jacob, 6th (01.44.07.36.58, www.huile-leblanc.com). M° St-Germain-des-Prés. **Open** 11am-1.30pm, 2.30-7.30pm Tue-Sat. Closed 2wks Aug. No credit cards. **Map** p131 C2 ㉝

The Leblanc family started making walnut oil before branching out to press pure oils from hazelnuts, almonds, pine nuts, grilled peanuts and olives. There are vinegars and mustards too.

La Hune

170 bd St-Germain, 6th (01.45.48.35.85). M° St-Germain-des-Prés. **Open** 10am-11.45pm Mon-Sat; 11am-7.45pm Sun. **Map** p131 B2 34

This Left Bank institution boasts a global selection of art and design books, and a truly magnificent collection of French literature and theory.

Jean-Paul Hévin

3 rue Vavin, 6th (01.43.54.09.85, www.jphevin.com). M° Notre-Dame-des-Champs or Vavin. **Open** 10am-7pm Tue-Sat. Closed Aug. **Map** p131 B4 35

Hévin specialises in the beguiling combination of chocolate with potent cheese fillings, which loyal customers serve with wine as an aperitif.

Lefranc.ferrant

22 rue de l'Echaudé, 6th (01.44.07.37.96, www.lefranc-ferrant.fr). M° St-Germain-des-Prés. **Open** 11am-7pm Tue-Sat and by appointment. **Map** p131 C2 36

Béatrice Ferrant and Mario Lefranc have a surreal approach to tailoring, as in a strapless yellow evening gown made like a pair of men's trousers – complete with flies.

Marie-Hélène de Taillac

8 rue de Tournon, 6th (01.44.27.07.07, www.mariehelenedetaillac.com). M° Mabillon. **Open** 11am-7pm Mon-Sat. **Map** p131 C3 37

Marie-Hélène de Taillac is a fine jeweller, using diamonds and emeralds in simple settings. This combination of precious stones and modern styling has made her popular with the fashion elite. They also adore her Left Bank shop.

Marie Mercié

23 rue St-Sulpice, 6th (01.43.26.45.83). M° Odéon. **Open** 11am-7pm Mon-Sat. **Map** p131 C3 38

Mercié's creations make you wish you lived in an era when hats were de rigueur. Step out in one shaped like curved fingers (with shocking-pink nail varnish and pink diamond ring) or a beret like a face with red lips and turquoise eyes. Ready-to-wear starts at about €30; *sur mesure* takes ten days.

Patrick Roger

108 bd St-Germain, 6th (01.43.29.38.42, www.patrickroger.com). M° Odéon. **Open** 10.30am-7.30pm daily. **Map** p131 B2 39

Whereas other *chocolatiers* aim for gloss, Roger may create a brushed effect on hens so realistic you almost expect them to lay (chocolate) eggs.

Paul & Joe

64 rue des Sts-Pères, 7th (01.42.22.47.01, www.paulandjoe.com). M° Rue du Bac or St-Germain-des-Prés. **Open** 10am-7pm Mon-Sat. **Map** p131 B2 40

Paul & Joe dresses leggy young things in a range of winter shorts, colourful mini dresses and voluminous trousers, with their intellectual paramours in slouchy woollens and chunky boots.

Peggy Huyn Kinh

9-11 rue Coëtlogon, 6th (01.42.84.83.82, www.phk.fr). M° St-Sulpice. **Open** 11am-7pm Mon-Sat. **Map** p131 B3 41

Once creative director at Cartier, Peggy Huyn Kinh now makes bags of boar skin and python, plus silver jewellery.

Pierre Hermé

72 rue Bonaparte, 6th (01.43.54.47.77). M° Mabillon, St-Germain-des-Prés or St-Sulpice. **Open** 10am-7pm Mon-Fri, Sun; 10am-8pm Sat. Closed 1st 3wks Aug. **Map** p131 B3 42

Pastry superstar Hermé attracts connoisseurs from near and far with his seasonal collections.

Poilâne

8 rue du Cherche-Midi, 6th (01.45.48.42.59, www.poilane.com). M° Sèvres Babylone or St-Sulpice. **Open** 7.15am-8.15pm Mon-Sat. **Map** p131 B3 43

Apollonia Poilâne runs the family shop, where locals queue for fresh country *miches*, flaky-crusted apple tarts and shortbread biscuits.

Richart

258 bd St-Germain, 7th (01.45.55.66.00, www.richart.com). Mº Solférino. **Open** 10am-7pm Mon-Sat. **Map** p131 A1 44

Each chocolate *ganache* has an intricate design, packages look like jewel boxes, and each purchase comes with a tract on how best to savour the stuff.

Ryst Dupeyron

79 rue du Bac, 7th (01.45.48.80.93, www.vintageandco.com). Mº Rue du Bac. **Open** 12.30-7.30pm Mon; 10.30am-7.30pm Tue-Sat. Closed 2wks Aug. **Map** p131 A2 45

The Dupeyrons have been selling armagnac for four generations, and still have bottles from 1868. Treasures here include 200 fine Bordeaux wines and an extensive range of vintage port.

Sonia Rykiel

175 bd St-Germain, 6th (01.49.54.60.60, www.soniarykiel.com). Mº St-Germain-des-Prés or Sèvres Babylone. **Open** 10.30am-7pm Mon-Sat. **Map** p131 B2 46

The queen of St-Germain's flagship store features a glamorous black and smoked glass look, perfect for narcissists. Menswear is located across the street, and two newer boutiques stock the Sonia by Sonia Rykiel range.

Vanessa Bruno

25 rue St-Sulpice, 6th (01.43.54.41.04, www.vanessabruno.com). Mº Odéon. **Open** 10.30am-7.30pm Mon-Sat. **Map** p131 C3 47

Bruno's mercerised cotton tanks, flattering trousers and tops have a Zen-like quality. She also makes great bags.

Yves Saint Laurent

6 pl St-Sulpice, 6th (01.43.29.43.00, www.ysl.com). Mº St-Sulpice. **Open** 11am-7pm Mon; 10.30am-7pm Tue-Sat. **Map** p131 C3 48

The memory of the founding designer, who died in 2008, lives on in this wonderfully elegant boutique, which was splendidly refitted in red in the same year. You'll find the menswear collection at 32 rue du Fbg-St-Honoré (8th).

Nightlife

Le Montana

28 rue St-Benoît, 6th (no phone). Mº St-Germain-des-Prés. **Open** 11pm-5am daily. **Admission** free. **Map** p131 B2 49

It's hard to believe that any place could out-hype Le Baron, but this exclusive club manages it. Revamped by über-cool graphic artist André, Le Montana is a VIP magnet – Lenny Kravitz, Vanessa Bruno and Kate Moss have all hit the floor here.

Wagg

62 rue Mazarine, 6th (01.55.42.22.01, www.wagg.fr). Mº Odéon. **Open** 11pm-6.45am Fri, Sat; 3.30pm-midnight Sun. **Admission** €12 Fri, Sat; €12 Sun (incl 1 drink). **Map** p131 C2 50

Wagg hosts a well-to-do Left Bank crowd. Expect funk, house and disco, plus salsa lessons on Sundays.

Arts & leisure

Le Lucernaire

53 rue Notre-Dame-des-Champs, 6th (01.42.22.26.50, www.lucernaire.fr). Mº Notre-Dame-des-Champs or Vavin. **Admission** €15-€30. **Map** p131 B4 51

Three theatres, three cinemas, a restaurant and a bar make up this versatile cultural centre. Molière and other classic playwrights get a good thrashing.

Odéon, Théâtre de L'Europe

Pl de l'Odéon, 6th (01.44.85.40.00, bookings 01.44.85.40.40, www.theatre-odeon.fr). Mº Odéon. **Box office** 11am-6pm Mon-Sat. **Admission** €6-€34. **Map** p131 C3 52

Highlights for 2014 include *As You Like It* and *Cyrano de Bergerac*. The theatre also plays host to the annual Impatience festival for young theatre companies in May.

Le Panthéon p146

The Latin Quarter & the 13th

The Latin Quarter

To many first-time visitors – especially those from the States – the Latin Quarter can be a big disappointment. Countless books have led them to believe that the area is somehow the quintessence of Paris, and they come with their heads stuffed with expat writers – Orwell, Hemingway, Henry Miller – only to find a touristy jam of bad restaurants and uninspiring shops. Granted, many of the narrow, crooked streets (like the Marais, the Latin Quarter was another part of Paris largely untouched by Haussmann) are charming, and there are some real architectural glories, especially ecclesiastical ones; but the crowds can make the experience of seeing them rather dispiriting.

The 'Latin' in the area's name probably derives from the fact that it has been the university quarter since medieval times, when Latin was the language of instruction. The district's long association with learning began in about 1100, when a number of renowned scholars, including Pierre Abélard, began to live and teach on Montagne Ste-Geneviève, independent of the established cathedral school of Notre-Dame. This loose association of scholars came to be referred to as a 'university'. The Paris schools attracted students from all over Europe and the 'colleges' multiplied, until the University of Paris was given official recognition with a charter from Pope Innocent III in 1215.

Sights & museums

Arènes de Lutèce

Rue Monge, rue de Navarre or rue des Arènes, 5th. M° Cardinal Lemoine or Place Monge. **Open** *Summer*

9am-9.30pm daily. *Winter* 8am-5.30pm daily. **Admission** free. **Map** p143 B4 ❶

This Roman arena, where wild beasts and gladiators fought, could seat 10,000 people. It was still visible during the reign of Philippe-Auguste in the 12th century, then disappeared under rubble. The site now attracts skateboarders, footballers and boules players.

Eglise St-Etienne-du-Mont

Pl Ste-Geneviève, 5th (01.43.54.11.79, www.saintetiennedumont.fr). M° Cardinal Lemoine/RER Luxembourg. **Open** 8.45am-7.45pm Tue-Fri; 8.45am-noon, 2-7.45pm Sat; 8.45am-12.15pm, 2-7.45pm Sun. *July, Aug* 10am-noon, 4-7.45pm Tue-Sun. **Map** p143 B4 ❷

Geneviève, patron saint of Paris, is credited with having miraculously saved the city from the ravages of Attila the Hun in 451, and her shrine has been a site of pilgrimage ever since. The present church was built in an amalgam of Gothic and Renaissance styles between 1492 and 1626, and the interior is wonderfully tall and light, with soaring columns and a classical balustrade. The stunning Renaissance rood screen, with its double spiral staircase and ornate stone strapwork, is the only surviving one in Paris. At the back of the church (reached through the sacristy), the catechism chapel constructed by Baltard in the 1860s has a cycle of paintings relating the saint's life story.

Eglise St-Séverin

3 rue des Prêtres-St-Séverin, 5th (01.42.34.93.50, www.saint-severin.com). M° Cluny La Sorbonne or St-Michel. **Open** 11am-7.30pm Mon-Sat; 9am-8.30pm Sun. **Map** p143 A3 ❸

Built on the site of the chapel of the hermit Séverin, itself set on a much earlier Merovingian burial ground, this lovely Flamboyant Gothic edifice was long the parish church of the Left Bank. The church dates from the 15th century, though the doorway, carved with foliage, was added in 1837 from the demolished Eglise St-Pierre-aux-Boeufs on Ile de la Cité. The double ambulatory is famed for its forest of 'palm tree' vaulting, which meets at the end in a unique spiral column that inspired a series of paintings by Robert Delaunay. The bell tower, a survivor from one of the earlier churches on the site, has the oldest bell in Paris (1412).

Eglise du Val-de-Grâce

Pl Alphonse-Laveran, 5th (01.40.51.51.92). RER Luxembourg or Port-Royal. **Open** noon-6pm Tue, Wed, Sat, Sun. **Admission** €5; free-€2.50 reductions. No credit cards. **Map** p143 A5 ❹

Anne of Austria, the wife of Louis XIII, vowed to erect 'a magnificent temple' if God blessed her with a son. She got two. The resulting church and surrounding Benedictine monastery – these days a military hospital and the Musée du Service de Santé des Armées – were built by François Mansart and Jacques Lemercier. This is the most luxuriously baroque of the city's 17th-century domed churches. In contrast, the surrounding monastery offers the perfect example of François Mansart's classical restraint. Phone in advance if you're after a guided visit.

Grande Galerie de l'Evolution

36 rue Geoffroy-St-Hilaire, 2 rue Bouffon or pl Valhubert, 5th (01.40.79.56.01). M° Gare d'Austerlitz or Jussieu. **Open** *Grande Galerie* 10am-6pm Mon, Wed-Sun. *Other galleries* 10am-5pm Mon, Wed-Fri; 10am-6pm Sat, Sun. **Admission** *Grande Galerie* €7; free-€5 reductions. *Other galleries* (each) €7; free-€5 reductions. No credit cards. **Map** p143 C5 ❺

One of the city's most child-friendly attractions, this is guaranteed to bowl adults over too. Located within the Jardin des Plantes, this 19th-century iron-framed, glass-roofed structure has been modernised with lifts, galleries and false floors, and filled with

The Latin Quarter

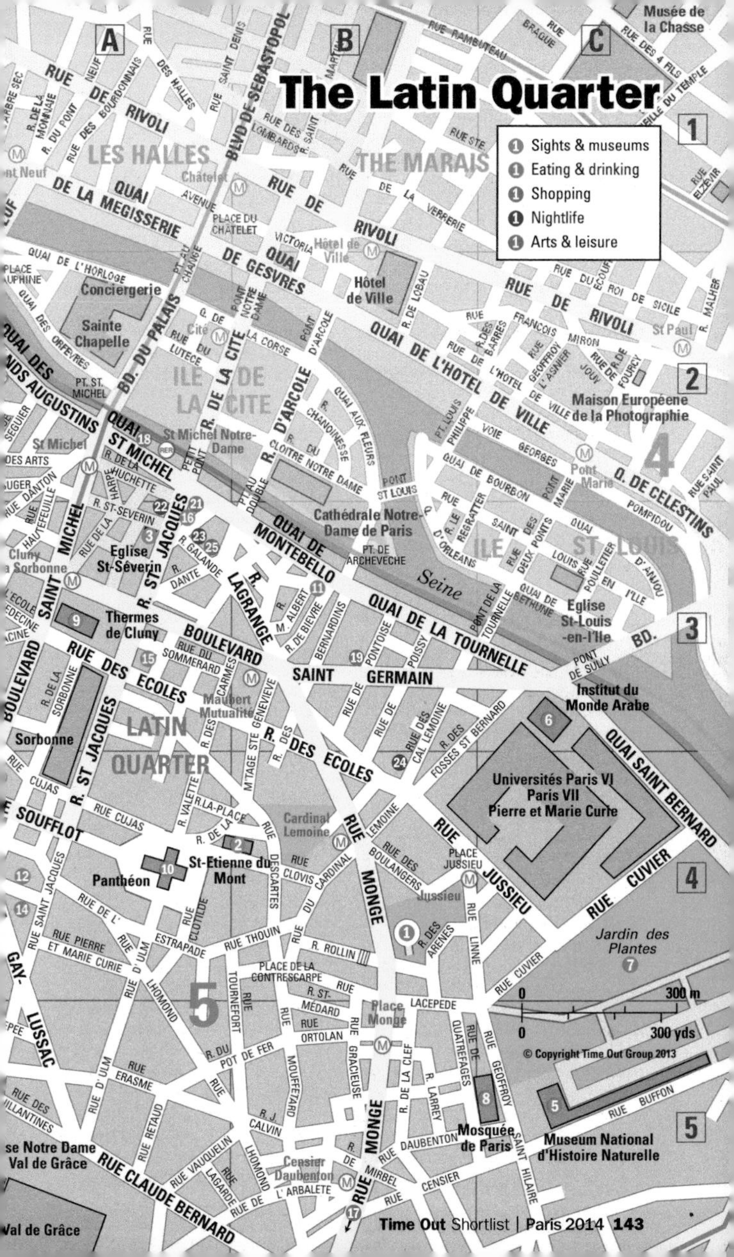

life-size models of tentacle-waving squid, open-mawed sharks and monkeys swarming down from the ceiling. The centrepiece is a procession of African wildlife across the first floor that resembles the procession into Noah's Ark. Glass-sided lifts take you up through suspended birds to the second floor, which deals with man's impact on nature (crocodile into handbag). The third floor focuses on endangered species.

Institut du Monde Arabe

1 rue des Fossés-St-Bernard, 5th (01.40.51.38.38, www.imarabe.org). M° Jussieu. **Open** *Museum* 10am-6pm Tue-Thur; 10am-9.30pm Fri; 10am-7pm Sat, Sun. *Library* 1-8pm Tue-Sat (July, Aug 1-6pm). *Tours* 3pm Tue-Fri; 3pm & 4.30pm Sat, Sun. **Admission** *Museum* €8; free-€6 reductions. *Library* free. *Exhibitions* varies. **Map** p143 C3 ❻

See box p145.

Jardin des Plantes

36 rue Geoffroy-St-Hilaire, 2 rue Bouffon, pl Valhubert or 57 rue Cuvier, 5th. M° Gare d'Austerlitz or Place Monge (01.40.79.56.01, www.jardindesplantes.net). **Open** *Main garden* Winter 8am-5.30pm daily. Summer 7.30am-7.45pm daily. *Alpine garden* Apr-Oct 8am-4.40pm Mon-Fri; 1.30-6pm Sat; 1.30-6.30pm Sun. Closed Nov-Mar. *Ménagerie* 9am-6pm Mon-Sat; 9am-6.30pm Sun. **Admission** *Alpine garden* free Mon-Fri; €2 Sat, Sun. *Jardin des Plantes* free. *Ménagerie* €10; free-€8 reductions. **Map** p143 C4 ❼

The Paris botanical garden – which contains more than 10,000 species and includes tropical greenhouses and rose, winter and Alpine gardens – is an enchanting place. Begun by Louis XIII's doctor as the royal medicinal plant garden in 1626, it opened to the public in 1640. The formal garden, which runs between two avenues of trees, is like something out of *Alice in Wonderland*. There's also a small zoo and the terrific Grande Galerie de l'Evolution. Ancient trees on view include a false acacia planted in 1636. A plaque on the old laboratory declares that this is the spot where Henri Becquerel discovered radioactivity in 1896.

La Mosquée de Paris

2 pl du Puits-de-l'Ermite, 5th (01.45.35.97.33, tearoom 01.43.31.38.20, baths 01.43.31.18.14, www.mosquee-de-paris.net). M° Monge. **Open** *Tours* 9am-noon, 2-6pm Mon-Thur, Sat, Sun (closed Muslim hols). *Tearoom* 10am-11.30pm daily. *Restaurant* noon-2.30pm, 7.30-10.30pm daily. *Baths* (women) 10am-9pm Mon, Wed, Sat; 2-9pm Fri; (men) 2-9pm Tue, Sun. **Admission** €3; free-€2 reductions. *Tearoom* free. *Baths* €15-€35. **Map** p143 C5 ❽

This vast Hispano-Moorish construct is the spiritual heart of France's Algerian-dominated Muslim population. In plan and function it divides into three sections: religious (grand patio, prayer room and minaret, all for worshippers and not curious tourists); scholarly (Islamic school and library); and, via rue Geoffroy-St-Hilaire, commercial (café and domed hammam). La Mosquée café is delightful – a courtyard shaded beneath green foliage and scented with the sweet smell of sheesha smoke.

Musée National du Moyen Age – Thermes de Cluny

6 pl Paul-Painlevé, 5th (01.53.73.78.00, www.musee-moyenage.fr). M° Cluny La Sorbonne. **Open** 9.15am-5.45pm Mon, Wed-Sun. **Admission** €8; free-€6 reductions. **Map** p143 A3 ❾

The national museum of medieval art is best known for the beautiful, allegorical *Lady and the Unicorn* tapestry cycle, but it also has important collections of medieval sculpture and enamels. The building itself, commonly known as Cluny, is also a rare example of 15th-century secular Gothic architecture, with its foliate Gothic doorways,

Brave new world

The Institut du Monde Arabe marked its 25th year in style.

One of Paris's most innovative museums reopened to the public in 2012, after a three-year, €5 million revamp. The beautiful museum of the **Institut du Monde Arabe** (see left), dedicated to the development of Islamic art and the history and culture of the Arab world, has been transformed, and reopened in time to mark its 25th anniversary. Collections from the 22 Arab countries that co-founded the museum can now be enjoyed once again, in an exciting and dynamic new interior.

A clever blend of high-tech and Arab influences, this Seine-side *grand projet* was constructed between 1980 and 1987 to a design by architect Jean Nouvel, who sought to build a modern interpretation of a Moorish palace.

Some 600 items are on display here, from places as diverse as Damascus, Aleppo, Latakia, Amman, Kairouan and Manama, as well as the Musée du Louvre, the Musée du Quai Branly and the Bibliothèque Nationale de France. And where before the collection was limited to art, the new museum has widened its scope (as well as its physical space), showcasing the Arab world in thematic ways, covering its ethno-linguistic, historical, cultural, anthropological and geographical diversity. Roberto Ostinelli's subtle but dynamic staging – conceived as a pathway dotted with bridges between past and present – works on both an emotional and an intellectual level.

What's more, there's a lively programme of events (exhibitions, film screenings, music and dance) and an excellent Middle East bookshop on the ground floor, and the views from the roof terrace (to which access is free) are fabulous.

And if your thirst for Arab culture is still unquenched after a visit here, head to the Louvre to check out its new Islamic arts wing.

hexagonal staircase jutting out of the façade and vaulted chapel. It was built from 1485 to 1498 – on top of a Gallo-Roman baths complex. The baths, built in characteristic Roman bands of stone and brick masonry, are the finest Roman remains in Paris. The vaulted *frigidarium* (cold bath), *tepidarium* (warm bath), *caldarium* (hot bath) and part of the hypocaust heating system are all still visible. A themed garden fronts the whole complex.

Le Panthéon

Pl du Panthéon, 5th (01.44.32.18.00). M° Cardinal Lemoine/RER Luxembourg. **Open** 10am-6pm (until 6.30pm summer) daily. **Admission** €8.50; free-€5.50 reductions. **Map** p143 A4 ⑩

Soufflot's neoclassical megastructure was the architectural *grand projet* of its day, commissioned by a grateful Louis XV to thank Sainte Geneviève for his recovery from illness. But by the time it was ready in 1790, a lot had changed; during the Revolution, the Panthéon was rededicated as a 'temple of reason' and the resting place of the nation's great men. The barrel-vaulted crypt now houses Voltaire, Rousseau, Hugo and Zola. New heroes are installed but rarely: Pierre and Marie Curie's remains were transferred here in 1995; Alexandre Dumas in 2002. Mount the steep spiral stairs to the colonnade encircling the dome for superb views.

Eating & drinking

Atelier Maître Albert

1 rue Maître-Albert, 5th (01.56.81. 30.01, www.ateliermaitrealbert.com). M° Maubert Mutualité or St-Michel. **Open** noon-2.30pm, 6.30-11pm Mon-Wed; noon-2.30pm, 6.30pm-1am Thur, Fri; 6.30pm-1am Sat; 6.30-11.30pm Sun. **€€**. **Bistro**. **Map** p143 B3 ⑪

This Guy Savoy outpost in the fifth has slick decor by Jean-Michel Wilmotte. The indigo-painted, grey marble-floored dining room with open kitchen and rôtisseries on view is attractive but very noisy at night. The short menu lets you have a Savoy classic or two to start with, including oysters in seawater *gelée* or more inventive dishes such as the ballotine of chicken, foie gras and celery root in a chicken-liver sauce. Next up, perhaps, tuna served with tiny iron casseroles of dauphinois potatoes, and cauliflower in béchamel sauce.

Le Crocodile

6 rue Royer-Collard, 5th (01.43.54. 32.37). RER Luxembourg. **Open** 6pm-2am Mon-Sat. Closed Aug. **Bar**. **Map** p143 A4 ⑫

Ignore the apparently boarded-up windows at Le Crocodile; if you're here late, then it's open. Friendly young regulars line the sides of this small, narrow bar and try to decide what to drink – not easy, given the length of the cocktail list: at last count there were 317 varieties. The generous €6-per-cocktail happy hour (Monday to Thursday before midnight) will allow you to start with a champagne *accroche-coeur*, followed up with a Goldschläger (served with gold leaf) before moving on to one of the other 316.

Lapérouse

51 quai des Grands-Augustins, 6th (01.43.26.68.04, www.laperouse.com). M° St-Michel. **Open** noon-2.30pm, 7.30-11pm Mon-Fri; 7.30-11pm Sat. Closed 2wks Aug. **€€€€**. **Brasserie**. **Map** p143 A2 ⑬

Lapérouse was formerly a clandestine rendezvous for French politicians and their mistresses; the tiny private dining rooms upstairs used to lock from the inside. Chef Alain Hacquard does a reasonable take on classic French cooking: his beef fillet is smoked for a more complex flavour; a tender saddle of rabbit is cooked in a clay crust, flavoured with lavender and rosemary and served with ravioli of onions. The only snag is the cost, especially of the wine – a half-bottle of Pouilly-Fuissé will set you back around €35.

Le Pantalon

7 rue Royer-Collard, 5th (no phone). RER Luxembourg. **Open** 3pm-2am daily. No credit cards. **€. Café.** **Map** p143 A4 ⑭

Le Pantalon is a local café that seems familiar yet is utterly surreal. It has the standard fixtures, including the old soaks at the bar – but the regulars and staff are enough to tip the balance into eccentricity. Friendly, funny French grown-ups and foreign students chat in a mishmash of languages; drinks are cheap enough to make you tipsy without the worry of a cash hangover.

Le Pré Verre

8 rue Thénard, 5th (01.43.54.59.47, www.lepreverre.com). M° Maubert Mutualité. **Open** noon-2pm, 7.30-10.30pm Tue-Sat. Closed 24 Dec-1 Jan. **€€. Bistro. Map** p143 A3 ⑮

Philippe Delacourcelle knows how to handle spices like few other French chefs. Salt cod with cassia bark and smoked potato purée is a classic: what the fish lacks in size it makes up for in rich, cinnamon-like flavour and crunchy texture, and smooth potato cooked in a smoker makes a startling accompaniment. Spices have a way of making desserts seem esoteric rather than decadent, but the roast figs with olives are an exception to the rule.

Ribouldingue

10 rue St-Julien-le-Pauvre, 5th (01.46.33.98.80, www.restaurant-ribouldingue.com). M° St-Michel. **Open** noon-2pm, 7.30-11pm Mon-Sat. **€€. Bistro. Map** p143 A3 ⑯

This bistro facing St-Julien-le-Pauvre church is the creation of Nadège Varigny, who spent ten years working with Yves Camdeborde before opening a restaurant inspired by the food of her childhood in Grenoble. It's full of people, including critics and chefs, who love simple, honest bistro fare, such as *daube de boeuf* or seared tuna on a bed of melting aubergine. If you have an appetite for offal, then you might want to opt for the gently sautéed brains with new potatoes or veal kidneys with a perfectly prepared potato gratin. For dessert, try the fresh ewe's cheese with bitter honey.

Shopping

Le Boulanger de Monge

123 rue Monge, 5th (01.43.37.54.20, www.leboulangerdemonge.com). M° Censier Daubenton. **Open** 7am-8.30pm Tue-Sun. **Map** p143 B5 ⑰

Dominique Saibron uses spices to give wonderful flavour to his organic sourdough *boule*. Every day about 2,000 bread-lovers visit this boutique, which also produces one of the city's best baguettes.

Bouquinistes

Along the quais, especially quai de Montebello & quai St-Michel, 5th. M° St-Michel. **Open** times vary from stall to stall, generally Tue-Sun. No credit cards. **Map** p143 A2 ⑱

The green, open-air boxes along the *quais* are one of the city's institutions. As well as the inevitable postcards and tourist tat, most sell a good selection of second-hand books – rummage through boxes packed with ancient paperbacks for something existential.

Diptyque

34 bd St-Germain, 5th (01.43.26.77.44, www.diptyqueparis.com). M° Maubert Mutualité. **Open** 10am-7pm Mon-Sat. **Map** p143 B3 ⑲

Diptyque's divinely scented candles are the quintessential gift from Paris. They come in 48 varieties and are probably the best you'll ever find. Prices aren't cheap, but with 50 to 60 hours' burn time, they're worth every euro.

Princesse Tam-Tam

52 bd St-Michel, 6th (01.40.51.72.99, www.princessetamtam.com). M° Cluny La Sorbonne. **Open** 1.30-7pm Mon; 10am-7pm Tue, Thur-Sat; 10am-1.30pm, 2-7pm Wed. **Map** p143 A4 ⑳

Paradis Latin

This fun, inexpensive underwear and swimwear brand has traffic-stopping promotions. Bright colours and sexily transparent gear rule.

Shakespeare & Company

37 rue de la Bûcherie, 5th (01.43.25. 40.93, www.shakespeareandcompany. com). M° St-Michel. **Open** 10am-11pm Mon-Fri; 11am-11pm Sat, Sun. **Map** p143 A3 ㉑

Unequivocably the best bookshop in Paris, the ramshackle Shakespeare & Co is always packed to the rafters with expat and tourist book lovers. There is a large second-hand section, along with antiquarian books next door.

Nightlife

Caveau de la Huchette

5 rue de la Huchette, 5th (01.43.26. 65.05, www.caveaudelahuchette.fr). M° St-Michel. **Open** 9.30pm-2.30am Mon-Wed, Sun; 9.30pm-6am Thur-Sat. *Concerts* 10.15pm. **Admission** €12 Mon-Thur, Sun; €14 Fri, Sat; €10 reductions. **Map** p143 A2 ㉒

This medieval cellar has been a mainstay for 60 years. The jazz shows are followed by early-hours performances in a swing, rock, soul or disco vein.

Caveau des Oubliettes

52 rue Galande, 5th (01.46.34.23.09, www.caveaudesoubliettes.fr). M° St-Michel. **Open** 5pm-2am Mon, Tue, Sun; 5pm-4am Wed-Sat. *Concerts* 10pm Wed-Sun. **Admission** free. **Map** p143 A3 ㉓

Atmosphere abounds in this former dungeon, a tiny space complete with instruments of torture and underground passages. There are various jam sessions in the week, and on Sundays.

Paradis Latin

28 rue Cardinal Lemoine, 5th (01.43. 25.28.28, www.paradislatin.com). M° Cardinal Lemoine. **Dinner** 8pm. **Show** 9.30pm daily. **Admission** *9.30pm show* (incl champagne) €88. *Dinner & show* €127-€185. **Map** p143 B4 ㉔

This is the most authentic of the cabarets, not only because it's family-run (the men run the cabaret, the daughter does the costumes), but also because the clientele is mostly French, something which has a direct effect on the prices (this is the cheapest revue) and the cuisine, which tends to be high quality. Show-wise you can expect the usual fare: generous doses of glitter, live singing and cheesy *entr'acte* acts.

Arts & leisure

Studio Galande

42 rue Galande, 5th (01.43.54.72.71, www.studiogalande.fr). M° Cluny La Sorbonne or St-Michel. **Admission** €8; €6 reductions. No credit cards. **Map** p143 A3 ㉕

Some 20 different films are screened in subtitled versions at this venerable Latin Quarter venue every week: international arthouse fare, combined with the occasional instalment from the *Matrix* series. On Friday and Saturday nights, dedicated fans of *The Rocky Horror Picture Show* turn up in drag, equipped with rice and water pistols.

The 13th

The construction in the mid-1990s of the **Bibliothèque Nationale de France** breathed life into the desolate area now known as the ZAC Rive Gauche, between Gare d'Austerlitz and the Périphérique. The long-term ZAC project includes a new university quarter, housing projects and a tramway providing links to the suburbs. This is one of the city's fastest rising quarters.

Sights & museums

Bibliothèque Nationale de France François Mitterrand

10 quai François-Mauriac, 13th (01.53. 79.59.59, www.bnf.fr). M° Bibliothèque François Mitterrand. **Open** 2-7pm

Mon; 9am-7pm Tue-Sat; 1-7pm Sun. **Admission** *1 day* €3.50. *1 year* €38; €20 reductions. **Map** p151 E2 26

Opened in 1996, the new national library was the last and costliest of Mitterrand's *grands projets*. Its architect, Dominique Perrault, was criticised for his curiously dated design. He also forgot to specify blinds to protect books from sunlight; they had to be added afterwards. The library houses over ten million volumes. Much of the library is open to the public: books, newspapers and periodicals are accessible to anyone over 18, and you can browse through photographic, film and sound archives in the audio-visual section.

Chapelle St-Louis-de-la-Salpêtrière

47 bd de l'Hôpital, 13th (01.42.16.04.24). M° Gare d'Austerlitz. **Open** 8.30am-6pm Mon-Fri, Sun; 11am-6pm Sat. **Admission** free. **Map** p151 C2 27

This austerely beautiful chapel, designed by Bruand and completed in 1677, features an octagonal dome in the centre and eight naves in which the sick were separated from the insane, the destitute from the debauched. Around the chapel sprawls the vast Hôpital de la Pitié-Salpêtrière, which became a centre for research into mental illness in the 1790s, when renowned doctor Philippe Pinel began to treat some of the inmates as sick rather than criminal; Charcot later pioneered neuropsychology here. Salpêtrière is one of the city's main teaching hospitals.

PARIS BY AREA

Docks en Seine

NEW *28-36 quai d'Austerlitz, 13th (www.paris-docks-en-seine.fr). M° Chevaleret or Gare d'Austerlitz.* **Map** p151 D1 28

Since 2005, the apple-green caterpillar of Docks en Seine has been pupating on the banks of the river between Gare d'Austerlitz and the BnF. It finally, belatedly opened its doors in 2012, transforming an industrial wasteland into a futuristic vision of culture and entertainment as imagined by architects Dominique Jakob and Brendan MacFarlane. From now on, its future is assured. A grassy terrace runs down to the water, there's a spanking new restaurant on the roof (the Moon Roof) and a bar/club (Wanderlust) on the first floor, and there are open-air screenings and exhibitions at the Cité de la Mode et du Design. The resurrection was completed with the opening of another club, Nüba, in late 2012. See also p152.

Manufacture Nationale des Gobelins

42 av des Gobelins, 13th (tours 01.44.08.53.59). M° Les Gobelins. **Open** 11am-6pm Tue-Sun. **Admission** €6; free-€4 reductions. No credit cards. **Map** p151 B2 29

The royal tapestry factory, which was founded by Colbert, is named after Jean Gobelin, a dyer who owned the site. Tapestries are still made here (mainly for French embassies), and visitors can watch weavers at work. The tour (in French; €7.50-€10) through the 1912 factory takes in the 18th-century chapel and the Beauvais workshops. Arrive 30 minutes before the start.

Eating & drinking

Le Bambou

70 rue Baudricourt, 13th (01.45.70.91.75). M° Olympiades or Tolbiac. **Open** 11.30am-3.30pm, 7-10.30pm Tue-Sun. **€. Vietnamese. Map** p151 C3 30

The Vietnamese fare here is a notch above what is normally served in Paris. Seating is elbow to elbow and, should you come on your own, the waiter will draw a line down the middle of the paper tablecloth and seat a stranger on the other side. That stranger might offer pointers on how to eat certain dishes, such as the no.42: grilled marinated pork to be wrapped in lettuce with beansprouts and herbs and eaten by hand, dipped into the accompanying sauce (no.43 is the same thing, but with pre-soaked rice paper wrappers).

The 13th

Sights & museums
Eating & drinking
Shopping
Nightlife
Arts & leisure
5
13
Plantes
Museum National d'Histoire Naturelle
Mosquée de Paris
Eglise Notre Dame de Val de Grâce
Val de Grâce
Hôpital Cochin
Maison d'Arrêt de la Santé
Gare d'Austerlitz
Hôpital La Pitié Salpêtrière
Seine
Ministère des Finances
Gare de Lyon
Bercy
Gare de Paris Bercy
Palais Omnisports de Paris Bercy
Bibliothèque Nationale de France
Bibliothèque F. Mitterrand
Quai de la Gare
Chevaleret
Nationale
Campo Formio
St Marcel
Les Gobelins
Place d'Italie
Tolbiac
Glacière
Censier Daubenton
Place Monge
Place Valhubert
Place Jeanne d'Arc
BD SAINT MICHEL
BOULEVARD DE PORT ROYAL
BOULEVARD ARAGO
BOULEVARD SAINT MARCEL
BOULEVARD DE L'HOPITAL
BOULEVARD VINCENT AURIOL
BOULEVARD AUGUSTE BLANQUI
BD ST JACQUES
RUE CLAUDE BERNARD
AVENUE DES GOBELINS
AVENUE D'ITALIE
AVENUE DE CHOISY
RUE NATIONALE
RUE JEANNE D'ARC
RUE MONGE
QUAI D'AUSTERLITZ
QUAI DE LA RAPÉE
QUAI DE LA GARE
QUAI FRANÇOIS MAURIAC
QUAI DE BERCY
BOULEVARD DE BERCY
PT. DE BERCY
PONT CHARLES DE GAULLE
PONT DE TOLBIAC
PASSERELLE SIMONE-DE-BEAUVOIR
RUE DE TOLBIAC
RUE DU CHAYEAU DES RENTIERS
RUE DE LA SANTE
RUE DE LA GLACIERE
RUE DE LA BUTTE AUX CAILLES
RUE DES CINQ DIAMANTS
RUE DU MOULIN DES PRES
RUE MOUFFETARD
RUE BUFFON
RUE POLIVEAU
RUE GEOFFROY SAINT HILAIRE
RUE DU CHEVALERET
RUE LOUISE WEISS
RUE DE DOMREMY
RUE THOMAS MANN
26
27
28
29
30
31
32
33
34
35
36
37
A
B
C
D
E
1
2
3
0
500 m
500 yds
© Copyright Time Out Group 2013

L'Ourcine

92 rue Broca, 13th (01.47.07.13.65). M° Glacière or Les Gobelins. **Open** noon-2pm, 7-10.30pm Tue-Thur; noon-2.30pm, 7-11pm Fri, Sat. Closed Aug. €. **Bistro**. **Map** p151 B2 ㉛

This restaurant near Gobelins is a wonderful bistro stop. Start with *pipérade*, succulent chorizo or a spread of sliced beef tongue with piquillo peppers; then try the sautéed baby squid with parsley, garlic and Espelette peppers, or the *piquillos* stuffed with puréed cod.

Petit Bain

7 port de la Gare, 13th (01.80.48.49.81, www.petitbain.org). M° Bibliothèque François Mitterrand or Quai de la Gare. **Open** 6pm-2am Wed-Sat; noon-5.30pm Sun (later in summer). **Map** p151 E2 ㉜

Petit Bain looks like a fluorescent green barge with a cubist wooden tree house plonked on top, and harbours an excellent line-up of concerts and exhibitions, plus a coveted terrace that doubles as a bar and restaurant. Below deck, a stage hosts gigs with everything from indie folk to rock on the playlist.

Sputnik

14 rue de la Butte aux Cailles, 13th (01.45.65.19.82, www.sputnik.fr). M° Place d'Italie. **Open** 2pm-2am Mon-Sat; 4pm-midnight Sun. **Café**. **Map** p151 B3 ㉝

A hip crowd gathers in this rock bar, which doubles as a sports bar during important football and rugby fixtures, and trebles as an internet café at other times. Ever-changing art exhibitions add interest to the walls, and bands once a month draw an indie crowd.

Nightlife

Batofar

Opposite 11 quai François-Mauriac, 13th (09.71.25.50.61, www.batofar.org). M° Quai de la Gare. **Open** 11pm-6am Mon-Sat; 6am-noon 1st Sun of mth. **Admission** free-€12. **Map** p151 E2 ㉞

In recent years, the Batofar has gone through a rapid succession of management teams. The current managers have helped revive the venue's tradition of playing cutting-edge music, including electro, dub step, techno and dancehall nights featuring international acts.

Nüba

NEW *36 quai d'Austerlitz, 13th (www.nuba-paris.fr). M° Chevaleret or Gare d'Austerlitz.* **Open** 11pm-6am Wed-Sat. **Map** p151 D1 ㉟

This hotly anticipated rooftop club at Docks en Seine has finally opened, adding another layer of excitement to a site that already houses Wanderlust. A vast terrace offers a superb view over the quays, along with DJs playing chill-out music, deckchairs, communal tables and table football. Inside, coloured lights reveal rooms done out in copper and stone. There are live concerts in the evenings, punctuated by clubby electro sets and inventive dance shows from the House of Drama collective.

Wanderlust

NEW *32 quai d'Austerlitz, 13th (www.wanderlustparis.com). M° Quai de la Gare.* **Open** 6pm-6am Wed-Sun. **Map** p151 D1 ㊱

Declared 2012's 'place to be' by Paris's fashionistas. Expect the cream of new-generation electronic dance music, plus excellent fashion-themed nights on Fridays (documentary screenings, catwalk shows and performances). Check the website for the full programme.

Arts & leisure

Piscine Josephine-Baker

Quai François-Mauriac, 13th (01.56.61.96.50). M° Quai de la Gare. **Open** times vary. **Admission** €3; €1.70 reductions. **Map** p151 E2 ㊲

Moored by the Bibliothèque Nationale, the Piscine Josephine-Baker complex boasts a 25m main pool (with sliding glass roof), a paddling pool and café, and a busy schedule of exercise classes.

Tour Montparnasse p154

Montparnasse

Montparnasse's heyday was short, but for a few years between the two world wars it was the emblematic 'gay Paree' district of after-dark merriment and fruitful artistic exchange. A great number of its most prominent figures were expats (including its finest chronicler, the Hungarian photographer Brassaï), and the late-night bars and artists' studios formed a bubble of cordial international relations that was irreparably popped in 1939.

The local atmosphere soured further with the completion of the Tour Montparnasse in the 1970s, a dark monolith that cast an ominous spell over the whole quarter. The dismay with which its construction was greeted prompted a change in building regulations in the city. Granted, this is rich territory for art museums, but with the exception of the Fondation Cartier, they're all about past glories.

Sights & museums

Les Catacombes

1 av Colonel Henri-Rol-Tanguy, 14th (01.43.22.47.63, www.catacombes-de-paris.fr). M°/RER Denfert Rochereau. **Open** 10am-5pm Tue-Sun (last entry 4pm). **Admission** €8; free-€6 reductions. **Map** p155 C3 ❶

This is the official entrance to the 3,000km (1,864-mile) tunnel network that runs under much of the city. With public burial pits overflowing in the era of the Revolutionary Terror, the bones of six million people were transferred to the *catacombes*. The bones of Marat, Robespierre and their cronies are packed in with wall upon wall of their fellow citizens. A damp, cramped tunnel takes you through a series of galleries before you reach the ossuary, the entrance to which is announced by a sign engraved in the stone: 'Stop! This is the empire of death.' The tour lasts approximately 45 minutes.

Cimetière du Montparnasse

3 bd Edgar-Quinet, 14th (01.44.10.86.50). M° Edgar Quinet or Raspail. **Open** *16 Mar-5 Nov* 8am-6pm Mon-Fri; 8.30am-6pm Sat; 9am-6pm Sun. *6 Nov-15 Mar* 8am-5.30pm Mon-Fri; 8.30am-5.30pm Sat; 9am-5.30pm Sun. **Admission** free. **Map** p155 B2 ❷

As with much of the Left Bank, this boneyard has literary clout: Beckett, Baudelaire, Sartre, Maupassant and Ionesco all rest here. There are also artists, including Brancusi, Frédéric Bartholdi and Man Ray. The impressive celebrity roll-call continues with Serge Gainsbourg, André Citroën, Coluche and Jean Seberg.

Fondation Cartier pour l'Art Contemporain

261 bd Raspail, 14th (01.42.18.56.50, www.fondation.cartier.fr). M° Denfert Rochereau or Raspail. **Open** 11am-10pm Tue; 11am-8pm Wed-Sun. **Admission** €9.50; free-€6.50 reductions. **Map** p155 C2 ❸

Jean Nouvel's glass and steel building, an exhibition centre with Cartier's offices above, is as much a work of art as the installations inside. Shows by artists and photographers have wide-ranging themes. Live events around the shows are called Soirées Nomades.

Event highlights America Latina: Latin American Photography 1963-2013 (Oct 2013-Mar 2014).

Fondation Henri Cartier-Bresson

2 impasse Lebouis, 14th (01.56.80.27.00, www.henricartierbresson.org). M° Gaîté. **Open** 1-6.30pm Tue, Thur, Fri, Sun; 1-8.30pm Wed; 11am-6.45pm Sat. Closed Aug & between exhibitions. **Admission** €6; €4 reductions. No credit cards. **Map** p155 A2 ❹

This two-floor gallery is dedicated to the work of acclaimed photographer Henri Cartier-Bresson. It consists of a tall, narrow *atelier* in a 1913 building with a minutely catalogued archive open to researchers, and a lounge on the fourth floor screening films. In the spirit of Cartier-Bresson, who assisted on three Jean Renoir films and drew and painted all his life (some drawings are also found on the fourth floor), the Fondation opens its doors to other disciplines with three annual shows.

Musée Bourdelle

16-18 rue Antoine-Bourdelle, 15th (01.49.54.73.73, www.bourdelle.paris.fr). M° Falguière or Montparnasse Bienvenüe. **Open** 10am-6pm Tue-Sun. **Admission** free. *Exhibitions* €7; free-€5.50 reductions. **Map** p155 A1 ❺

The sculptor Antoine Bourdelle (1861-1929), a pupil of Rodin, produced a number of monumental works, including the relief friezes at the Théâtre des Champs-Elysées. Set around a garden, the museum includes the artist's apartment and studios. A 1950s extension tracks the evolution of Bourdelle's equestrian monument to General Alvear in Buenos Aires, Argentina, and his masterful *Hercules the Archer*. A modern wing houses bronzes.

Musée du Montparnasse

21 av du Maine, 15th (01.42.22.91.96,www.museedumontparnasse.net). M° Montparnasse Bienvenüe. **Open** 12.30-7pm Tue-Sun. **Admission** €6; free-€5 reductions. No credit cards. **Map** p155 A1 ❻

Set in one of the last surviving alleys of studios, this was home to Marie Vassilieff, whose own academy and cheap canteen welcomed poor artists Picasso, Cocteau and Matisse. Shows focus on present-day artists and the area's creative past.

Tour Montparnasse

33 av du Maine, 15th (01.45.38.52.56, www.tourmontparnasse56.com). M° Montparnasse Bienvenüe. **Open** *Oct-Mar* 9.30am-10.30pm Mon-Thur, Sun; 9.30am-11pm Fri, Sat. *Apr-Sept* 9.30am-11.30pm daily. **Admission** €13; free-€9.50 reductions. **Map** p155 A1 ❼

PARIS BY AREA

Built in 1974 on the site of the old station, this 209m (686ft) steel-and-glass monolith is shorter than the Eiffel Tower, but better placed for fabulous views of the city. A lift whisks you up in 38 seconds to the 56th floor, where you'll find a display of aerial scenes of Paris, an upgraded café-lounge, a souvenir shop – and lots and lots of sky.

Eating & drinking

La Cerisaie

70 bd Edgar Quinet, 14th (01.43.20.98.98, www.restaurantlacerisaie.com). M° Edgar Quinet or Montparnasse. **Open** noon-2pm, 7-10pm Mon-Fri. Closed Aug & 1wk Dec. **€€. Bistro.** **Map** p155 A1 ❽

Nothing about La Cerisaie's unprepossessing red façade hints at the talent that lurks inside. On the daily changing blackboard menu you might find *bourride de maquereau*, a thrifty take on the garlicky French fish stew, or *cochon noir de Bigorre*, an ancient breed of pig that puts ordinary pork to shame. *Baba à l'armagnac*, a variation on the usual rum cake, comes with great chantilly.

Cobéa

NEW *11 rue Raymond Losserand, 14th (01.43.20.21.39, www.cobea.fr). M° Gaîté or Pernety.* **Open** 12.15-1.45pm, 7.15-9.45pm Tue-Sat. **€€€. Haute cuisine. Map** p155 A2 ❾

Cobéa is a slick restaurant launched by Jerome Cobou and Philippe Bellissent, who won a Michelin star when he was head chef at L'Hôtel. The ethos here is gastronomy without the snobbery. Set in a renovated 1920s house with big windows overlooking a green space, it feels peaceful and cosy, while touches such as silverware and Bernardaud porcelain add a luxury feel. The set menus are a treasure chest of reworked classics, plus a daily-changing 'chef's surprise'. Each dish is accompanied by a well-sourced wine recommendation.

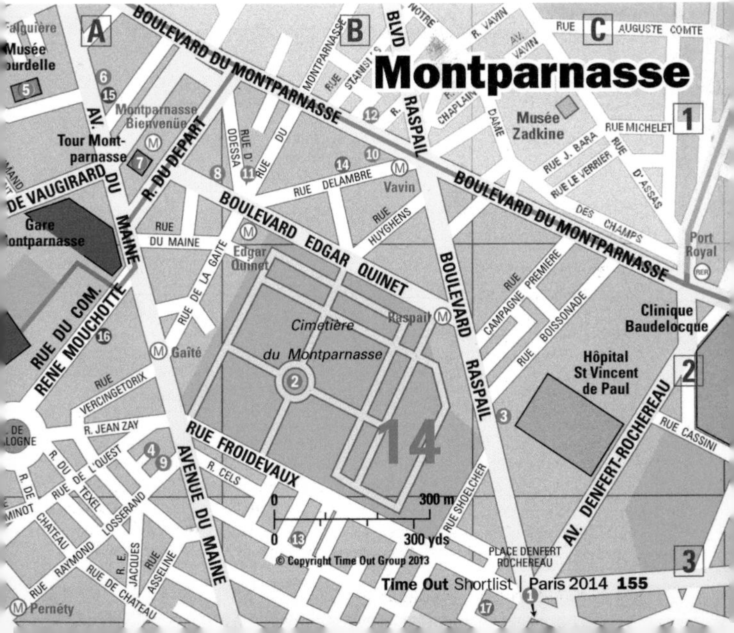

Storie

La Coupole

102 bd du Montparnasse, 14th (01.43. 20.14.20, www.lacoupole-paris.com). M° Vavin. **Open** 8.30am-midnight Mon-Wed, Sun; 8.30am-1am Thur-Sat. **€€. Brasserie. Map** p155 B1 ⑩

La Coupole still glows with some of the old glamour. The people-watching remains superb, inside and out, and the long ranks of linen-covered tables, mosaic floor and sheer scale of the operation still make coming here an event. The set menu offers steaks, foie gras, fish and game stews, but the real treat is the shellfish.

Josselin

67 rue du Montparnasse, 14th (01.43. 20.93.50). M° Edgar Quinet. **Open** 11.15am-3.15pm, 6-11.30pm Tue-Fri; 11.30am-midnight Sat; 11.30am-11.30pm Sun. Closed 1st wk Jan & Aug. **€.** No credit cards. **Crêperie. Map** p155 B1 ⑪

Josselin is the star *crêperie* of the area, and the one with the longest queues. The speciality is the Couple – two layers of galette with the filling in the middle. Wash it all down with bowls of cider, of which the brut is best.

Le Select

99 bd du Montparnasse, 6th (01.45. 48.38.24). M° Vavin. **Open** 7am-2am Mon-Thur, Sun; 7am-4am Fri, Sat. **€. Café. Map** p155 B1 ⑫

For a decade between the wars, this area was where Man Ray, Cocteau and Lost Generation Americans hung out in the vast, glass-fronted cafés. Eight decades on, Le Select is the best of these inevitable tourist haunts.

Shopping

Madame de

NEW *65 rue Daguerre, 14th (01.77. 10.59.46, www.madamede.net). M° Denfert-Rochereau.* **Open** 11am-7.30pm Tue-Sat. **Map** p155 B3 ⑬

This delightful second-hand shop only stocks pieces 'that are like new' – even better, the prices wouldn't look out of place in the sales: a taupe Vanessa Bruno bag for €187, APC jeans for €66, a checked Zara dress for €40.

Storie

NEW *20 rue Delambre, 14th (01.83.56. 01.98, www.storieblog.com). M° Vavin.* **Open** 11am-2pm, 3-8pm Tue-Sat; 5-8pm Sun. **Map** p155 B1 ⑭

A magical shop selling a mix of objects from around the world – from Korean coffee cups to wooden deer heads.

Nightlife

Mix Club

24 rue de l'Arrivée, 15th (01.56. 80.37.37, www.mixclub.fr). M° Montparnasse Bienvenüe. **Open** 11pm-6am Thur-Sat. **Admission** free-€20. **Map** p155 A1 ⑮

The Mix Club has one of the city's biggest dancefloors. Regular visitors include Erick Morillo's Subliminal and Ministry of Sound parties.

Le Petit Journal Montparnasse

13 rue du Commandant-René-Mouchotte, 14th (01.43.21.56.70, www.petitjournalmontparnasse.com). M° Gaîté. **Open** 7pm-2am Mon-Sat. *Concerts* 9.30pm Mon-Thur; 10pm Fri, Sat. **Admission** prices vary. **Map** p155 A2 ⑯

Two-level jazz brasserie in the shadow of the Tour Montparnasse with Latin sounds, R&B and soul-gospel.

Arts & leisure

Le Chaplin Denfert

24 pl Denfert-Rochereau, 14th (01.43. 21.41.01, www.cinemadenfert.fr). M° Denfert Rochereau/RER Denfert Rochereau. **Admission** €8; €6-€7 reductions. No credit cards. **Map** p155 C3 ⑰

This charming little cinema offers a nicely eclectic repertory selection that ranges from François Ozon and Hayao Miyazaki to shorts and animation.

Château de Versailles p162

Worth the Trip

North

Basilique St-Denis

1 rue de la Légion-d'Honneur, 93200 St-Denis (01.48.09.83.54). M° St-Denis Basilique/tram 1. **Open** *Apr-Sept* 10am-6.15pm Mon-Sat; noon-6.15pm Sun. *Oct-Mar* 10am-5pm Mon-Sat; noon-5.15pm Sun. **Tours** 10.30am, 3pm Mon-Sat; 12.15pm, 3pm Sun. **Admission** €7.50; free-€4.50 reductions.

Legend has it that when St Denis was beheaded, he picked up his noggin and walked with it to Vicus Catulliacus (now St-Denis) to be buried. The first church, parts of which can be seen in the crypt, was built over his tomb in around 475. The present edifice was begun in the 1130s. It is considered to be the first example of Gothic architecture. In the 13th century, mason Pierre de Montreuil erected the spire and rebuilt the choir nave and transept. St-Denis was the burial place for all but three French monarchs between 996 and the end of the *ancien régime*, so the ambulatory is a museum of French funerary sculpture. It includes a fanciful Gothic tomb for Dagobert, the austere effigy of Charles V, and the Renaissance tomb of Louis XII and his wife Anne de Bretagne. In 1792, these tombs were desecrated, and the royal remains thrown into a pit.

Musée de l'Air et de l'Espace

Aéroport de Paris-Le Bourget, 93352 Le Bourget Cedex (01.49.92.70.00, www.mae.org). M° Gare du Nord, then bus 350/RER Le Bourget, then bus 152. **Open** *Apr-Sept* 10am-6pm Tue-Sun. *Oct-Mar* 10am-5pm Tue-Sun. **Admission** free. *With 1-3 animations* €8-€16; free-€12 reductions.

The impressive air and space museum is set in the former passenger terminal at Le Bourget airport. The collection begins with the pioneers, including fragile-looking biplanes and the command cabin of a Zeppelin airship. On the runway are Mirage fighters, a US

Thunderchief, and Ariane launchers 1 and 5. A hangar houses the prototype Concorde 001 and wartime survivors.

East

104

104 rue d'Aubervilliers, 19th (01.53.35.50.00, www.104.fr). M° Riquet. **Open** noon-8pm Tue-Fri; 11am-8pm Sat, Sun. **Admission** free. *Exhibitions* prices vary.

It's more than a century since tourist-choked Montmartre was the centre of artistic activity in Paris. But now the north-east of Paris is again where the action is, in a previously neglected area of bleak railway goods yards and dilapidated social housing. 104, described as a 'space for artistic creation', occupies a vast 19th-century building on the rue d'Aubervilliers that used to house Paris's municipal undertakers. There aren't any constraints on the kind of work the resident artists do – 104 is open to 'all the arts' – but they're expected to show finished pieces in one of four annual 'festivals'.

Every month, 104 opens its doors to Omnivore, a dynamic culinary movement that supports and promotes France's most exciting young chefs. Omnivore selects two chefs a month to concoct themed food nights for 100 hungry punters. Dates are announced online (www.omnivore.com).

La Cité des Sciences et de l'Industrie

La Villette, 30 av Corentin-Cariou, 19th (01.40.05.70.00, www.cite-sciences.fr). M° Porte de la Villette. **Open** 10am-6pm Tue-Sat; 10am-7pm Sun. **Admission** €8; free-€6 reductions.

This ultra-modern science museum pulls in five million visitors a year. Explora, the permanent show, occupies the upper two floors, whisking visitors through 30,000sq m (320,000sq ft) of space, life, matter and communication: scale models of satellites including the Ariane space shuttle, planes and robots, plus the chance to experience weightlessness, make for an exciting trip. In the Espace Images, try the delayed camera and other optical illusions, draw 3D images on a computer or lend your voice to the *Mona Lisa*. The hothouse garden investigates developments in agriculture and bio-technology. The brilliant Cité des Enfants runs workshops for younger children.

Disneyland Paris/Walt Disney Studios Park

Marne-la-Vallée (www.disneylandparis.com). 32km E of Paris. RER A or TGV Marne-la-Vallée-Chessy. By car, A4 exit 14. **Open** Times vary, see website for details. **Admission** Prices vary, see website for details.

Young ones will get a real kick out of Fantasyland, with its Alice maze, Sleeping Beauty's castle and teacup rides. Walt Disney Studios focuses on special effects and the tricks of the animation trade. Thrill-seekers should head for the Twilight Zone Tower of Terror, which sends daredevils plummeting down a 13-storey lift shaft.

South

Maison de Jean Cocteau

15 rue du Lau, 91490 Milly-la-Forêt (01.64.98.11.50, www.jeancocteau.net). 60km S of Paris. RER D Maisse, then 7km taxi ride. By car, A6 exit 13. **Open** *Mar-Oct* 10am-7pm Wed-Sun. *Nov-mid Jan* 2-6pm Sat, Sun (Wed-Sun 19 Dec-1 Jan). Closed mid Jan-Feb. **Admission** €7; free-€4.50 reductions.

Thanks to the hefty financial input of Pierre Bergé (partner of the late Yves Saint Laurent) and five years of refurbishment, Cocteau's old country house has been transformed into a fascinating museum. The living room is wonderfully flamboyant, with antique furniture and gold palm trees framing a Bérard painting of Oedipus. The bedroom, meanwhile, with its four-poster bed and a mural of a castle, boasts a fairytale quality that's reminiscent of Cocteau's romantic fantasy *La Belle et la Bête*. Finally the study, with its leopard print walls and erotic memorabilia, offers the most intimate glimpse into the artist's creative process. The rest of the house has been converted into exhibition space with two galleries: one a collection of portraits of Cocteau by artists such as Picasso, Warhol and Modigliani; the other dedicated to temporary collections. Cocteau's body rests nearby, in the Chapelle Saint-Blaise-des Simples (rue de l'Amiral de Graville, Milly-la-Forêt, 01.64.98.84.94, open 10am-12.30pm, 2-6pm Wed-Sun).

Musée Fragonard

7 av du Général de Gaulle, 94704 Maisons-Alfort (01.43.96.71.72, http://musee.vet-alfort.fr). Mº Ecole Vétérinaire de Maisons-Alfort. **Open** 2-6pm Wed, Thur; 1-6pm Sat, Sun. Closed Aug. **Admission** €7; free reductions.

In 18th-century French medical schools, study aids were produced in one of two ways. They were either painstakingly sculpted in coloured wax or made from the real things – organs, limbs, tangled vascular systems – dried or preserved in formaldehyde. Veterinary surgeon Honoré Fragonard (cousin of the famous rococo painter) was a master of the second method, and many of his most striking works are now on display here. *Tête humaine injectée* is a human head whose blood vessels were injected with coloured wax, red for arteries and blue for veins. *Cavalier de l'apocalypse* is a flayed man on the back of a flayed horse, inspired by a painting by Dürer.

Parc André Citroën

Rue Balard, rue St-Charles or quai Citroën, 15th. Mº Balard or Javel. **Open** 8am-dusk Mon-Fri; 9am-dusk Sat, Sun, public hols.

This park is a fun, postmodern version of a French formal garden, designed by Gilles Clément and Alain Prévost. It comprises glasshouses, computerised fountains, waterfalls, a wilderness and themed gardens with different coloured plants and even sounds. The tethered Eutelsat helium balloon takes visitors up for panoramic views. If the weather looks unreliable, call 01.44.26.20.00.

West

Bois de Boulogne

16th. Mº Les Sablons or Porte Dauphine. **Admission** free.

Covering 865 hectares, the Bois was once the Forêt de Rouvray hunting grounds. It was landscaped in the 1860s, when artificial grottoes and waterfalls were created around the Lac Inférieur. The Jardin de Bagatelle is famous for its roses, daffodils and water lilies. The Jardin d'Acclimatation is a children's amusement park, complete with miniature train, farm, rollercoaster and boat rides.

Musée Belmondo

14 rue de L'Abreuvoir, 92100 Boulogne-Billancourt (01.55.18.69.01, www.museepaulbelmondo.fr). Mº Boulogne Jean Jaurès, then bus 123. **Open** 2-6pm Tue-Fri; 11am-6pm Sat, Sun. **Admission** €5; free-€3.70 reductions.

Jean-Paul Belmondo's father, Paul, was one of France's most important 20th-century sculptors, and one of the last to use neoclassical, academic techniques. The space, revamped by architects Chartier-Corbasson, is an interior designer's dream – the mix of stark white, black and timber materials lends a different mood to each section, and several rooms harbour alcoves in which Belmondo's sculptures sit enticingly.

Musée Marmottan – Claude Monet

2 rue Louis-Boilly, 16th (01.44.96.50.33, www.marmottan.com). Mº La Muette. **Open** 10am-6pm Tue, Wed, Fri-Sun; 10am-8pm Thur. **Admission** €10; free-€5 reductions.

This old hunting pavilion has become a famed holder of Impressionist art thanks to two bequests: the first by the

PARIS BY AREA

Starck service

The designer's new restaurant in the Puces de St-Ouen.

It's official: Philippe Starck has finally got over 'baroque modern' with not a single Perspex Louis XVI chair in sight at his new 250-seat restaurant, **Ma Cocotte** (106 rue des Rosiers, St-Ouen, 01.49.51.70.00, www.macocotte-lespuces.com), in the vast Marché aux Puces de St-Ouen flea market.

Housed in a handsome red-brick loft building at the entrance to the gorgeous Serpette antiques market, it has rather more in common with Terence Conran's taste for steel open kitchens and tiles, although perhaps that's no accident. Surfing on the current retro vogue for 1960s and '70s furniture, Habitat is planning to open up a 'vintage space' (77-81 rue des Rosiers, St-Ouen, www.habitat.fr/vintage) just down the road for owners of old Habitat classics to re-sell their vintage pieces.

On a wet Sunday afternoon soon after its launch, Ma Cocotte was bustling with families and young couples queuing for a seat at the high communal tables or regular Formica ones, umbrellas dripping on the decorative encaustic floor tiles. On the menu, conviviality is the order of the day, with litre pitchers of Starck (champagne, passionfruit, cucumber, ginger and mint); sharing plates of radish, foie gras or caviar; and mains such as rôtisserie farm chicken for four (€80) or côte de boeuf for two or three (€89), prepared by head chef Yannick Papin and a vast army of kitchen staff all decked out in Chairman Mao-style blue cap and overalls.

After years in the doldrums, the Puces is starting to show signs of life again, and the weekend crowds are sure to fancy a post-browse brunch at Ma Cocotte.

daughter of the doctor of Manet, Monet, Pissarro, Sisley and Renoir; the second by Monet's son Michel. Its Monet collection, the largest in the world, numbers 165 works, plus sketchbooks, palette and photos. Upstairs are works by Renoir, Manet, Gauguin, Caillebotte and Berthe Morisot, a Sèvres clock and a collection of First Empire furniture.

Versailles

Centuries of makeovers have made Versailles the most sumptuously clad château in the world. Architect Louis Le Vau first embellished the original building – a hunting lodge built during Louis XIII's reign – after Louis XIV saw Vaux-le-Vicomte, the impressive residence of his finance minister, Nicolas Fouquet. After Le Vau's death in 1670, Jules Hardouin-Mansart took over as principal architect, transforming Versailles into the château we know today.

Château de Versailles

78000 Versailles (01.30.83.78.00, advance tickets 08.92.68.46.94, www.chateauversailles.fr). **Open** *Apr-Oct* 9am-6.30pm Tue-Sun. *Nov-Mar* 9am-5.30pm Tue-Sun. **Admission** €15; free-€13 reductions.

Versailles is a masterpiece – and it's almost always packed with visitors. Allow yourself a whole day to appreciate the sumptuous State Apartments and the Hall of Mirrors, the highlights of any visit and mainly accessible with a day ticket. The Grand Appartement, where Louis XIV held court, consists of six gilded salons (Venus, Mercury, Apollo and so on). No less luxurious, the Queen's Apartment includes her bedroom, where royal births took place in full view of the court. Hardouin-Mansart's showpiece, the Hall of Mirrors, where a united Germany was proclaimed in 1871 and the Treaty of Versailles was signed in 1919, is flooded with light from its 17 windows.

Domaine de Versailles

Gardens **Open** *Apr-Oct* 7am-dusk daily. *Nov-Mar* 8am-dusk daily. **Admission** *Winter* free (statues covered over). *Summer* €3; free-€1.50 reductions. *Grandes Eaux Musicales* (01.30.83.78.88). **Open** *Apr-Oct* Sat, Sun. **Admission** €8.50; free-€6.50 reductions. *Park* **Open** dawn-dusk daily. **Admission** free.

The sprawling gardens consist of formal parterres, ponds, elaborate statues and a series of fountains. On weekend afternoons from spring to autumn, the fountains are set to music for the Grandes Eaux Musicales.

Event highlights Le Nôtre in Perspective 1613-2013 (until 24 Feb 2014)

Grand Trianon/Petit Trianon/Domaine de Marie-Antoinette

Open *Apr-Oct* noon-6.30pm Tue-Sun. *Nov-Mar* noon-5.30pm Tue-Sun. **Admission** €10; free-€6 reductions.

In 1687, Hardouin-Mansart built the pink marble Grand Trianon in the north of the park. Here Louis XIV and his children's governess and secret second wife, Madame de Maintenon, could admire the intimate gardens from the colonnaded portico. The Petit Trianon, built for Louis XV's mistress Madame de Pompadour, is a wonderful example of neoclassicism. It later became part of the Domaine de Marie-Antoinette, an exclusive hideaway located beyond the canal in the wooded parkland. Given to Marie-Antoinette as a wedding gift by her husband Louis XVI in 1774, the domain also includes the chapel adjoining the Petit Trianon, plus a theatre, a neoclassical 'Temple d'Amour', and Marie-Antoinette's fairytale farm and dairy.

Getting there

By car 20km (12.5 miles) from Paris by the A13 or D10. *By train* For the station nearest the château, take the RER C5 (VICK or VERO trains) to Versailles-Rive Gauche.

Essentials

Buddha Bar Hotel

Hotels

After a slew of major hotel openings in the last couple of years, the big news during 2012/13 was all about closures, with two of the city's most famous palace hotels shutting their doors for major renovations. The **Ritz** and the **Crillon** will both be out of action until at least 2014, as they freshen up to try to contend with the influx of Asian super-luxury from the **Shangri-La**, **Royal Monceau**, **Mandarin Oriental** and, from late 2013, **Peninsula Paris**. In the meantime, these new five-star arrivals have taken service and design to a different level, although the accompanying rack rates can be eye-watering.

For something a little less luxe, the city's burgeoning boutique hotel selection means that you can still afford good design, as long as you can make do without the uniformed doormen. You can be soothed by fine linen, marble baths and a dreamy pool and hammam at **Le Metropolitan**, walk through silk taffeta curtains to your own terrace at **Le Petit Paris**, gaze across the Marais rooftops from the cool new **Jules et Jim**, and fraternise at the trendy cava bar of the Spanish-owned **Banke**.

Further down the scale, there is now a wide choice of moderately priced and even budget design hotels, especially around the hip east and north-east of the city, such as **Mama Shelter**, **Standard Design Hotel**, **Le Quartier Bastille**, **20 Prieuré** and **Hôtel Crayon**. And shoestring travellers should also consider booking a bed at **St Christopher's Inn** on the Canal d'Ourcq, whose façade is lit up like an art installation at night (or, more centrally, at their brand new outpost opposite the Gare du Nord).

Classification

We've divided the hotels by area, then listed them in four categories, according to the standard prices (not including seasonal offers or discounts) for one night in a double room with en suite shower/bath. For deluxe hotels (**€€€€**), you can expect to pay more than €350; for properties in the expensive bracket (**€€€**), €220-€350; for moderate properties (**€€**), allow €130-€219; while budget rooms (**€**) go for less than €130.

In the know

All hotels in France charge a room tax (*taxe de séjour*) of around €1 per person per night, although this is sometimes included in the rate.

Champs-Elysées & Western Paris

Buddha Bar Hotel

NEW *4 rue d'Anjou, 8th (01.83.96.88.88, www.buddhabarhotelparis.com). Mº Concorde or Madeleine.* **€€€€**.

Opened in June 2013, this latest instalment in the Buddha Bar empire is a wonderful mix of French style and neo-Asian extravagance set in a handsome 18th-century *hôtel particulier*. The Le Vraymonde restaurant is headed by acclaimed Senegalese chef Rougui Dia.

Four Seasons George V

31 av George V, 8th (01.49.52.70.00, www.fourseasons.com/paris). Mº Alma Marceau or George V. **€€€€**.

There's no denying that the George V is serious about luxury: chandeliers, marble and tapestries, over-attentive staff, glorious flower arrangements, divine bathrooms, and ludicrously comfortable beds in some of the largest rooms in Paris. The spa area includes whirlpools, saunas and treatments; non-guests can reserve appointments.

SHORTLIST

Best newcomers
- Auberge Flora (see p175)
- Buddha Bar Hotel (see left)
- Hotel O (see p171)
- St Christopher's Inn Gare du Nord (see p175)

Best spa splurge
- Four Seasons George V (see left)
- Hôtel Fouquet's Barrière (see p167)
- Le Meurice (see p172)

Best alfresco breakfast
- Hôtel de l'Abbaye Saint-Germain (see p179)
- Mama Shelter (see p175)

Best bars
- Hôtel Plaza Athénée (see p167)
- Royal Monceau (see p168)

Best for fashion week
- L'Hôtel (see p179)
- Le Montalembert (see p177)

Best bathrooms
- Four Seasons George V (see left)
- Renaissance Paris Arc de Triomphe (see p168)

Best bargain beds
- Mama Shelter (see p175)
- St Christopher's Inn (see p175)

Chic sleeps
- Hôtel La Belle Juliette (see p179)
- Hôtel Amour (see p172)

Lap of luxury
- Hôtel le Bristol (see p167)
- Hôtel W Paris-Opéra (see p171)
- Shangri-La Paris (see p168)

AVIATIC HOTEL

Hôtel le Bristol

112 rue du Fbg-St-Honoré, 8th (01.53.43.43.00, www.hotel-bristol.com). M° Champs-Elysées Clémenceau. **€€€€**.

Set on the exclusive rue du Faubourg St-Honoré, the Bristol is a luxurious 'palace' hotel with a loyal following of fashionistas and millionaires drawn by the location, impeccable service, larger than average rooms and a three Michelin-starred restaurant with Eric Fréchon at the helm.

Hôtel Daniel

8 rue Frédéric-Bastiat, 8th (01.42.56.17.00, www.hoteldanielparis.com). M° Franklin D. Roosevelt or St-Philippe-du-Roule. **€€€€**.

This romantic hideaway is decorated in chinoiserie and a palette of rich colours, with 26 rooms (free Wi-Fi) cosily appointed in *toile de Jouy* and an intricately hand-painted restaurant that feels like a courtyard. At about €50 a head, the gastronomic restaurant, run by chef Jérôme Bonnet, is a good deal for this neighbourhood.

Hôtel Fouquet's Barrière

46 av George V, 8th (01.40.69.60.00, www.fouquets-barriere.com). M° George V. **€€€€**.

This grandiose five-star is built around the fin-de-siècle brasserie Le Fouquet's. Five buildings form the hotel complex, with 81 rooms (including 33 suites), upmarket restaurant Le Diane, the U Spa, indoor pool and a roof terrace for hire. Jacques Garcia was responsible for the interior design, which retains the Empire style of the exterior while incorporating luxurious touches inside – flatscreen TVs and mist-free mirrors in the marble bathrooms. And, of course, it's unbeatable for location – right at the junction of avenue George V and the Champs-Elysées.

Hôtel Plaza Athénée

25 av Montaigne, 8th (01.53.67.66.65, www.plaza-athenee-paris.com). M° Alma Marceau. **€€€€**.

This palace is ideally placed for power shopping at Chanel, Louis Vuitton, Dior and other avenue Montaigne boutiques. Material girls and boys will enjoy the high-tech room amenities, such as remote-controlled air con, internet and video-game access on the TV via infrared keyboard, and mini hi-fi. Make time for a drink in the Bar du Plaza, a cocktail bunny's most *outré* fantasy.

Hôtel Square

3 rue de Boulainvilliers, 16th (01.44.14.91.90, www.hotelsquare.com). M° Passy/RER Avenue du Pdt Kennedy. **€€€€**.

This courageously modern hotel has a dramatic yet welcoming interior, and attentive service that comes from having to look after only 22 rooms. They're decorated in amber, brick or slate colours, with exotic woods, quality fabrics and bathrooms seemingly cut from one huge chunk of Carrara marble. View exhibitions in the atrium gallery or mingle with media types at the hip Zebra Square restaurant and DJ bar.

Les Jardins de la Villa

5 rue Bélidor, 17th (01.53.81.01.10, www.jardinsdelavilla.com). M° Porte Maillot. **€€€**.

Behind a sober frontage, the 33-room Jardins de la Villa is a playful affair, with a couture theme and a penchant for fuchsia pink. It's dotted with surreal touches – not least a high heel-shaped couch in reception. The beautifully appointed rooms pair modern luxuries (Nespresso machines, free Wi-Fi, sleek flatscreen TVs) with old-fashioned attention to detail. The location is off the tourist trail, but close to the métro and perfect for a little peace and quiet.

Jays Paris

6 rue Copernic, 16th (01.47.04.16.16, www.jays-paris.com). M° Kléber or Victor Hugo. **€€€€**.

Jays is a luxurious *boutique-apart* hotel that trades on a clever blend of antique furniture, modern design and high-tech equipment. The marble staircase, lit entirely by natural light filtered through the glass atrium overhead, gives an instant feeling of grandeur, and leads to five suites, each with a fully equipped kitchenette and free Wi-Fi. A cosy salon is available.

Le Metropolitan

10 pl de Mexico, 16th (01.56.90. 40.04, www.radissonblu.com). Mº Trocadero. **€€€**.

This 40-room offering from Radisson Blu is supremely sleek. The discreet entrance is only a few metres wide, but inside the triangular structure opens out into a surprisingly large area, with a monumental art deco-style fireplace, and cream leather and black granite reminiscent of New York in the 1930s. The first floor contains a swank insiders' cocktail bar, but the biggest surprise of all is the breathtaking view of the Eiffel Tower from the front façade, best enjoyed through the huge oval window while lying on the four-poster bed of the sixth floor suite. Below ground are a sublime swimming pool and hammam reserved for guests.

Opéra Diamond

4 rue de la Pépinière, 8th (01.44.70. 02.00, www.paris-hotel-diamond.com). Mº St-Lazare. **€€€€**.

This sparkling hotel lives up to its name with a night-sky decor made up of black granite resin punctuated with crystals and LEDs. The 30 rooms are equally splendid, with Swarovski crystal touches to the furniture, black bathrooms and satin curtains that close to become a photomontage of a female nude crossed with architectural imagery. The Executive rooms have iPod stations, Nespresso machines, and speakers in the bathrooms.

Renaissance Paris Arc de Triomphe

39 av de Wagram, 17th (01.55.37. 55.37, www.marriott.com). Mº Ternes. **€€€**.

You can't miss it. This six-storey undulating glass façade is like no other part of the neighbourhood. All rooms are stylishly done out in pale greys, charcoals and dark wood, with Eames-style furniture. Nice high-tech touches include an iPod dock on the bedside radio and a flatscreen TV with Wi-Fi keyboard. Bathrooms are a glory of polished metal, tasteful tiles and gleaming glass. The Makassar restaurant serves delicate and delicious Franco-Asian fusion food.

Royal Monceau

37 av Hoche, 8th (01.42.99.88.00, www.leroyalmonceau.com). Mº Charles de Gaulle Etoile. **€€€€**.

The Royal Monceau is a supremely classy retreat. This is a hotel that takes art appreciation seriously, with its own art agenda blog and an art concierge. Philippe Starck was in charge of the refit, and his cheeky touches are everywhere. The bedrooms are a studied jumble, with beds in the middle of the room, pictures leaned up against the wall, a guitar waiting to be strummed and a lampshade decked with scribbled notes. But beyond all this designer frippery there lie some gorgeous treats, including vast walk-in wardrobes, spacious bathrooms with twin sinks, and huge mirrors that magically transform into TVs.

Le Sezz

6 av Frémiet, 16th (01.56.75.26.26, www.hotelsezz.com). Mº Passy. **€€€**.

Le Sezz has 26 sleek, luxurious rooms and suites. The understated decor represents a refreshingly modern take on luxury, with black parquet flooring, rough-hewn stone walls and bathrooms partitioned off with sweeping glass façades. The bar and public areas are equally sleek and chic. Free Wi-Fi.

Shangri-La Paris

10 av d'Iéna, 16th (01.53.67.19.98, www.shangri-la.com). Mº Iéna. **€€€€**.

Pierre-Yves Rochon's design at the Shangri-La is an ode to French imperialism, with colonial-style paintings,

Bed and board

Book in at the wonderful Auberge Flora.

There's nothing better after an exceptional meal than being able to slip between cool white sheets without even having to leave the building. Flora Mikula, the hugely talented chef behind Les Olivades and Les Saveurs de Flora, left the smart 8th for the more boho 11th to pursue her dream of creating an urban inn – the **Auberge Flora** (see p175).

'It's a restaurant with rooms rather than a hotel with a restaurant,' she says, but as much care has gone into the decor and comfort of the rooms as goes into her Mediterranean cuisine. From the laughter behind the kitchen hatch to the unique decorative touches – Bernardaud china on the restaurant walls, watering cans lining the stairs – everything is imbued with Flora's ebullient personality.

The fabulously affordable *bistronomie*-style menu features a course of French tapas served on a three-tier cake stand and rich main courses that manage to be both satisfying and refined. And with Flora herself in the kitchen, it feels almost like you're being invited into the chef's home.

Upstairs, the 21 bedrooms are spread across three floors and themed around *bohème* (brocade throws, fringed lampshades, vivid colours), *potager* (aubergine-coloured walls, vast pumpkin pictures as headboards), and *nature* (stone sinks, mirrors framed with tiny rounds of wood). All the rooms have iPod docks and flatscreen TVs, and the top two categories offer bathrobes too.

As you would expect, breakfast is a treat, and it's made all the more enjoyable by the steady stream of locals popping in for coffee and pastries at the bar. Unsnobbish, warm and welcoming, feminine and joyful, Auberge Flora is a unique place to stay with a real heart.

ATELIER 103
RIVE GAUCHE
A stylish aparthotel in the heart of Paris
www.atelier103.fr
Tel: +33 (0)1 53 63 25 50
welcome@atelier103.fr
Saint Germain-des-Prés

knick-knacks and light fittings mixed with century-old marble floors, stained-glass windows and thick fabrics. Half of the 81 rooms and suites look out on to Eiffel's filigree tower, and the top-floor Suite Panoramique provides what could be Paris's best panorama over the Left Bank. The mansion, built in 1896 by botanist Roland Bonaparte (Napoleon Bonaparte's great-nephew), drips in Napoleonic carvings and gilding; and there's a Louis XIV-style salon whose splendour rivals Versailles. Dining-wise, expect the best of France and Asia, including Shang Palace, a gourmet Cantonese restaurant.

Opéra to Les Halles

Hôtel Brighton

218 rue de Rivoli, 1st (01.47.03.61.61, www.esprit-de-france.com). M° Tuileries. **€€**.

With several of the bedrooms looking out over the Tuileries gardens, the Brighton is great value, so ask for a room with a view. Recently restored, it has a classical atmosphere, from the high ceilings in the rooms to the faux-marble and mosaic decor downstairs.

Hôtel Chopin

10 bd Montmartre or 46 passage Jouffroy, 9th (01.47.70.58.10, www.hotel-chopin.com). M° Grands Boulevards. **€**.

Handsomely set in a historic, glass-roofed arcade next door to the Grévin museum, the Chopin's original 1846 façade adds to its old-fashioned appeal. The 36 rooms are quiet and functional, done out in salmon and green or blue.

Hôtel Concorde Opéra Paris

108 rue St-Lazare, 8th (01.40.08.44.44, www.concorde-hotels.com). M° St-Lazare. **€€€**.

Guests here are cocooned in sound-proofed luxury. The 19th-century lobby with jewel-encrusted granite columns is a historic landmark: the high ceilings, walls and sculptures look much as they have for over a century. Rooms are spacious, with double entrance doors and exclusive Annick Goutal toiletries; the belle époque brasserie, Café Terminus, and sexy Golden Black Bar were designed by Sonia Rykiel. Guests have access to a nearby fitness centre.

Hôtel Crayon

NEW *25 rue du Bouloi, 1st (01.42.36.54.19, www.hotelcrayon.com). M° Les Halles.* **€€**.

Hôtel Crayon offers colour therapy with rooms painted top to toe in a choice of 16 hues. Each also features a life-size hand-drawn nude pencilled on the wall in a Matisse style, a white bathroom with colour accents where vintage furniture has been adapted to support contemporary sinks, silky smooth cotton bedlinen and random vintage holiday snaps collected from flea markets and mounted in frames. You can order a selection of meals via room service, and a copious breakfast is served in the vaulted breakfast room.

Hotel O

NEW *19 rue Hérold, 1st (01.42.36.04.02, www.hotel-o-paris.com). M° Palais Royal-Musée du Louvre or Les Halles.* **€€**.

The new Hotel O is a sleek, 29-room venture that adds some welcome hip to the arrondissement accommodation options. Rooms (styled by cool young design company Ora-Ito, hence the 'O' in the hotel's name) are small but exquisite, with retro-futuristic features that make you feel like you're on board a 1970s spaceship, with clean lines, gracious curves and blocks of pink, grey, purple and dark turquoise.

Hôtel W Paris-Opéra

4 rue Meyerbeer, 9th (01.77.48.94.94, www.wparisopera.fr). M° Opéra/RER Auber. **€€€€**.

The Starwood hotel group's latest venture took two and a half years to finish, but it was worth the wait, with

91 rooms that ooze NYC style from every nook and cranny. For an all-out treat, the 'Extreme Wow' suite will set you back a whopping €2,300 (don't worry, standard doubles start at €340), but you'll get 88sq m of smart modern design all to yourself, and the feeling that you've walked on to the set of a James Bond movie.

Hôtel Westminster

13 rue de la Paix, 2nd (01.42.61.57.46, www.warwickwestminsteropera.com). M° Opéra/RER Auber. **€€€€**.

This luxury hotel has more than a touch of British warmth about it, no doubt owing to the influence of its favourite 19th-century guest, the Duke of Westminster (after whom the hotel was named; the current Duke reportedly stays here as well). The hotel fitness centre has an enviable top-floor location, with a beautiful tiled steam room and views over the city, and the cosy bar features deep leather chairs, a fireplace and live jazz at weekends.

InterContinental Paris Le Grand

2 rue Scribe, 9th (01.40.07.32.32, www.paris.intercontinental.com). M° Opéra. **€€€€**.

This 1862 hotel is the chain's European flagship – the landmark establishment occupies the entire block (three wings, almost 500 rooms) next to the opera house; some 80 of the honey-coloured rooms overlook the Palais Garnier. The space under the vast *verrière* is one of the best oases in town, and the hotel's restaurant and elegant coffeehouse, the Café de la Paix, poached its chef, Laurent Delarbre, from the Ritz. For a relaxing daytime break, head to I-Spa.

Mandarin Oriental

251 rue St-Honoré, 1st (01.70.98.78.88, www.mandarinoriental.com). M° Tuileries. **€€€€**.

Set in a 1930s building on rue St-Honoré, the MO has a wonderfully indulgent location – and the interior doesn't disappoint either, with 138 luxurious rooms, fusion restaurants, a vast interior garden, and a smart spa with pool and seven spa suites with private hammams. Chef Thierry Marx's gastronomic offering is the Sur Mesure restaurant, an all-white affair with Asian-influenced delights.

Le Meurice

228 rue de Rivoli, 1st (01.44.58.10.10, www.lemeurice.com). M° Tuileries. **€€€€**.

With its extravagant Louis XVI decor, intricate mosaic tiled floors and clever, modish restyling by Philippe Starck, Le Meurice is looking grander than ever. All 160 rooms (kitted out with iPod-ready radio alarms) are done up in distinct historical styles; the Belle Etoile suite on the seventh floor provides stunning views from its terrace. You can relax in the Winter Garden to the strains of jazz performances; for some more intensive intervention, head over to the lavish spa complex.

Montmartre & Pigalle

Hôtel Amour

8 rue Navarin, 9th (01.48.78.31.80, www.hotelamourparis.fr). M° St-Georges. **€€**.

This boutique hotel is a real hit with the in crowd. Each of the 20 rooms (with free Wi-Fi) is unique, decorated on the theme of love or eroticism by a coterie of contemporary artists and designers such as Marc Newson and Sophie Calle. Seven of the rooms contain artists' installations, and two others have their own private bar and a large terrace on which to hold your own party. The late-night brasserie has a coveted outdoor garden.

Hôtel Banke

20 rue La Fayette, 9th (01.55.33.22.22, www.derbyhotels.com). M° Le Peletier. **€€€**.

The Banke may well have the most eye-popping lobby in the city, a huge two-storey space done in outrageous belle époque style, all crimson, black pillars and gold leaf beneath a whopping glass roof. After such opulence, the rooms are perhaps something of a let-down; but they are stylish and comfortably equipped. The mezzanine bar partakes of the lobby's *luxe*, and the Josefin restaurant serves nouvelle Med cuisine.

Hôtel Particulier Montmartre

23 av Junot, 18th (01.53.41.81.40, www.hotel-particulier-montmartre.com). M° Lamarck Caulaincourt. **€€€€**.
Visitors lucky (and wealthy) enough to manage to book a suite at the Hôtel Particulier Montmartre will find themselves in one of the city's hidden gems. Nestled in a quiet passage off rue Lepic, this sumptuous *Directoire*-style house is dedicated to art, with each of the five luxurious suites personalised by an avant-garde artist. Free Wi-Fi.

Hôtel Royal Fromentin

11 rue Fromentin, 9th (01.48.74.85.93, www.hotelroyalfromentin.com). M° Blanche or Pigalle. **€€**.
Wood panelling, art deco windows and a vintage glass lift echo the hotel's origins as a 1930s cabaret hall; its theatrical feel attracted Blondie and Nirvana. Many of its 47 rooms have views of Sacré-Coeur. Rooms have been renovated in French style, with bright fabrics and an old-fashioned feel.

Kube Hotel

1-5 passage Ruelle, 18th (01.42.05.20.00, www.kubehotel.com). M° La Chapelle. **€€€**.
The younger sister of the Murano Urban Resort, Kube is a more hip and affordable design hotel. Like the Murano, it sits behind an unremarkable façade in an unlikely neighbourhood, the ethnically diverse Goutte d'Or. The Ice Kube bar serves vodka in glasses that, like the bar itself, are carved from ice. Access to the 41 rooms is by fingerprint identification technology and there's free Wi-Fi access.

North-east Paris

Hôtel Garden Saint-Martin

35 rue Yves Toudic, 10th (01.42.40.17.72, www.hotel-gardensaintmartin-paris.com). M° Jacques Bonsergent. **€**.
The shops, cafés and bars along the Canal St-Martin draw visitors to this hotel, where creature comforts are guaranteed at an excellent rate. No prizes will be won for the ordinary decor, but there is a very pleasant patio garden, and the staff are helpful.

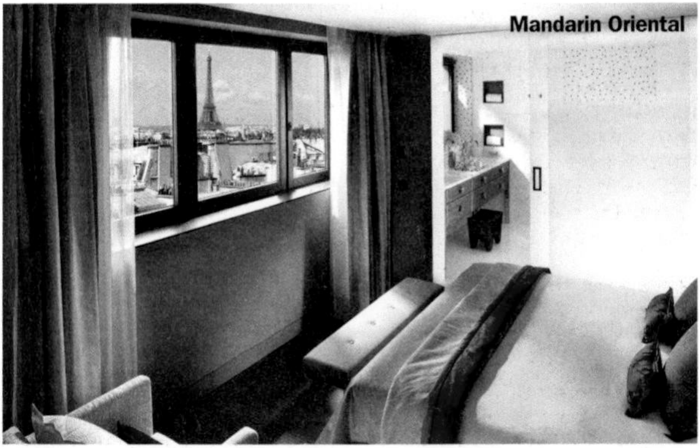
Mandarin Oriental

LE MARCEAU BASTILLE ★★★★

Hôtel-Gallery
13 rue Jules César
75012 Paris
Tél: 00.33(0)1 43 43 11 65
Fax: 00.33(0)1 43 41 67 70
infos@hotelmarceaubastille.com
Géneral Manager: Christophe Diallo

Le Marceau Bastille – Hotel gallery is a charming and contemporary 4 stars hotel, located nearly a few steps away from the Bastille square, as well "Gare de Lyon" train station and the historic Marais neighbourhood. The hotel interiors denote a characteristically contemporary style.

Le Marceau Bastille Hotel offers 55 rooms of two kinds: First, the "urban" option guarantees a cozy and resolutely avant-garde type atmosphere swathed in vibrant color, still seeped in elegance. The "ecological" option provides calm and sunny rooms set off by bright yet soft tones, natural materials, organic forms and sleek lines. The furnishings are contemporary and combine delicacy with modern technology. The living room and the breakfast room walls are dedicated to the Art with the permanent collections of contemporary artists.

Hotel Facilities

General

Bar, 24-Hour Front Desk, Newspapers, Non-Smoking Rooms, Rooms/Facilities for Disabled Guests, Elevator, free Safety Deposit Box, Heating, Design Hotel, Luggage Storage, Air-conditioning, Fitness room.

Services

Massage, Room Service, Laundry, Dry Cleaning, Breakfast in the Room, Fax/Photocopying.
Free! All children under 2 years stay free of charge for cots.
Free! Wi-Fi is available in the entire hotel and is free of charge.
Free! Pets are allowed on request. No extra charges.
Extra beds are available on request only. Any type of extra bed or baby cot is upon request and needs to be confirmed by the hotel. Public parking is possible at a location nearby.

Hotel Policies

Check-in 13:00 & Check-out 12:00

Accepted credit cards

American Express, Visa, Euro/MasterCard, Carte Bleue, Diners Club, JCB

Area Information

Architect, Historic and Art Area.
Place de la Bastille - L'Opéra Bastille - L'Hôtel Sully - L'Hôtel Carnavalet - L'Institut du Monde Arabe et la Mosquée de Paris - Le Pavillon de l'Arsenal. Le Quartier du Marais - La Place des Vosges - Cour Saint - Emilion

Stroll and Walk Area

La Promenade Plantée - Le Port de Plaisance de Paris Arsenal - Le Jardin des Plantes and Muséum National d'Histoire Naturelle - L'Ile Saint Louis.

Mama Shelter

109 rue de Bagnolet, 20th (01.43.48.48.48, www.mamashelter.com). M° Alexandre Dumas, Maraîchers or Porte de Bagnolet. **€**.

Philippe Starck's design commission is a stone's throw east of Père Lachaise, and its decor appeals to the young-at-heart with Batman and Incredible Hulk light fittings, dark walls, polished wood and splashes of bright fabrics. Every room comes with an iMac computer, TV, free internet access and a CD and DVD player; and when hunger strikes, there's a brasserie with a romantic terrace. If you're sure of your dates, book online and take advantage of the saver's rate.

St Christopher's Inn

159 rue de Crimée, 19th (01.40.34.34.40, www.st-christophers.co.uk/paris-hostels). M° Crimée, Jaurès, Laumière or Stalingrad. **€**.

If you don't mind bunking up with others, you could try this Paris branch of the English youth hostel chain. The decor in the bedrooms has a sailor's cabin feel, with round, colourful mirrors, bubble-pattern wallpaper and 1950s-inspired cabin furniture. The hostel really comes into its own in its bar, Belushi's, where the usual backpack brigade are joined by Parisians bent on taking advantage of the canal-side setting, satellite sports, lunchtime brasserie and some of the cheapest drinks in the capital. A second branch, located next to Gare du Nord, opened in spring 2013.

The Marais & Eastern Paris

Le 20 Prieuré Hôtel

20 rue du Grand Prieuré, 11th (01.47.00.74.14, www.hotel20prieure.com). M° République. **€**.

This young, funky and affordable place benefits from particularly welcoming staff. Each room has a huge blow-up of a Paris landmark covering the entire wall behind the bed, giving you the illusion that you are sleeping halfway up the Eiffel Tower, or on Bir-Hakeim bridge as the métro speeds by. Bathrooms are mundane in comparison, but things brighten up again in the light-flooded breakfast room, with pop art portraits and a reworked 1970s look.

L'Auberge Flora

NEW *44 bd Richard Lenoir, 11th (01.47.00.52.77, www.aubergeflora.fr). M° Richard Lenoir.* **€**.

See box p169.

Grand Hôtel Jeanne d'Arc

3 rue de Jarente, 4th (01.48.87.62.11, www.hoteljeannedarc.com). M° Chemin Vert. **€**.

The Jeanne d'Arc's strong point is its lovely location on a quiet road close to pretty place du Marché-Ste-Catherine. Refurbishment has made the reception area striking. The bedrooms are simple but comfortable.

Hôtel Bourg Tibourg

19 rue du Bourg-Tibourg, 4th (01.42.78.47.39, www.hotelbourgtibourg.com). M° Hôtel de Ville. **€€€**.

The Bourg Tibourg has the same owners as Hôtel Costes and the same interior decorator – but don't expect this jewel box of a boutique hotel to look like a miniature replica. Aside from its enviable location in the heart of the Marais and its fashion-pack fans, here it's all about Jacques Garcia's neo-Gothic-cum-Byzantine decor – impressive and imaginative. Exotic, scented candles, mosaic-tiled bathrooms and luxurious fabrics in rich colours create the perfect escape from the outside world. There's no restaurant or lounge – posing is done in the neighbourhood bars. Free Wi-Fi.

Hôtel de la Bretonnerie

22 rue Ste-Croix-de-la-Bretonnerie, 4th (01.48.87.77.63, www.bretonnerie.com). M° Hôtel de Ville. **€€**.

With a combination of wrought ironwork, exposed stone and ancient wooden beams, the labyrinth of corridors and passages in this 17th-century *hôtel particulier* are full of atmosphere. Tapestries, rich colours and the occasional four-poster bed give the 29 suites and bedrooms individuality. Location is convenient too. Free Wi-Fi.

Hôtel Gabriel

25 rue du Grand Prieuré, 11th (01.47.00.13.38, www.gabrielparis marais.com). M° République. **€€.**

Paris's first 'detox hotel' is a shrine to quality kip. The air-conditioned, pure white rooms are not short on techno wizardry: there's an iPod station; free Wi-Fi, of course; and the sine qua non of sleep aids, the NightCove device. This white box is easily programmed to emit sounds and light that stimulate melatonin: choose between sleep, nap or wake-up programmes. If you're still feeling rundown, then head downstairs for a detox massage. A partner gym, suggested jogging routes and green taxis complete the healthy vibe.

Hôtel Jules & Jim

11 rue des Gravilliers, 4th (01.44.54. 13.13, www.hoteljulesetjim.com). M° Arts et Métiers. **€€€.**

Located in the heart of the Marais, this modern hotel is surrounded by two paved courtyards and has lovely rooftop views. Guest rooms are comfortable, with all mod cons, while a continental buffet breakfast is served in the chic dining area. Guests can enjoy cocktails at the bar or on the terrace.

Hôtel du Petit Moulin

29-31 rue de Poitou, 3rd (01.42.74. 10.10, www.hoteldupetitmoulin.com). M° St-Sébastien Froissart. **€€.**

Within striking distance of the hip shops on rue Charlot, this listed, turn-of-the-century façade masks what was once the oldest *boulangerie* in Paris, lovingly restored as a boutique hotel by Nadia Murano and Denis Nourry. The couple recruited Christian Lacroix for the decor, and the result is a riot of colour, trompe l'oeil effects and a savvy mix of old and new. Each of its 17 exquisitely appointed rooms is unique, and the walls in rooms 202, 204 and 205 feature swirling, extravagant drawings and scribbles taken from Lacroix's sketchbook. Free parking.

Murano Urban Resort

13 bd du Temple, 3rd (01.42.71.20.00, www.muranoresort.com). M° Filles du Calvaire or Oberkampf. **€€€€.**

Behind this unremarkable façade is a super cool and supremely luxurious hotel, popular with the fashion set for its slick lounge-style design, excellent restaurant and high-tech flourishes – including coloured light co-ordinators that enable you to change the mood of your room at the touch of a button. The handsome bar has a mind-boggling 140 varieties of vodka to sample, which can make the fingerprint access to the hotel's 43 rooms and nine suites (two of which feature private pools) a late-night godsend. Free Wi-Fi.

The Seine & Islands

Hôtel des Deux-Iles

59 rue St-Louis-en-l'Ile, 4th (01.43.26.13.35, www.deuxiles-paris-hotel.com). M° Pont Marie. **€€.**

This peaceful 17th-century townhouse offers 17 soundproofed, air-conditioned rooms kitted out in toned-down stripes, *toile de Jouy* fabrics and neo colonial-style furniture. Its star features are a tiny courtyard off the lobby and a vaulted stone breakfast area. All the rooms and bathrooms were freshened up in recent years. There's free Wi-Fi.

Hôtel du Jeu de Paume

54 rue St-Louis-en-l'Ile, 4th (01.43.26. 14.18, www.jeudepaumehotel.com). M° Pont Marie. **€€€.**

With a discreet courtyard entrance, 17th-century beams, private garden and a unique timbered breakfast room that was once a real tennis court built under Louis XIII, this is a charming and romantic hotel. These days, it is filled with an attractive array of modern and classical art, and has a coveted billiards table. A dramatic glass lift and catwalks lead to the rooms and two self-catering apartments, which are simple and tasteful.

The 7th & Western Paris

Le Bellechasse

8 rue de Bellechasse, 7th (01.45.50. 22.31, www.lebellechasse.com). M° Assemblée Nationale or Solférino/ RER Musée d'Orsay. €€€€.

This former *hôtel particulier* was transformed by Christian Lacroix into a trendy boutique hotel. Only a few steps away from the Musée d'Orsay, it offers 34 splendid – though small – rooms, in seven decorative styles. Book early, as the Bellechasse is very popular.

Hôtel Duc de Saint-Simon

14 rue de St-Simon, 7th (01.44.39. 20.20, www.hotelducdesaintsimon.com). M° Rue du Bac. €€€.

A lovely courtyard leads the way into this popular hotel on the edge of St-Germain-des-Prés. Of the 34 bedrooms, four have terraces over a closed-off, leafy garden. It's perfect for lovers, though if you can do without a four-poster bed there are more spacious rooms than the Honeymoon Suite.

Hôtel Eiffel Rive Gauche

6 rue du Gros-Caillou, 7th (01.45.51. 51.51, www.hotel-eiffel.com). M° Ecole Militaire. €.

The Provençal decor and warm welcome make this a nice retreat. All 29 rooms feature Empire-style bedheads and modern bathrooms. Outside, there's a tiny, tiled courtyard with a bridge. If this is fully booked, try sister hotel Eiffel Villa Garibaldi (48 bd Garibaldi, 15th, 01.56.58.56.58).

Hôtel Lenox

9 rue de l'Université, 7th (01.42.96. 10.95, www.lenoxsaintgermain.com). M° St-Germain-des-Prés. €€.

Its location may be in the seventh arrondissement, but this venerable literary and artistic haunt is unmistakably part of St-Germain-des-Prés. The art deco-style Lenox Club Bar, which is open to the public, features supremely comfortable leather club chairs and an array of jazz instruments on the walls. Bedrooms, which are reached by an astonishing glass lift, have traditional decor and city views.

Le Montalembert

3 rue Montalembert, 7th (01.45.49. 68.68, www.montalembert.com). M° Rue du Bac. €€€.

Grace Leo-Andrieu's impeccable boutique hotel is a benchmark of quality and service. It has everything that *mode* maniacs could want: bathrooms stuffed with Molton Brown toiletries, a set of digital scales and plenty of mirrors with which to keep an eye on their figure. Decorated in pale lilac, cinnamon and olive tones, the entire hotel has Wi-Fi access, and each room is equipped with a flatscreen TV. Clattery two-person stairwell lifts are a nice nod to old-fashioned ways.

Sublim Eiffel

94 bd Garibaldi, 15th (01.40.65.95.95, www.sublimeiffel.com). M° Sèvres-Lecourbe. €€.

Some Barry White on your iPod is essential for this luuurve hotel not far from the Eiffel Tower. Carpets printed with paving stones and manhole covers lead to the rooms, where everything has been put in place for steamy nights. It's all to do with the lighting effects, which include a starry Eiffel Tower or street-scene lights above the bed and sparkling LEDs in the showers, filtered by coloured glass doors. All guests get the use of the mini-gym and hammam, and there is a massage room too. The bar adds a bit of jazz.

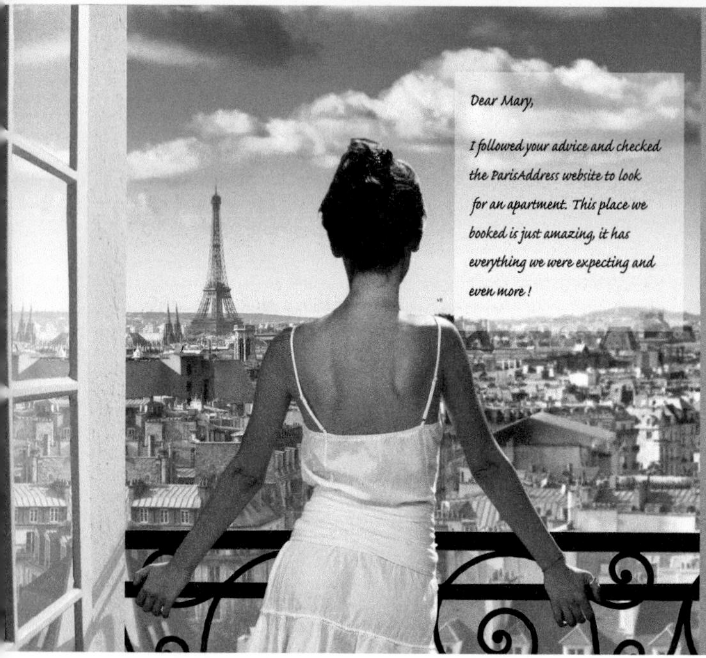
Dear Mary,
I followed your advice and checked the ParisAddress website to look for an apartment. This place we booked is just amazing, it has everything we were expecting and even more !

- > Instant availability
- > Instant booking
- > Easy process
- > Prices all included, no hidden fees !
- > Personal greeting
- > Assistance 7/7

WWW.PARISADDRESS.COM

You wish to live like a true Parisian ?
Saint-Germain-Des-Prés, the Latin Quarter, St Louis Island, the Marais, Eiffel Tower and so many other great areas for you to discover !
To make your next trip in Paris an unique and unforgettable experience, rent an apartment and discover Paris from 'within'.
ParisAddress invites you to discover picturesque and fully furnished apartments !

www.parisaddress.com - booking@parisaddress.com - +33 1 43 20 91 57

Parisaddress

St-Germain-des-Prés & Odéon

Artus Hotel

34 rue de Buci, 6th (01.43.29.07.20, www.artushotel.com). M° Mabillon. €€.
The Artus is the ideal spot for a classic taste of Paris – you couldn't be any closer to the heart of the Left Bank action. Inside the look is chic boutique, with 27 individually designed rooms ranging from cosy to capacious. Staff are eager to help and full of local tips.

Le Clos Médicis

56 rue Monsieur-le-Prince, 6th (01.43.29.10.80, www.closmedicis.com). M° Odéon/RER Luxembourg. €€.
More like a stylish, private townhouse than a hotel, Le Clos Médicis is located by the Luxembourg gardens. The hotel's decor is refreshingly modern, with rooms done out with taffeta curtains and chenille bedcovers, and antique floor tiles in the bathrooms. The lounge has a working fireplace.

L'Hôtel

13 rue des Beaux-Arts, 6th (01.44.41.99.00, www.l-hotel.com). M° Mabillon or St-Germain-des-Prés. €€€.
Guests at the sumptuously decorated L'Hôtel are more likely to be models and film stars than the starving writers who frequented it during Oscar Wilde's last days (the playwright died in a room on the ground floor in November 1900). Under Jacques Garcia's restoration, each room has a theme: Mistinguett's *chambre* retains its art deco mirror bed, and Wilde's tribute room is appropriately clad in green peacock murals. In the basement is a small pool, which is wonderfully private – only two people are allowed down here at a time.

Hôtel de l'Abbaye Saint-Germain

10 rue Cassette, 6th (01.45.44.38.11, www.hotelabbayeparis.com). M° Rennes or St-Sulpice. €€€.
A monumental entrance opens the way through a courtyard into this tranquil hotel, originally part of a convent. Wood panelling, well-stuffed sofas and an open fireplace in the drawing room make for a relaxed atmosphere, but, best of all, there's a surprisingly large garden where breakfast is served in the warmer months. The 43 rooms and duplex apartment are tasteful and luxurious.

Hôtel La Belle Juliette

92 rue du Cherche-Midi, 6th (01.42.22.97.40, www.hotel-belle-juliette-paris.com). M° Vaneau. €€€.
Juliette Récamier was the great society beauty of the Napoleonic era, and is the inspiration for this hotel. Designer Anne Gelbard has filled the 34 rooms with the colours of the Napoleonic era and of Juliette's famous portrait by Gérard – pale yellow, eau-de-nil, duck-egg blue, slate and Augustan red. It's classical without being constricting, as there are also high-tech gadgets and luxury bathrooms. The Talma bar is named after a romantic actor of the time and offers organic breakfasts, lunches and Italian tapas at night.

Hôtel du Globe

15 rue des Quatre-Vents, 6th (01.43.26.35.50, www.hotel-du-globe.fr). M° Odéon. €€.
The Hôtel du Globe has managed to retain much of its 17th-century character – and very pleasant it is too. Gothic wrought-iron doors open into the florid corridors, and an unexplained suit of armour supervises guests from the tiny salon. The bedrooms with baths are somewhat larger than those with showers, and if you're an early booker you might even get the room with the four-poster bed.

Hôtel des Saints-Pères

65 rue des Sts-Pères, 6th (01.45.44.50.00, www.espritfrance.com). M° St-Germain-des-Prés. €€.
Built in 1658 by one of Louis XIV's architects, this hotel has an enviable

L'Hôtel p179

location near St-Germain-des-Prés' boutiques. It boasts a charming garden and a sophisticated, if small, bar. The most coveted room is no.100, with its fine 17th-century ceiling by painters from the Versailles School; it also has an open bathroom, so you can gaze at scenes from the myth of Leda and the Swan while you scrub.

Hôtel Villa Madame

44 rue Madame, 6th (01.45.48.02.81, www.hotelvillamadameparis.com). M° St-Sulpice. **€€€.**

This revamped hotel (formerly called the Regents), located in a quiet street, is a lovely surprise, with its courtyard garden used for breakfast during the summer. Honey- and chocolate-coloured woods mix with warm-toned velvets to make the rooms (which all feature plasma TVs) feel cosy and inviting; some even have small balconies with loungers.

Relais Saint-Germain

9 carrefour de l'Odéon, 6th (01.44.27.07.97, www.hotel-paris-relais-saint-germain.com). M° Odéon. **€€€.**

The wood-beamed ceilings remain intact at the Relais Saint-Germain, a 17th-century hotel renovated by acclaimed chef Yves Camdeborde (originator of the *bistronomique* dining trend) and his wife Claudine. Each of the 22 rooms has a different take on eclectic Provençal charm, and the marble bathrooms are positively huge by Paris standards. Another major plus: guests get first dibs on highly sought-after seats in the 15-table Le Comptoir restaurant next door.

The Latin Quarter & the 13th

Familia Hôtel

11 rue des Ecoles, 5th (01.43.54.55.27, www.hotel-paris-familia.com). M° Cardinal Lemoine or Jussieu. **€.**

This old-fashioned Latin Quarter hotel has balconies hung with tumbling plants and walls draped with replica French tapestries. Owner Eric Gaucheron extends a warm welcome, and the 30 rooms have personalised touches such as sepia murals, cherry-wood furniture and stone walls. The Gaucherons also own the Minerve next door – book in advance for both.

Five Hôtel

3 rue Flatters, 5th (01.43.31.74.21, www.thefivehotel.com). M° Les Gobelins or Port Royal. **€€€.**

The rooms in this stunning boutique hotel may be small, but they're all exquisitely designed, with Chinese lacquer and velvety fabrics. Fibre optics built into the walls create the illusion of sleeping under a starry sky, and you can choose from four fragrances to subtly perfume your room. Guests staying in the suite have access to a private garden with a jacuzzi.

Hôtel les Degrés de Notre-Dame

10 rue des Grands-Degrés, 5th (01.55.42.88.88, www.lesdegreshotel.com). M° Maubert-Mutualité or St-Michel. **€€**.
On a tiny street across the river from Notre-Dame, this vintage hotel is an absolute gem. Its ten rooms are full of character, with original paintings, antique furniture and exposed wooden beams (nos.47 and 501 have views of the cathedral). It has an adorable restaurant and, a few streets away, two studio apartments that the owner rents to preferred customers only.

Hôtel du Panthéon

19 pl du Panthéon, 5th (01.43.54.32.95, www.hoteldupantheon.com). M° Cluny La Sorbonne or Maubert Mutualité/RER Luxembourg. **€€**.
The 36 rooms of this elegant hotel are beautifully decorated with classic French *toile de Jouy* fabrics, antique furniture and painted woodwork. Some enjoy impressive views of the Panthéon; others squint out on to a hardly less romantic courtyard, complete with chestnut tree.

Hôtel Résidence Henri IV

50 rue des Bernardins, 5th (01.44.41.31.81, www.residencehenri4.com). M° Cardinal Lemoine. **€€**.
This belle époque-style hotel has a mere eight rooms and five apartments, so guests are assured of the staff's full attention. Peacefully situated next to leafy square Paul-Langevin, it's just minutes away from Notre-Dame. The four-person apartments come with a mini-kitchen featuring a hob, fridge and microwave. Free Wi-Fi available.

Hôtel de la Sorbonne

6 rue Victor-Cousin, 5th (01.43.54.58.08, www.hotelsorbonne.com). M° Cluny La Sorbonne/RER Luxembourg. **€€**.
It's out with the old at this charming, freshly renovated hotel, whose new look is very much a modern take on art nouveau, with bold wallpapers, floral prints, lush fabrics and quotes from French literature woven into the carpets. Rooms are all equipped with iMac computers.

Le Petit Paris

214 rue St-Jacques, 5th (01.53.10.29.29, www.hotelpetitparis.com). M° Maubert Mutualité/RER Luxembourg. **€€€**.
This new venture is a dynamic exercise in taste and colour. The 20 rooms, designed by Sybille de Margerie, are arranged by era, running from the puce and purple of the medieval rooms to the wildly decadent orange, yellow and pink of the swinging '60s rooms. Luxury abounds with finest silks, velvets and taffetas. Some of the rooms have small terraces, and those with baths have a TV you can watch while soaking. An honesty bar in the lounge and jukebox encourage conviviality.

Montparnasse

Hôtel Aviatic

105 rue de Vaugirard, 6th (01.53.63.25.50, www.aviatic.fr). M° Duroc or Montparnasse Bienvenüe. **€€**.
This historic hotel has masses of character, from the Empire-style lounge and garden atrium to the bistro-style breakfast room and marble floor in the lobby. New decoration throughout, in beautiful steely greys, warm reds, elegant, striped velvets and *toile de Jouy* fabrics, lends an impressive touch of glamour to proceedings.

Getting Around

Airports

Roissy-Charles-de-Gaulle

01.70.36.39.50, www.adp.fr. 30km (19 miles) north-east of Paris.

For most international flights. The three main terminals are some way apart; check which one you need for your flight back. The terminals are linked by the CDGVAL free driverless train. The **RER B** line (36.58, www.transilien.com) is the quickest way to central Paris (40mins to Gare du Nord; 45mins to RER Châtelet-Les Halles; €9.10 single). RER trains run every 10-15mins, 4.58am-11.58pm daily.

Air France buses (08.92.35.08.20, www.cars-airfrance.com; €15 single, €24 return) leave every 20-30mins, 6am-11pm daily, and stop at Porte Maillot and place Charles-de-Gaulle (35-50min trip). Buses also run to Gare Montparnasse and Gare de Lyon (€16.50 single, €27 return) every 30mins (45-60min trip), 6am-10pm daily; a bus between Roissy and Orly (€19) runs every 30mins, 5.55am-10.30pm daily from Roissy.

RATP Roissybus (32.46, www.ratp.fr; €10) runs every 15-20mins, 5.45am-11pm daily, between the airport and the corner of rue Scribe/rue Auber (at least 45mins); buy your tickets on the bus.

Paris Airports Service is a 24-hour door-to-door minibus service between airports and hotels, seven days a week. Roissy prices go from €26 for one person to €99 for eight people, 6am-8pm (minimum €42, 4-6am, 8-10pm); you can reserve a place on 01.55.98.10.80, www.parisairportservice.com. A **taxi** into central Paris from Roissy-Charles-de-Gaulle airport should take 30-60mins and costs €40-€50, plus €1 per luggage item.

Orly

01.70.36.39.50, www.adp.fr. About 18km (11 miles) south of Paris.

Orly-Sud terminal is mainly international and Orly-Ouest is mainly domestic.

Air France buses (08.92.35.08.20, www.cars-airfrance.com; €11.50 single, €18.50 return) leave both terminals every 30mins, 6am-11.30pm daily, and stop at Invalides and Montparnasse (30-45mins).

The **RATP Orlybus** (32.46, www.ratp.fr) runs to Denfert-Rochereau every 15mins, 5.35am-11.30pm (30mins); buy tickets (€6.90) on the bus. High-speed **Orlyval** shuttle trains (www.orlyval.fr) run every 4-7mins (6am-11pm daily) to RER B station Antony (€10.75 to Châtelet-les-Halles); allow about 35mins for central Paris.

Orly prices for the Paris Airports Service (*see left*) are €25 for one and €5-€12 per passenger depending on the number. A **taxi** takes 20-40mins and costs €16-€26.

Paris Beauvais

08.92.68.20.66, www.aeroportbeauvais.com. 70km (43 miles) north of Paris.

This is Paris's budget hub, used by the likes of Ryanair and Wizz Air. **Buses** (€15) to/from Porte Maillot leave 15-30mins after each arrival and 3hrs 15mins before each departure. Tickets from Arrivals or buy tickets on the bus.

Arriving by car

Options for crossing the Channel with a car include: **Eurotunnel** (08.10.63.03.04, www.eurotunnel.com); **Brittany Ferries** (08.25.82.88.28, www.brittanyferries.com), **P&O Ferries** (08.25.12.01.56, www.poferries.com) and **My Ferry Link** (0044.8442. 482100, www.myferrylink.com).

Arriving by coach

International coaches arrive at **Gare Routière Internationale Paris-Galliéni** at Porte de Bagnolet, 20th. For tickets (in English) call Eurolines on 08.92.89.90.91 or 0044.1582.404 511, or visit www.eurolines.fr.

Arriving by rail

Eurostar from London St Pancras International (0044.8432.186186, www.eurostar.com) to Paris Gare du Nord (08.92.35.35.35) takes 2hrs 15mins direct. Check in at least 30mins before departure. Fares start at £69 return.

Cycles can be taken as hand luggage if they are dismantled and carried in a bike bag (check dimensions with Eurostar). You can also check them in at the EuroDespatch depot at St Pancras (Esprit Parcel Service, 0044.844.822 5822) or Sernam depot at Gare du Nord (01.48.74.14.80). Check-in must be done 24hrs ahead; a Eurostar ticket must be shown. The service costs £20/€25.

Maps

Free maps of the métro, bus and RER systems are available at airports and métro stations.

Public transport

RATP (32.46, www.ratp.fr) runs the bus, métro and suburban tram routes, as well as lines A and B of the RER express railway, which connects with the métro inside Paris. State rail **SNCF** (36.35, www.sncf.com) runs RER lines C, D and E for the suburbs.

Fares & tickets

Paris and its suburbs are divided into six travel zones, with 1 and 2 covering the city centre. RATP tickets and passes are valid on the métro, bus and RER. Tickets and *carnets* can be bought at métro stations, tourist offices and tobacconists; single tickets can be bought on buses. Retain your ticket in case of spot checks; you'll also need it to exit from RER stations.

A ticket is €1.70, a carnet of ten €12.50. A Mobilis day pass is €6.40 for zones 1 and 2 and €15.20 for zones 1-5 (not including airports).

Métro & RER

The Paris **métro** is the fastest way of getting around. Trains run 5.30am-12.40am Mon-Thur, 5.30am-1.30am Fri-Sun. Numbered lines have their direction named after the last stop. Follow the orange *Correspondance* signs to change lines. The five **RER** lines run 5.30am-1am daily across Paris and into commuterland. Métro tickets are valid for RER journeys within zones 1 and 2.

Buses

Buses run 6.30am-8.30pm, with some routes continuing until 12.30am, Mon-Sat; limited services operate on selected lines Sun and public holidays. You can use a métro ticket, a ticket bought from the driver (€1.90) or a travel pass. Tickets should be punched in the machine next to the driver; passes should be shown to the driver.

Night buses

The 47 **Noctilien** lines run from place du Châtelet to the suburbs (hourly 12.30am-5.30am Mon-Thur; half-hourly 1am-5.35am Fri, Sat);

look out for the Noctilien logo or the N in front of the route number. A ticket costs €1.70 (€1.90 from the driver); travel passes are valid.

River transport

Batobus
08.25.05.01.01, www.batobus.com.
One-day pass €14 (€7, €9 reductions). River buses stop every 17-35mins at the Eiffel Tower, Musée d'Orsay, St-Germain-des-Prés (quai Malaquais), Notre-Dame, Jardin des Plantes, Hôtel de Ville, the Louvre, Champs-Elysées (Pont Alexandre III). Tickets are available from Batobus stops, RATP and tourist offices.

Rail travel

Versailles and Disneyland Paris are served by the RER. Most locations out of the city are served by the SNCF railway; the TGV high-speed train is steadily being extended to all the main regions. Tickets can be bought at any SNCF station, SNCF shops and travel agents. If you reserve online or by phone, you can pay and pick up your tickets from the station or have them sent to your home. SNCF automatic machines (*billeterie automatique*) only work with French credit/debit cards. Buy tickets in advance to secure the cheaper fare. Before you board any train, stamp your ticket in the orange *composteur* machines on the platforms, or you might have to pay a hefty fine.

SNCF
36.35, www.sncf.com.
Open 7am-10pm daily.

Taxis

Taxis are hard to find at rush hour or early in the morning. Ranks are indicated with a blue sign. A white light on a taxi's roof means it's free; an orange one means it's busy. You also pay for the time it takes your radioed taxi to arrive. Payment by credit card – mention when you book – is usually €15 minimum. Don't feel obliged to tip, although rounding up to the nearest euro is polite.

Alpha
01.45.85.85.85, www.alphataxis.fr.
G7
36.07, www.taxis-g7.fr.
Taxis Bleus
08.91.70.10.10, www.taxis-bleus.com.

Driving

If you're planning to bring your car to France, you should bring its registration and insurance documents with you.

Bison Futé
08.00.10.02.00, www.bison-fute.equipement.gouv.fr.
Infotrafic
08.92.70.77.66 (€0.34/min), www.infotrafic.fr.

Breakdown services

Beaking down in France can be an expensive business, so it's advisable to take out additional breakdown insurance cover before you travel, for example with a company such as the **AA** (www.theaa.com) or **Green Flag** (www.greenflag.com). **Dan Dépann Auto** (08.00.25.10.00, www.dandepann.fr) operates a 24-hour breakdown service in the Paris area.

Parking

There are still a few free on-street parking areas in Paris, but they're often full. If you park illegally, your car may be clamped or towed away.

Don't park in zones marked for deliveries (*livraisons*) or taxis. *Horodateurs*, pay-and-display machines, take a special card (*carte de stationnement* at €15 or €40, from tobacconists). Parking is often free at weekends, after 7pm and in August. Underground car parks cost around €2.50 per hour. Some have lower rates after 6pm. See www.parkingsdeparis.com.

Vehicle removal

If your car is impounded, contact the nearest police station. There are eight car pounds (*préfourrières*) in Paris; to find out where your car might be, visit www.prefecture-police-paris.interieur.gouv.fr.

Car hire

To hire a car you must be 25 or over and have held a licence for at least a year. Some agencies accept drivers aged 21-24, but a day fee of €20-€25 is usual. Take your licence and passport. Bargain firms may have a high charge for damage: read the small print before signing.

Ada
www.ada.fr.
Avis
08.21.23.07.60, www.avis.fr.
Budget
08.25.00.35.64, www.budget.fr.
EasyCar
www.easycar.com.
Europcar
08.25.35.83.58, www.europcar.fr.
Hertz
01.55.31.93.21, www.hertz.fr.
Rent-a-Car
08.91.70.02.00, www.rentacar.fr.

Cycling

In 2007, the mayor launched a municipal bike hire scheme – Vélib (www.velib.paris.fr). There are now over 20,000 bicycles available 24 hours a day, at nearly 1,800 'stations' across the city. Just swipe your travel card to release the bikes from their stands. The *mairie* actively promotes cycling in the city and the Vélib scheme is complemented by some 400km (250 miles) of bike lanes snaking their way around Paris.

A free *Paris à Vélo* map can be picked up at any *mairie* or from bike shops. Cycle lanes (*pistes cyclables*) run mostly N–S and E–W. N–S routes include rue de Rennes, av d'Italie, bd Sébastopol and av Marceau. E–W routes take in the rue de Rivoli, bd St-Germain, bd St-Jacques and av Daumesnil. You could be fined if you don't use them, which is a bit rich considering the lanes are often blocked by delivery vans. Cyclists are also entitled to use certain bus lanes (especially the new ones set off by a strip of kerb stones). Don't let the locals' blasé attitude to helmets and lights convince you it's not worth using them.

Cycle hire

Note that bike insurance may not cover theft: check before you sign.

Freescoot
63 quai de la Tournelle, 5th (01.44.07.06.72, www.freescoot.fr). Mº Maubert Mutualité or St-Michel.
Open 9am-1pm, 2-7pm daily; closed Sun Oct-mid Apr.
Bicycles (from €15 per day) and scooters (from €45 per day) for hire.

Left Bank Scooters
06.82.70.13.82, www.leftbank scooters.com.
This company hires out vintage-style Vespas (from €70 per day), with delivery and collection from your apartment or hotel. Various tours are also available.

Resources A-Z

For information on travelling to France from within the European Union, including details of visa regulations and healthcare provision, see the EU's travel website: http://europa.eu/travel.

Accident & emergency

In a medical emergency, you should call the Sapeurs-Pompiers, who have trained paramedics.

Ambulance (SAMU)	**15**
Police	**17**
Fire (Sapeurs-Pompiers)	**18**
Emergency (from a mobile phone)	**112**

Credit card loss

Call one of these 24hr services.

American Express *01.44.77.72.00*
Diners Club *08.20.82.01.43*
MasterCard *08.00.90.13.87*
Visa *08.92.70.57.05*

Customs

Non-EU residents can claim a tax refund or *détaxe* (around 12%) on VAT if they spend over €175 in one purchase and if they live outside the EU for more than six months in the year. At the shop ask for a *bordereau de vente à l'exportation.*

Dental emergencies

Look in the *Pages Jaunes* (www.pagesjaunes.fr) under *Dentistes*. For emergencies contact:

Hôpital de la Pitié-Salpêtrière
47-83 bd de l'Hôpital, 13th (01.42.16.00.00). M° Gare d'Austerlitz.
Open 24hrs.

SOS Dentaire
87 bd Port-Royal, 13th (01.43.37.51.00). M° Les Gobelins/RER Port-Royal.
Open by phone 9am-midnight daily.

Disabled

General information (in French) is available on the Secrétaire d'Etat aux Personnes Handicapées website: www.handicap.gouv.fr.

Electricity

France uses the standard 220-240V, 50-cycle AC system. Visitors with 240V British appliances need an adapter (*adaptateur*). US 110V appliances need an adapter and a transformer (*transformateur*).

Embassies & consulates

Australian Embassy
4 rue Jean-Rey, 15th (01.40.59.33.00, www.france.embassy.gov.au). M° Bir-Hakeim. **Open** *Consular services* 9am-noon, 2-4pm Mon-Fri. *Visas* 10am-noon Mon-Fri.

British Embassy
35 rue du Fbg-St-Honoré, 8th (01.44.51.31.00, www.ukinfrance.fco.gov.uk). M° Concorde. Consular services 18bis rue d'Anjou, 8th. M° Concorde.
Open 9.30am-12.30pm, 2.30-4.30pm Mon-Fri. *Visas 16 rue d'Anjou, 8th (01.44.51.31.01).* **Open** 9.30am-1pm, 2.30-6pm Mon-Fri.
British citizens wanting consular services (such as new passports) should ignore the queue at 16 rue d'Anjou and instead walk in at no.18bis.

Canadian Embassy
35 av Montaigne, 8th (01.44.43.29.00, www.amb-canada.fr).

ESSENTIALS

M° Franklin D Roosevelt. Consular services (01.44.43.29.02). **Open** 9am-noon, 2-5pm Mon-Fri. *Visas 37 av Montaigne, 8th (01.44.43.29.16).* **Open** 8.30-10.30am Mon-Fri.

Irish Embassy
12 av Foch, 16th. Consulate 4 rue Rude, 16th (01.44.17.67.00, www.embassyofireland.fr). M° Charles de Gaulle Etoile. **Open** *Consular/visas* 9.30am-noon Mon-Fri. *By phone* 9.30am-1pm, 2.30-5.30pm Mon-Fri.

New Zealand Embassy
7ter rue Léonard-de-Vinci, 16th (01.45.01.43.43, www.nzembassy.com/france). M° Victor Hugo. **Open** 9am-1pm Mon-Fri. *Visas* 9am-12.30pm Mon-Fri. Visas for travel to New Zealand can be applied for on the website www.immigration.govt.nz.

South African Embassy
59 quai d'Orsay, 7th (01.53.59.23.23, www.afriquesud.net). M° Invalides. **Open** 8.30am-5.15pm Mon-Fri. *Consulate/visas (01.47.53.99.70)* 9am-noon Mon-Fri.

US Embassy
2 av Gabriel, 8th (01.43.12.22.22, http://france.usembassy.gov). M° Concorde. Consulate/visas 4 av Gabriel, 8th (08.10.26.46.26). M° Concorde. **Open** *Consular services* 9am-12.30pm, 1-3pm Mon-Fri. *Visas 08.92.23.84.72.*

Internet

Milk
31 bd de Sébastopol, 1st (01.40.13.06.51, www.milklub.com). M° Châtelet or Rambuteau/RER Châtelet Les Halles. **Open** 24hrs daily.

Opening hours

Standard opening hours for shops are generally 9am/10am-7pm/8pm Mon-Sat. Some close on Mondays, some for lunch (usually 12.30-2pm) and some in August.

Pharmacies

All *pharmacies* sport a green neon cross. If closed, a pharmacy will have a sign indicating the nearest one open. Staff can provide basic medical services like disinfecting and bandaging wounds (for a small fee) and will indicate the nearest doctor on duty. The following are all open late:

Matignon
1 av Matignon, 8th (01.43.59.86.55). M° Franklin D Roosevelt. **Open** 8.30am-2am daily.

Pharmacie des Champs-Elysées
84 av des Champs-Elysées, 8th (01.45.62.02.41). M° George V. **Open** until 2am daily.

Pharmacie Européenne de la Place de Clichy
6 pl de Clichy, 9th (01.48.74.65.18). M° Place de Clichy. **Open** 24hrs daily.

Pharmacie des Halles
10 bd de Sébastopol, 4th (01.42.72.03.23). M° Châtelet. **Open** 9am-midnight Mon-Sat; 9am-10pm Sun.

Police

The French equivalent of 999/911 is **17** (**112** from a mobile), but don't expect a speedy response. If you're assaulted or robbed, report the incident as soon as possible. Make a statement (*procès verbal*) at the *point d'accueil* closest to the crime. To find it, contact the Préfecture Centrale (08.91.01.22.22) or go to www.prefecture-police-paris.interieur.gouv.fr. You'll need to obtain a statement for insurance purposes.

Post

Post offices (*bureaux de poste*) are open 8am-7.30pm Mon-Fri; 8am-1pm Sat, apart from the 24hr one listed below. All are listed in the phone book: under *Administration des PTT* in the *Pages Jaunes*; under *Poste* in the *Pages Blanches*. Most post offices have machines that weigh your letter, print out a stamp and give change, saving you from queuing. You can also buy stamps at a tobacconist.

Main Post Office
52 rue du Louvre, 1st (36.31). Mº Les Halles or Louvre Rivoli.
Open 24hrs daily.

Smoking

Smoking is prohibited in all enclosed public spaces. Hotels can still offer smoking rooms.

Telephones

All French phone numbers have ten digits. Paris and Ile-de-France numbers begin with 01; the rest of France is divided into four zones, 02 to 05. Mobile phone numbers start with 06. Numbers beginning with 08 can only be reached from inside France. The France country code is 33; leave off the first 0 at the start of the ten-digit number. Most public phones use *télécartes* (phonecards). These are sold at post offices and tobacconists, and they cost €7.50 for 50 units or €15 for 120 units.

Time

France is one hour ahead of GMT and uses the 24hr system (for example, 18h means 6pm).

Tipping

A service charge of ten to 15% is legally included in your bill at all restaurants, cafés and bars. However, it's polite to round up the final amount for drinks, or to leave a cash tip of €1-€2 or more for a meal, depending on service.

Toilets

The city's automatic street toilets are not as terrifying as they first appear. Each loo is washed down and disinfected after use. If a space age-style experience doesn't appeal, you could always nip into the toilets of a café; although theoretically reserved for customers, a polite request should win sympathy with the waiter.

Tourist information

Office de Tourisme et des Congrès de Paris
25 rue des Pyramides (08.92.68.30.00, www.parisinfo.com). Mº Pyramides.
Open *Summer* 9am-7pm daily. *Winter* 10am-7pm daily.
Info on Paris and the suburbs; tickets.
Other locations *Anvers, 72 bd Rochechouart, 9th. Gare de Lyon, 20 bd Diderot, 12th. Gare du Nord, 18 rue de Dunkerque, 10th. Porte de Versailles, 1 place de la Porte de Versailles, 15th.*

Visas

European Union nationals do not need a visa to enter France, nor do US, Canadian, Australian, New Zealand or South African citizens for stays of up to three months. Nationals of other countries should enquire at the nearest French embassy or consulate before leaving home. If you are travelling to France from one of the countries included in the Schengen agreement (most of the EU, but not Britain or Ireland), the visa from that country should be sufficient.

What's on

There are two listings magazines: *L'Officiel des Spectacles* (€0.50) and *Pariscope* (€0.40).

Vocabulary

General expressions

good morning/hello *bonjour*; **good evening** *bonsoir*; **goodbye** *au revoir*; **hi** *salut*; **OK** *d'accord*; **yes** *oui*; **no** *non*; **how are you?** *comment allez-vous?*; **how's it going?** *comment ça va?/ça va?*; **sir/Mr** *monsieur* (M); **madam/Mrs** *madame* (Mme); **miss** *mademoiselle* (Mlle); **please** *s'il vous plaît*; **thank you** *merci*; **thank you very much** *merci beaucoup*; **sorry** *pardon*; **excuse me** *excusez-moi*; **do you speak English?** *parlez-vous anglais?*; **I don't speak French** *je ne parle pas français*; **I don't understand** *je ne comprends pas*; **speak more slowly, please** *parlez plus lentement, s'il vous plaît*; **good** *bon/bonne*; **bad** *mauvais/mauvaise*; **small** *petit/petite*; **big** *grand/grande*; **beautiful** *beau/belle*; **well** *bien*; **badly** *mal*; **a bit** *un peu*; **a lot** *beaucoup*; **very** *très*; **with** *avec*; **without** *sans*; **and** *et*; **or** *ou*; **because** *parce que*; **who?** *qui?*; **when?** *quand?*; **what?** *quoi?*; **which?** *quel?*; **where?** *où?*; **why?** *pourquoi?*; **how?** *comment?*; **at what time?** *à quelle heure?*; **forbidden** *interdit/défendu*; **out of order** *hors service* (HS)/*en panne*; **daily** *tous les jours* (tlj)

Getting around

where is the (nearest) métro? *où est le métro (le plus proche)?*; **when is the next train for... ?** *c'est quand le prochain train pour...?*; **ticket** *un billet*; **station** *la gare*; **platform** *le quai*; **entrance** *entrée*; **exit** *sortie*; **left** *gauche*; **right** *droite*; **straight on** *tout droit*; **far** *loin*; **near** *pas loin/près d'ici*; **street map** *le plan*; **bank** *la banque*; **is there a bank near here?** *est-ce qu'il y a une banque près d'ici?*

Accommodation

do you have a room (for this evening/for two people)? *avez-vous une chambre (pour ce soir/pour deux personnes)?*; **full** *complet*; **room** *une chambre*; **bed** *un lit*; **double bed** *un grand lit*; **(a room with) twin beds** (*une chambre à*) *deux lits*; **with bath(room)/shower** *avec* (*salle de*) *bain/douche*; **breakfast** *le petit déjeuner*; **included** *compris*

At the restaurant

I'd like to book a table (for three/at 8pm) *je voudrais réserver une table (pour trois personnes/à vingt heures)*; **lunch** *le déjeuner*; **dinner** *le dîner*; **coffee** (espresso) *un café*; **white coffee** *un café au lait/café crème*; **tea** *du thé*; **wine** *du vin*; **beer** *la bière*; **mineral water** *eau minérale*; **fizzy** *gazeuse*; **still** *plate*; **tap water** *eau du robinet/une carafe d'eau*; **the bill, please** *l'addition, s'il vous plaît*

Numbers

0 *zéro*; **1** *un, une*; **2** *deux*; **3** *trois*; **4** *quatre*; **5** *cinq*; **6** *six*; **7** *sept*; **8** *huit*; **9** *neuf*; **10** *dix*; **11** *onze*; **12** *douze*; **13** *treize*; **14** *quatorze*; **15** *quinze*; **16** *seize*; **17** *dix-sept*; **18** *dix-huit*; **19** *dix-neuf*; **20** *vingt*; **21** *vingt-et-un*; **22** *vingt-deux*; **30** *trente*; **40** *quarante*; **50** *cinquante*; **60** *soixante*; **70** *soixante-dix*; **80** *quatre-vingts*; **90** *quatre-vingt-dix*; **100** *cent*; **1000** *mille*; **1,000,000** *un million*

Index

Sights & Areas

ESSENTIALS

LIDO
CHAMPS-ÉLYSÉES
PARIS
THE FAMOUS CABARET
OF THE CHAMPS-ÉLYSÉES:
70 artistes on stage,
600 sumptuous costumes,
23 monumental sets...
Extract of the show
Le Lido c'est Paris !
DINNER & SHOW from €160
CHAMPAGNE & SHOW from €95
116 bis avenue des Champs-Élysées 75008 Paris - Tel. : + 33 (0)1 40 76 56 10
E-mail: reservation@lido.fr
www.Lido.fr - facebook.com/lidodeparis.officiel